Proletarians and Protest

fm

Proletarians and Protest)

THE ROOTS OF CLASS FORMATION IN AN INDUSTRIALIZING WORLD

EDITED BY
MICHAEL HANAGAN
AND
CHARLES STEPHENSON

CONTRIBUTIONS IN LABOR STUDIES, NUMBER 17

GREENWOOD PRESS
NEW YORK • WESTPORT, CONNECTICUT • LONDON

Library of Congress Cataloging in Publication Data

Main entry under title:

Proletarians and protest.

(Contributions in labor studies, ISSN 0886-8239 ; no. 17)
  Bibliography: p.
  Includes index.
  1. Social classes—History—Addresses, essays, lectures.
2. Labor and laboring classes—History—Addresses, essays, lectures.   3. Urban-rural migration—History—Addresses, essays, lectures.   I. Hanagan, Michael P., 1947–   . II. Stephenson, Charles.   III. Series.
HT621.P74   1985   305.5   85–5596
ISBN 0–313–23217–2 (lib. bdg. : alk. paper)

Library of Congress Catalog Card number: 85–5596
ISBN: 0–313–23217–2
ISSN: 0886-8239

First published in 1986

Greenwood Press, Inc.
88 Post Road West
Westport, Connecticut 06881

Printed in the United States of America

The paper used in this book complies with the Permanent Paper Standard issued by the National Information Standards Organization (Z39.48–1984).

10 9 8 7 6 5 4 3 2 1

Michael Hanagan's Dedication:

To Nora

Charles Stephenson's Dedication:
To Ron Herlan, Paul Hehn, John Killigrew,
Fred Halley, and George Rentsch
and other friends at Brockport

Contents

Illustrations

Tables

Acknowledgments

We would like to thank Chuck Thomas for his invaluable help at the beginning of this project. Miriam Cohen, John Cumbler, Len Smith, Chuck Tilly, and Betty Stephenson provided valuable criticism, advice, and support. Chuck Sokolik provided much appreciated help in bringing this project to completion.

Proletarians and Protest

1

Introduction

Michael Hanagan and Charles Stephenson

The impact of industrialization and of the concomitant process of class formation on working-class social protest is one of the oldest themes of labor history. Karl Marx, J. L. and Barbara Hammond, Sidney and Beatrice Webb, John R. Commons, and many others assigned considerable analytical significance to the working-class response to the first stage of industrial development. More recently, the work of E. P. Thompson, a central influence on modern labor and social history, has contributed an important reinterpretation of the basic process of class formation and its relation to social protest.[1] Yet as the articles in this collection demonstrate, the present status of research in this field is as alive and vigorous as ever.

There are several reasons for the sustained level of interest in this topic. Perhaps most inspiring has been the very high quality of so much past work in this area. Almost all the papers in this collection, for example, whether written by historians, sociologists, or anthropologists, and whether written about South America, Europe, or Africa, reveal Thompson's influence. Practically alone of contemporary researchers in the field, his influence seems to reach everywhere. Thompson's classic *The Making of the English Working Class* argues that during the early years of the Industrial Revolution in England, a variety of pre-industrial traditions coalesced into a unified working-class culture. The central thrust of Thompson's work has been to link the actions of protestors to their daily experience in a manner that makes their protests plausible, comprehensible, and related to a larger and continuing tradition of resistance. The Thompsonian influence is revealed in the concern shown in almost all the essays here to uncover elements of continuity in working-class behavior and to relate working-class behavior to shared experiences.

Yet most of the essays in this collection pursue connections between workers' lives and protests that add new dimensions to the study of class formation begun by Thompson. In contrast to Thompson's emphasis on ideology as the mediating link between experience and protest, these essays portray class formation as a series of social solidarities that bind workers together and mark them off from other social groups. Class formation occurs when the social solidarities that organize daily life—the solidarities of participation in migrant communities, of family, and of neighborhood urban life and a similar position in a work hierarchy—increasingly shut the working class off from other social groups and draw its members together. Although the distinction is sometimes subtle, most essays in this collection stress the mediating role of social structures more than that of ideology; they show how pre-existing social groups and social structural conditions mediated between work experience and popular protest. They try to sort out the structural conditions that promoted continuity between the industrial working class and the milieux from which it originated.

The regional and comparative studies in this collection forcefully show the great variety and heterogeneity of the proletarianization process. These studies show that the influence of rural ideologies on the labor movement is more complicated than is generally assumed. Much modern labor history has stressed the rural background of the proletariat in terms of the transition from a "moral economy" to a capitalist economy; within this context, historians have shown how workers used moral terms of rural culture to forge a critique of urban industrial capitalism. Although the picture of rural culture drawn by these historians might seem too similar to the *gemeinschaft* so beloved by nineteenth-century sociologists to be fully credible, this attention to rural background has proved extremely valuable as far as it goes. But what of those newly proletarianized workers without a tradition of moral economy? The William Roseberry essay poses this question and addresses a central issue confronting students of proletarianizing population in many countries of the modern world.

Perhaps just as important to the evolution of worker protest as the culture of rural society was the nature of those rural and urban institutions that organized the movement of workers to the city. If the influence of rural ideologies on the labor movement cannot be taken for granted, a new alternative arises; it is possible that formally organized rural political movements acting through migration networks can influence urban working-class life. Much recent research suggests that the countryside provided far more than a cultural background for industrial workers. For decades, and perhaps for generations, workers continued to maintain ties with the countryside. Particularly in modern Third World nations, changes in political attitudes in the countryside continued to influence class formation among workers already established in the city. Conversely, the spread of militant ideas among workers and news of urban unrest could also have considerable effect on rural dwellers. In order to understand the circumstances under which political influences moved from country to city or the reverse, it is necessary first to explore the links by which workers moved to the industrial city, or the mechanisms through which they were recruited to urban industrial work. The essays by Leslie Page Moch, Florencia Mallon, and Sharon Stichter examine migration networks and suggest that the structure and form of migration networks were compelling determinants of migrant identification and consciousness in the urban community.

The close ties with the country maintained by so many urban proletarians raise key questions concerning the timing of class formation. A growing accumulation of evidence suggests that the rise of factory industry and the urbanization it produced did not so much result in the creation of a proletarian labor force as in its redistribution.[2] The number of proletarians, both in agriculture and in domestic industry, had expanded dramatically in the several centuries prior to the Industrial Revolution; these workers formed the basis of the early industrial proletariat. The articles by Louise Tilly and Flemming Mikkelsen deal primarily with the timing of class formation and with its consequences for working-class protest.

The transiency of the industrial worker is another aspect of the question concerning the timing of class formation. Everyone is familiar with the prevalence of child labor in the Industrial Revolution, and yet little has been done to find out what happened to child laborers when they were too old to work in the factory. Doubtless, answers to these questions differ greatly from one industrial region to another, but in some areas of Europe, children and young women may well have returned to rural homes to take up agricultural responsibilities as they grew older. When European labor historians look at industrial workers in the city perhaps they too easily assume that these workers represent the milieu from which the future industrial working class would be formed. More work needs to be done to ascertain the moment at which unskilled workers began to settle down permanently in the city and to have children destined for urban industry. The essay by Michael Hanagan deals primarily with this question of the formation of a permanent proletariat that expected to spend its entire worklife within urban industry.

A further reason for our contributors' interest in structural factors is the emergence of new ways to conceptualize structural influence on labor history. For a long time, the only detailed studies of the Industrial Revolution concentrated on England; now we have a rich body of scholarly literature about the onset of industrial transformation in most of Western and Central Europe. Now little remains of Arnold Toynbee's and Paul

Mantoux's initial vision of an "Industrial Revolution"—the rapid succession of commercial, agricultural, and industrial transformations resulting in the sudden appearance of a newly created proletariat.[3] Such scholars as Franklin Mendels and David Levine have traced the lineage of the industrial proletariat far back in history and have emphasized the disparate origins of the modern proletariat.[4] Still other scholars, including Raphael Samuel and Bruce Laurie, have emphasized the continuing importance of traditional methods of workplace organization and of artisanal influence well into the twentieth century.[5]

While recent students of European and United States history have challenged time-honored interpretations of the Industrial Revolution, other scholars have questioned whether models of European and North American industrial transformation, no matter how accurate, can ever have wide application to contemporary countries undergoing economic change. Andre Gunder Frank and Eric Wolf are among the best known scholars who early challenged the application of European and North American models to other continents, but this position has gained considerable support from the somewhat different arguments advanced by scholars such as Immanuel Wallerstein and Daniel Chirot.[6]

All these theorists have distinguished between those "core" nations of Western Europe and North America that industrialized in the early and mid-nineteenth century and the "non-core" nations that have attempted industrialization in the late nineteenth or twentieth century. They have all argued that the nature and pace of economic change in non-core countries will be different than in the core countries of advanced capitalism; the implications of these differences for the development of labor movements in the non-core countries remain a subject of considerable debate.[7] Also, we were fortunate to discover work under way on the question of *failed* proletarianization. More clearly than when we began assembling this collection, we can see now that workforce disintegration or successful resistance to proletarianization provides a valuable vantage point for discerning essential elements in the proletarianization process.

The major theme of this book, provided by the rich regional and national studies, is that it mattered a great deal to the emergence of an urban labor movement whether the workers came from one kind of rural environment or another, whether they came to the city by bands organized at the village level or under the auspices of private recruiters, or whether they planned to stay the whole of their lives or for only a few short years in urban industry.

Three questions run through this collection, and every contribution responds to at least one. First, where did the workforce come from and what was the effect of its origins on the evolution of worker militancy? Second, how did the proletarianizing population get to the industrializing city, and what was the effect of migration patterns on worker militancy? Third, what did proletarianizing populations find when they arrived in the industrializing city, and what factors influenced migrant workers to settle down permanently and make the factory town their home? Each one of these questions concerns a crucial stage in the formation of a *permanent* proletariat and will be discussed separately. Quite often, answers to these questions differ between the countries of advanced capitalism and those countries undergoing industrial transformation in the twentieth century.

First, let us consider how those areas that sent migrants to the industrializing city shaped the migrants' response to their new environment. Flemming Mikkelsen's comparative discussion of Denmark, Sweden, and Norway presents a version of the rural-to-urban transition that is similar to the picture drawn by Karl Marx for England. In the cases of the three Scandinavian countries, evidence suggests that landlords had already created a substantial agricultural proletariat in the seventeenth and eighteenth centuries. The advent of industrialization in Scandinavian cities drew agricultural proletarians to the city to become industrial proletarians. In these countries, proletarianization was a separate and prior step to membership in the urban industrial workforce. The process described by Mikkelsen probably is the quickest and most efficient manner of capitalist proletarianization. It was, so to speak, the "straight road," but it was not the only road.

A look at other essays reveals that there were many other paths that led to the formation of an urban industrial proletariat. In many countries, capitalism had not prepared an agricultural proletariat in the countryside before it took root in the cities. In most of the countries or regions under study here, for example, the countryside is dominated by petty-commodity production or by non-capitalist modes of production. Typically, the urban industrial proletariat had to be created out of a non- or quasi-proletarian rural workforce.

Recruitment of proletarians in rural regions often took place in areas in crisis. Early industrialization was a grim business almost everywhere; the attractions of the industrializing city exerted a very weak influence on those able to survive in the countryside. In the early period of industrialization, where rural non-proletarians had the choice, they generally elected to remain outside the industrial proletariat. Barbara Weinstein offers an example of such resistance in the 1920s and 1930s Amazon, where rubber tappers had the opportunity to become proletarians in Fordlandia. By themselves, the attractions of steady pay and regular work proved unappealing. Where resources such as land were not strapped to the limit and where the continued expansion of independent production were still possible (as in the Amazon region), there was not an economic or a social basis for the creation of an industrial workforce.

Variations in the nature of the rural crisis that produced proletarians may play an important role in determining the political issues that mobilize industrial workers. Rural crisis could be a product of the breakup of communal institutions such as peasant villages or tribal societies, but also it commonly was a product of the dissolution of individualist economic structures, such as small-scale commercial farming or domestic industry. Attempts to transform rural areas were not important solely to the extent that they produced industrial workers; differences in the cultural background of migrant workers might also have influenced the development of urban protest movements in positive or negative ways. William Roseberry's study of Venezuela, for example, makes it clear that the rural experience of migrant workers did not always provide a training in communal values that yielded a critique of the capitalism found in the city. Roseberry contrasts the Venezuelan rural experience with that of the Vietnamese peasants studied by James Scott. Addressing a very different setting, the peasantry of Southeast Asia, James Scott has argued that violations of the norms of a peasant moral economy provided the basis for peasant grievances and rebellion.[8] Scholars such as Scott have helped historians to understand how different varieties of communal tradition have influenced mass protest; the moral economy school, however, leaves us totally unprepared for occasions where proletarians emerge from pre-existing capitalistic economic formations. Roseberry's essay reminds us forcefully of the diverse origins of the proletariat and of the need for careful examination of the material origins of the working class in each setting.

Attempts among historians of Venezuela to uncover a "pre-industrial" tradition of communal values immediately prior to the growth of an urban proletariat are likely to prove fruitless. The proximate background of much of the Venezuelan urban population is coffee growing, in fact a highly competitive, profit-oriented, individualist agricultural occupation. Longing for the *gemeinschaft* of rural life on the part of Venezuelan city dwellers is a product of urban nostalgia. Because the basic premises on which this nostalgia is formed are myths, Roseberry argues that such shapeless sentimentality can easily be translated into conservative apologetics to cover up the capitulation of past governments to foreign economic pressures and narrow economic interests. As Roseberry points out, however, the agrarian community is not the only source available for critiquing existing society; for example, the socialist ideal is capable of mobilizing workers and providing a critique of capitalism, even when that ideal is not reinforced by a rural communitarian tradition. Simultaneously with capitalist penetration, new traditions of resistance developed that provide a far more useful framework than a mythical rural past, not only in moral terms, but for political action as well.

The case of Venezuela, like that of other non-core nations, poses challenging problems for students of proletarianization influenced by the classics of labor history; differences in the economic and political background between the core and non-core nations produced distinctive patterns of social solidarity and political organization in the non-core city. The background to industrialization differs in three important ways between the core and non-core nations. First of all, in the non-core nation the sector or sectors undergoing industrialization are more isolated from the overall national economy than was the case in the core nations of the nineteenth century. Second, the industrialized sectors of national economies of non-core nations have readily identifiable characteristics; these sectors are dependent on foreign capital and more subject to fluc-tuation than was the case among core nations. Finally, the rural crises that produce proletarianization in the non-core nations are more im-mediately linked to legal enactments and to national-level political de-cisions than was the case in the core nations of the nineteenth century. Let us look at these points separately.

The major reason for the economic isolation of the industrializing sectors in non-core nations is the absence of the systems of domestic industry and artisanal production that flourished in eighteenth- and nineteenth-century Europe. Even in the early nineteenth century, France, Scandinavia, and the German states produced a wide range of basic and luxury goods. Labor historians are always reminding us that the largest proportion of commodity production in nineteenth-century Europe was going on in sectors outside the coal, iron, and steel complex of the early Industrial Revolution.[9] In none of these countries or regions was com-modity production as closely identified with a small handful of goods in the way that Venezuela, Peru, Brazil, and Kenya are associated with such commodities as oil, minerals, rubber, and coffee. In the non-core coun-tries studied by Roseberry, Mallon, Weinstein, and Stichter, the prole-tarianized workforce is concentrated in a handful of large industries that produce for a worldwide market.

Numerous scholarly studies have revealed reasons for the weakness of the petty-commodity production sector in non-core countries. First of all (and most obviously), in the period before they were exposed to Western products, many countries had not developed the extensive de-gree of petty-commodity production that had emerged in the West. Other countries that possessed extensively developed petty-commodity production (such as China and much of Malaysia) perhaps lacked the institutional framework that might have produced a "breakthrough" to capitalist production. In any case, the result of this failure was what Clifford Geertz has labeled "involution," an endless refinement and in-tensification of petty-commodity production that entailed a *breakdown* of capital accumulation as the division of labor became ever more elabo-rate.[10] Another powerful cause for the failure of capitalism to develop outside Europe was simply the success of capitalism in Europe. Once Europeans had advanced to the stage of capitalist development, they worked to destroy the ladder on which others might climb to reach their newly achieved position. The flow of cheap European industrial products to the colonial or semi-colonial market destroyed or transformed petty-commodity production in these markets.

Of great significance in the understanding of European development is the dramatic industrial transformation that occurred before the outbreak of the Industrial Revolution in the nineteenth century. From their meager beginnings in the fifteenth century, the forces of petty-commodity production reached such a highly developed state that they helped to promote a capital accumulation sufficient to permit full-scale industrialization. The "putting-out" system and the growing subordination of rural artisans to urban-centered merchants, two trends produced by the leasing of looms and other instruments of production, already had broken the bonds of simple-commodity production before the introduction of new technologies. In the non-core nations, both independent and colonized, the occupations of those engaged in domestic industry and in urban artisanal occupations were destroyed without these people ever having had the opportunity to join an urban proletariat. Often, this process inadvertently reinforced the power of non-capitalist modes of production within the non-core economy.

Not only was the industrial sector more isolated in the non-core nations, but the characteristics of the industrial sector differed between core and non-core nations. In this collection, for example, the essays dealing with the core countries focus on workers who produce textiles, machine products, iron, and coal. In contrast, the essays concentrating on the non-core countries show workers who produce oil, coffee, rubber, and copper. Because of the inadequacies of their internal economic development or of the influence of European capitalism on their economies, nations outside the core (such as Brazil, Peru, and Venezuela) that were able to retain their political independence seldom were able to retain control over their own economies. The very fact that they managed to retain their political independence made them risky investments.

Foreign investment was attracted especially to high-profit areas in colonized non-core nations such as Kenya. Core investment occurred particularly frequently in industries that depended on the exploitation of natural resources or in plantation agriculture; but such investment excluded long-term, capital-intensive assets. The specialized sectors that underwent development resulted in the "boom-bust" cycle of development. When international demand collapsed in a leading industrial sector, the alternative sources of industrial employment necessary to absorb the unemployed were extremely limited. Work for the unemployed could be found only in agriculture or in another specialized industrial sector, if more than one existed in a non-core country. In such countries, the massive recruitment of labor from one failing specialized industrial sector to another growing specialized industrial sector occurs frequently. The instability of the labor force revealed in the essays by Roseberry and Mallon is bound up with the conditions of non-core industrial development.

Besides economic factors such as the isolation of the industrial sector in the non-core nations and its special composition, the primacy of politics in the proletarianization process in non-core nations needs to be noted. Where rural dwellers in Scandinavia, Germany, France, and Italy might have seen the pressure of heartless entrepreneurs and ruthless city dwellers as the driving force behind their proletarianization, country people in Venezuela, Kenya, Peru, and Brazil were more likely to see the heavy hand of colonial administrators, foreign investors, and *comprador* governments. In those countries where capitalism came from outside, the transformation of the countryside occurred in a far more politicized context than it did in the countries of today's advanced capitalism.

In some cases the state's active role in proletarianization has politicized rural populations; in these cases it is not memories of a traditional moral economy, but organized rural political movements that have exerted influence on urban working-class politics. Outside the advanced industrial countries, rural protest often has been the cutting edge of resistance to capitalism. In these cases, not simply the moral economy, but powerful movements opposing capitalism and colonialism, have been one legacy from the countryside to the urban working class. Labor movements have sometimes assimilated political lessons from insurgent rural dwellers, and working-class militancy has followed in the wake of rural protest. Typically, in nineteenth-century industrializing Europe, the direction of influence was the other way; but even in Europe, the ability of workers to coordinate and form coalitions with rural rebels surely was one important reason for the massive character of popular protest in the first half of the nineteenth century.[11]

Marxist historians always have stressed the importance of politics in proletarianization. Even in Western Europe, capitalist industrialization required a redefinition of property rights that necessitated state support for proletarianization. But outside the countries of advanced capitalism, almost all scholars admit the political aspects of proletarianization and that it is its social and economic aspects that require more attention. Outside the West, native capitalists neither expected nor depended on proletarian observance of bourgeois law. In those newly industrializing states that maintained their formal political independence, foreign supplies of capital backed up their investments with military pressure on existing governments. In the colonies, administrators legislated rural economic revolutions aimed expressly at proletarianizing the rural population just as surely as, but far more consciously than, the British enclosure acts of the nineteenth century.

It is no accident that African labor historians have provided some of the most interesting writings on the proletarianization process. As the study by Sharon Stichter shows, the African continent became a laboratory for experiments in proletarianization. The continent was dominated by colonial administrators, men who felt little need to explain themselves to the populations they governed. Also, the late date of African colonization and the identity of the colonial powers were of crucial significance. The colonization of Africa came after the Industrial Revolution in Europe and the creation of a modern proletariat there; obviously, conditions in Europe strongly influenced the aims of European administrators. Moreover, the major African colonial powers—England, France, Belgium, and (far behind) Germany—also were major industrial powers that wanted to integrate the colonies into their home-based economy.

Outside the advanced industrial nations physical coercion seems to have been a very important force in labor recruitment. In Kenya, railway officials introduced the *corvée* to obtain a labor force. New legislation forced workers to stay on the job, and village councils of elders cooperated with authorities in locating deserting workers and sending them back to work. In the central highlands of Peru, indebted peasants were forced into the mines in order to work off their debts. In these cases, rural dwellers found themselves suddenly thrust into an unfamiliar world of urban industrial labor in which few felt motivated to participate. In the case of indebted peasants, the best they could do was to preserve their position on the land. They could not better it. Most of these laborers thought more about escaping back to the countryside than about trying to ameliorate their position on the job. In any case, this legally decreed process of proletarianization helped increase the hostility to colonialism and foreign capitalism among many sectors of the rural population.

If their dependence on the countryside renders urban migrants in non-core countries impervious to urban ideologies, it can still contribute to their politicization by making them subject to movements of rural protest. In Kenya, Stichter shows that a rural protest movement, the Mau Mau, exerted influence on the unskilled urban working class; yet, in Europe, the frustration and hatred that erupted occasionally among workers in domestic industry in the countryside reached the city only indirectly. In Europe, memories of a rural moral economy may sometimes have helped to shape the political outlook of urban working-class movements, but rural protest movements never directly affected the shaping of urban politics. European historians often lament the inability of socialist movements to provide leadership for such rural protest movements as the Italian fasci of 1893, the Silesian weavers of 1844, the rural insurgents in southern France in 1851; but they seldom inquire why these rural movements had so little influence on the urban working class.

European labor historians do not expect rural political movements to influence urban political movements, but labor historians in the non-core countries are often confronted with this circumstance. How can we explain the divergent historical experiences at the root of this historiographical difference? Here we want to look at the second of our themes, how the workers got to the city; it is the nature of the migration process itself that requires investigation. Unskilled workers will seldom leave the home community, however impoverished or desolate, without some prior link to their new destination. After all, at home prospective migrants have at least some claims on family, kin, friends, or community. However inadequate, something is better than nothing, and in an unfamiliar city migrants will likely fear that they will be surrounded by hostile strangers. Indeed, such fears often have justification, despite much evidence of existing communities willing to embrace strangers.

The importance of "chain migration" in both core and non-core nations means that the ongoing ties between rural sending areas and the industrial "receiving" areas need careful attention. Chain migration was a form of migration that made aid, information, and encouragement available in the industrial city to kin or fellow villagers who migrated there.[12] In Europe, the continuing ties between city and countryside may have served mainly to coordinate protests in the countryside with struggles launched in the urban centers. Outside Europe, the possibility that urban workers might be influenced by rural insurrection loomed larger.

The chapter by Leslie Page Moch presents a classic example of chain migration among industrial workers in Western Europe. Membership in the chain linking rural migrants and urban workers brought advantages, sometimes substantial ones, and it helped to determine the urban position occupied by migrant groups. In the early twentieth century, rural migrants poured into the southern French city of Nîmes. Although most observers probably would not have distinguished the physical setting or the occupational structure of the Cévenol villages from those in the Lozère, the migrants from the two regions found very different employment in Nîmes. The Cévenols ended up in white-collar jobs, the Lozèriens in blue-collar jobs. The basic explanation for this difference is less one of skill (although Cévenol Protestants were somewhat more literate), and more one of chain migration networks. In the past, Cévenol Protestants had established links within the white-collar workforce. As new migrants from these villages came, their friends and relatives found what space for them they could. Lozèriens had the same urge to help neighbors and kin, but their networks were blue-collar ones. Thus, identical patterns of migration yielded very different social results.

The very frequency of chain migration among unskilled and semi-skilled migrants to the industrializing city means that enduring channels of communication between sending areas and receiving areas usually exist; less certain are the nature and the direction of the communications exchanged. For example, under what circumstances might we expect rural values and attitudes to be transmitted to urban migrants? Under what circumstances might urban attitudes be conveyed back to the sending area? In Western Europe during the Industrial Revolution, the role of the worker in rural industry deserves particularly careful attention. The Hanagan, Moch, and Tilly essays all show the importance of rural industry in the formation of the European industrial proletariat. In the case of cottage industry, the interaction of the forces of rural economic crisis and expanding urban opportunity was particularly intimate. In Europe, the initial industrialization that populated the cities often destroyed jobs in cottage industry. While the jobs that rural workers lost rarely were the same as those they found in the city to which they migrated, the connection between rural push and urban pull was direct.

The essay by Michael Hanagan suggests that urban workers with a background in domestic industry who returned to their rural roots in time of economic crisis may have helped ignite rebellion in the countryside. He shows that the presence of workers in rural industry in the Stéphanois region of France created the possibility for a sharing of collective interests between city and country. In 1848 in Saint-Bonnet-le-Château, the demands of urban workers penetrated into the countryside, as migrant workers from Saint-Etienne returned to seek shelter in the rural industrial milieu from which they had come. The presence of domestic laborers in the countryside provided a vehicle for the transmission of urban influence. Although the great tragedy of the 1848 revolution was that it took the countryside many months to coordinate itself with the revolutionary demands advanced in the cities, the presence of a large rural industrial force may explain at least partially why the years between 1848 and 1851 witnessed the last French uprisings in which urban and rural protestors managed any coordination at all. After 1851, rural and urban protest would follow different rhythms.

Outside Europe, however, the rural world could exert even greater influence on the urban world of the industrial working classes. The Peruvian miners studied by Florencia Mallon present a particularly interesting example of the interplay of rural and urban networks. In this case, chain migration became institutionalized in the recruitment policies of the coal company. Systems of recruitment such as the *enganche* or the *contradori* bound up village loyalties with workplace loyalties. Since many workers planned to retire to their villages, and since committees to aid those remaining in sending villages were an important mining community social group, the ties between mining community and village were continually reinforced. When bad times hit the mining community, these ties proved very useful. Laid-off miners or those miners fired for labor militancy could expect to find memories of them still fresh in the villages from which they had come.

The Stichter essay shows a different dynamic in the relationship between temporary migration and militancy in Kenya, with the strong influence of Mau Mau protest among unskilled and semi-skilled urban workers. Many skilled workers long resident in the city shunned Mau Mau because they feared that membership in a revolutionary movement would have a deleterious effect on their painfully constructed union movement. Here, temporary migrants had less concern; many expected to return permanently to the countryside and identified with the deep commitment to the rebellion by their rural relations. In this case, and undoubtedly in others, unskilled and industrial workers received an impetus to militancy from the countryside.

Whenever urban migrants had reason to suppose that their eventural destiny was to return to the countryside, it might be expected that they would pay particular attention to maintaining their ties there. We have good reason to suspect that the ties of unskilled and semi-skilled workers to the rural community might be closer in modern non-core nations undergoing industrial change than was the case in Western Europe or North America. Indeed, the precarious condition of industrial employment in many modern-day countries has reinforced the workers' need to maintain ties to their village and to attempt to maintain their esteem in the eyes of acquaintances there. The cyclical economic fluctuations that hit non-core economies with such devastating impact meant that workers in the non-core countries were especially exposed to unemployment and that the opportunities for finding alternative industrial employment were not very good.

Several interesting arguments appear in this collection that show why revolutionary movements have a greater tendency to flow from country to city in the modern world than was the case in nineteenth-century Europe. Now more than ever, the connection between rural and urban worlds is a two-way street. Some rural migrants bring revolutionary ideas with them to the city, and in some cases the unskilled segment of the industrial working class may be the most revolutionary section of the urban economy precisely because it is so imperfectly integrated into the city and so closely linked to the rural world. Finally, the influence of domestic industry in promoting solidarity between protestors in the city and the country may apply in the European case. This difference between Europe and the rest of the world may be explained by Europe's rich heritage of petty-commodity production and the multiple links between city and country.

The heritage of petty-commodity production is of key importance in understanding why urban labor movements played such an active role in class formation in European countries. The nature of the crisis in rural domestic industry helps explain why the rural protest had so little influence on urban workers, and the crisis of urban artisans explains why militant political leadership could be found in the city.

Typically, in Europe, rural protest followed from urban unrest, or it occurred separately; in general, rural movements did not influence urban politics. In time of crisis, workers who returned to rural families may have helped coordinate militant activity across town and country, but European industrial workers relatively rapidly forged a class identity separate from that of the rural population. The militance occasionally demonstrated by cottage laborers in the countryside generally vanished when they arrived in the city; rural rebellion did not greatly influence urban class formation. Louise Tilly's study of Milan and Lyon shows that the presence of large numbers of former domestic workers in the urban workforce hardly served to radicalize the local population. Indeed, the reverse was the case. The entry of large numbers of domestic workers into a newly emerging industrial proletariat generally entailed a decline of urban militancy, at least for a substantial period of time. Why? Certainly not because the domestic workers were stunned by their initial contact with industrial work: the rural worker in domestic industry was well prepared for the urban industrial world. While cottage industry ran the gamut from small, independent producers to dispersed proletarian production, the clear drift was toward proletarianized production. The domestic laborer entering nineteenth-century urban industry typically had been employed in industries with a very extensive division of labor. Had the rural worker not been forced to move to the tick of the factory clock or the rhythm of the morning whistle, he or she might often have found the tempo of work governed by the fear of starvation. The former domestic industrialist employed at factory labor was not likely to feel as ill at ease in the factory environment as a worker without domestic experience.

In contrast to the skilled artisans who might be his or her neighbors, what the domestic worker turned industrial proletarian lacked was bargaining strength and membership in the urban community. Factory workers generally lacked skills that might have enabled them to stand together in an urban labor market flooded with other unskilled domestic workers like themselves. Also, it took time to establish social contacts in the industrial city, to find out the cafes, taverns, laundries, and fountains where other workers congregated, to establish the credit at local stores that gave workers margin to maneuver, and to get to know other workers in the shop.

Lack of skill and the time needed to form new social ties were not, however, the only explanations for the quiescence of the new workforce. Many domestic workers desperately needed to make good in the city because they could not go home again. The long-term decline of rural industry meant that little chance existed for the cottage laborer ever to recover a position in the countryside. The rural industrialist who migrated to the city was in a position to help other fellow domestic laborers come to the city later on, but seldom were the rural dwellers in a position to help the urban worker to return permanently to the countyside. In some ways, domestic industry helped prepare a capitalist workforce for factory industry in the same ways as did the creation of a rural agricultural proletariat. Both domestic industrialist and rural proletarian learned the discipline of capitalist industry in the countryside. Domestic industry may have been even more effective in forming a factory proletariat, because, unlike rural proletarians or tribalists, domestic industrialists knew that they could not go home again.

While the quiescent migrant from domestic industry explains the feeble influence of rural protest on European workers, the key factor in the dynamic labor movements formed in nineteenth-century European cities was the urban artisans. These urban skilled workers possessed strong organization and a wide range of skills. When threatened with the introduction of machines, these workers possessed a unity and a determination that served as a basis for militant actions. The battles between urban artisans and urban capitalists were unavoidable because the mechanization of industry was in the mainstream of capitalist development in the nineteenth century. Everywhere in Europe, these artisans led the militant struggles and played key roles in the formation of mass urban labor movements.[13] The non-existence of urban artisans or their early destruction in non-core countries is surely one of the most important reasons for the failure of independent labor movements to develop in the non-core countries and for the impact of rural protest on urban protest.

In Europe, a key issue on the agenda of class formation is the examination of the conditions under which militant urban artisans were willing and able to coalesce with less politically active, industrial workers who had recently migrated to the city. The essays in this collection provide new insight into this topic by exploring the circumstances in which the industrial working class settled in the city and became ready to respond to the political initiatives of artisans. The urban socialist movements described in the essays by Moch, Hanagan, Mikkelsen, and Tilly presume large numbers of urban workers who identified themselves as lifetime factory proletarians. Permanent urban residence marks a definitive break with the rural countryside and a recognition of permanent membership in the urban polis. After all, the benefits of participation in urban politics and joint action with urban artisans might depend heavily on whether workers viewed their stay in the city as temporary or permanent. While the political consequences of breaking ties with the countryside and identifying with the urban scene are not necessarily radicalizing, that process did signal an important change in orientation. It meant the true beginnings of the working class that modern labor historians study.

In summary, this collection presents a new way of conceptualizing how rural society and migration shaped the process of class formation. The comparison of proletarianization in core and non-core nations shows that some of our common assumptions about the relationship between communal tradition and political militancy leave out of consideration a large proportion of the migrants who enter the urban workforce. The extent to which the development of a socialist ideology relies on a prior schooling in communitarian traditions such as that of the moral economy seems doubtful, and the question of the relationship between rural values and urban political movements appears in a new light. A look outside Europe shows that the influence of *rural ideologies* on industrial workers becomes problematic, while the influence of *rural political movements* on urban labor movements becomes indisputable. The comparison between core and non-core nations also underlines the need to look at the nature of the social linkages between city and country. Historians in Western Europe have generally taken for granted that, in some form or other, the industrial working classes are the major actors in industrializing society; but elsewhere politicized rural movements have stimulated the growth and shaped the direction of the urban working-class movement. An understanding of migration patterns and the economic situation of sending and receiving communities can help historians understand why political influence has passed exclusively from city to country in the West and why the political road between city and country has been a two-way street outside the West.

Finally, a comparison between core and non-core nations highlights some neglected aspects of the proletarianization process in Europe. The comparison emphasizes the uniqueness of developed petty-commodity production in Europe and helps historians understand how the heritage of domestic industry and urban artisanal production distinctively molded the course of the European labor movement. The scholars who have contributed to this collection will themselves pursue these exciting new areas, but they also issue an appeal to others to join them in researching and in discussing these aspects of class formation.

NOTES

1. E. P. Thompson, *The Making of the English Working Class* (New York: Vintage Books, 1963). For some comments on Thompson's work, see Perry Anderson, *Arguments within English Marxism* (London: New Left Books, 1980); Craig Calhoun, *The Question of Class Struggle: Social Foundations of Popular Radicalism during the Industrial Revolution* (Chicago: University of Chicago Press, 1982); and Ellen Kay Trimberger, "E. P. Thompson: Understanding the Process of History," in *Vision and Method in Historical Sociology*, ed. Theda Skocpol (Cambridge, England: Cambridge University Press, 1984), pp. 211–243.

2. See Yves Lequin, *Les ouvriers de la région lyonnaise*, 2 vols. (Lyon: Presses Universitaires de Lyon, 1977); and Charles Tilly, "Flows of Capital and Forms of Industry in Europe, 1500–1900," *Theory and Society* 12 (1983): 123–142.

3. David Levine, *Family Formation in an Age of Nascent Capitalism* (New York: Academic Press, 1977); and Franklin F. Mendels, "Proto-Industrialization: The First Phase of Industrialization," *Journal of Economic History*, 32:1 (1972): 241–261.

4. Peter Kriedte et al., *Industrialization before Industrialization: Rural Industry in the Genesis of Capitalism* (Cambridge, England: Cambridge University Press, 1981).

5. Raphael Samuel, "Workshop of the World: Steam Power and Hand Technology in Mid-Victorian Britain," *History Workshop*, Issue 3 (Spring 1977): 6–72.

6. Immanuel Wallerstein, *The Origins of the European World Economy in the Sixteenth Century* (New York: Academic Press, 1979); and Daniel Chirot, *Social Change in the Twentieth Century* (New York: Harcourt Brace Jovanovich, 1977).

7. Immanuel Wallerstein, *The Modern World System II: Mercantilism and the Consolidation of the European World Economy, 1600–1750* (New York: Academic Press, 1980). For some important and telling criticisms of the "dependency theorists" see Robert Brenner, "Agrarian Class Structure and Economic Development in Pre-Industrial Europe," *Past and Present*, 70 (1976): 30–74; and idem, "The Origins of Capitalist Development: A Critique of Neo-Smithian Marxism," *New Left Review* n. 104 (1977): 25–92. See also Frederick Cooper, "The Problem of Slavery in African Studies," *Journal of African History*, 20: (1979): 103–125, and idem, "Africa and the World Economy," *African Studies Review*, 24:2–3 (1981): 1–93.

8. James C. Scott, *The Moral Economy: Rebellion and Subsistence in Southeast Asia* (New Haven: Yale University Press, 1976).

9. Besides Samuels, "Workshop of the World," see also François Caron, *An Economic History of Modern France* (New York: Columbia University Press, 1979); Tihomir Markovitch, "Le revenu industriel et artisanal sous la monarchie de Juillet et le Second Empire," *Economies et sociétés*, ser. AF, vol. 4 (Apr. 1967); and Patrick O'Brien and Caglar Keyder, *Economic Growth in Britain and France* (London: Routledge and Kegan Paul, 1978).

10. See Mark Elvin, *The Pattern of the Chinese Past* (Stanford: Stanford University Press, 1973); and Clifford Geertz, *Agricultural Involution: The Process of Ecological Change in Indonesia* (Berkeley: University of California Press, 1963).

"Petty-commodity production" takes place when each producer owns the requisite means of production for the performance of his labor.

11. See John Merriman, *The Agony of the Republic: The Repression of the Left in Revolutionary France, 1848–1851* (New Haven: Yale University Press, 1978); and Charles Tilly, *The Vendée* (Cambridge, Mass.: Harvard University Press, 1964). See also Tony Judt, *Socialism in Provence: A Study in the Origins of the Modern French Left 1871–1914* (Cambridge, England: Cambridge University Press, 1979). While Judt stresses the independence of his peasant socialists, still it is an urban industrial doctrine to which they have pledged their allegiance.

12. Charles Tilly, "Migration in Modern European History," in *Human Migration, Patterns and Policies*, ed. William H. McNeill and Ruth S. Adams, pp. 48–72 (Bloomington: Indiana University Press, 1978).

13. See Michael Hanagan, *The Logic of Solidarity: Artisans and Industrial Workers in Three French Towns, 1871–1914* (Urbana: University of Illinois Press, 1980).

2
Workers and Industrialization in Scandinavia, 1750–1940

Flemming Mikkelsen

Between 1750 and 1940 Denmark, Sweden, and Norway slowly evolved from agrarian forms of production, including recurring subsistence crises, and feudal conditions to an industrial mode of production combined with an emerging democratic welfare state. This transition can be neither described nor explained as a gradual, continuous process of modernization; rather, it was characterized by crisis, class conflicts, and changing constellations of power. Capitalism and statebuilding as dominant forms of economy and politics inevitably changed the structure of production and class positions, including the internal forms of social organization under which people mobilized and protested to defend and to advance their own interests.

The following analysis of similarities and contrasts among these countries relies primarily on newly developed demographic, economic, and social-historical literature. There are strengths and weaknesses in this chapter that reflect differences in states of research of the three countries. In addition, this chapter is an effort to construct hypotheses, ask questions, and connect links according to a general synthesis even where the empirical basis is thin or, at times, lacking.

The first section is a descriptive overview of the basic demographic, economic, and political stages of development throughout the period. This is followed by an explanation of how capital concentration and resource mobilization changed profoundly the fundamental structure of people's everyday lives—how they ate, looked for employment and worked, married, raised families, and even how they related to other people. The third section, "From Social Protest to Class Conflict," takes these problems a step further to focus on how oppressed groups of people managed to protect collectively and to support their demands against opposing interests, groups, and classes in a way which, over time, changed the structure of production and power in the society.

DEMOGRAPHIC, ECONOMIC, AND POLITICAL TRENDS IN DENMARK, SWEDEN, AND NORWAY, 1800–1940

The populations in Denmark, Sweden, and Norway rose respectively from 1.4, 3.5, and 1.4 million in 1850 to 2.8, 5.5, and 2.4 million in 1910, and to 3.8, 6.3, and 2.9 million in 1939.[1] At the same time, they had passed from a condition of high birthrate and high mortality—both on the order of 30–40 per thousand—to a situation where both of these magnitudes had fallen to around 15–20 per thousand for the birth rate and to around 10–15 per thousand for the death rate.[2]

The demographic transition, however, had not taken place at a smooth or uniform rate. Denmark's population growth was more gradual than those of the other Scandinavian countries. Influenced by the large waves of emigration that characterized the Swedish and Norwegian societies from the mid-1860s until around 1910, the growth rates in both Sweden and Norway fluctuated together; Danish emigration was of less importance.[3] The inter-war period bore witness to another problem, namely, a fall in the excess of births over deaths as the net reproduction rate fell below replacement level. The fall was most pronounced in Sweden but was also experienced by the other Scandinavian countries. Further differentiation between the countries can be found in their patterns of urbanization and occupational development (See Table 2.1). As early as 1800, Denmark had a sizeable urban population, and it maintained its comparative position throughout the period. Sweden's urban population increased relatively steadily up to the turn of the century, followed by strong growth, quite in contrast to the urbanization in Norway, which rose until about 1900 and thereafter stagnated.

This pattern of development repeats itself in the distribution of the labor force (see Table 2.2). Reasons for the clear differences in these nations between rural and urban areas and between primary, secondary, and tertiary occupational sectors relate to differences between the countries with regard to internal population movements and industrial development. The most pronounced structural change appeared in Sweden. Based on a predominant agrarian sector and some industrialization that occurred in small waves in 1850 and during the 1870s, the industrial breakthrough occurred around 1890 and lasted throughout the interwar period. The workforce was primarily employed in industry, but the service sector also expanded strongly. In contrast to Swedish industry, which was export-oriented and based on large production units, Danish industry produced in small units in order to provide the home market with consumer goods.

Year	Denmark	Sweden	Norway
1800	20.9	9.8	7.4
1835	20.8	9.7	10.9
1850	20.8	10.1	12.8
1860	23.6	11.3	14.5
1870	24.8	13.0	16.9
1880	28.1	15.1	20.0
1890	33.3	18.8	23.7
1900	38.3	21.5	28.2
1910	40.3	24.8	28.9
1920	43.2	29.5	29.8
1930	44.2	32.5	28.5
1940	47.7	37.4	28.6

Source: Stein Kuhnle: Patterns of Social and Political Mobilization (Lond. 1975), Table 3.

Table 2.1 Percentage of Total Population Living in Urban Areas in Denmark, Sweden, and Norway, 1800-1940

Except for some smaller leaps forward in the beginning of the 1870s and 1890s, the progress of Danish industry was very steady. For a long time, the workforce preserved its artisanal character structured accordingly to trade. Unlike Denmark, however, industrialization in Norway was characterized by peaks and troughs. The preliminary phase of industrialization took place during the 1890s, but it was between 1905 and 1920, with the construction of hydroelectrical and chemical industry in connection with its large resources of water power, that Norway first

Year	Agriculture			Industry/Handicraft			Otherwise		
1870	54	69	56	24	13	16	22	18	28
1880	52	65		24	15		24	20	
1890	47	62	49	26	19	22	27	19	29
1900	42	54	41	28	27	26	30	19	33
1910	37	44	39	28	29	25	35	27	36
1920	35	40	38	27	31	27	38	29	35
1930	35	37	37	27	31	25	38	32	38
1940	28	25	30	32	37	32	40	38	38

Source: W. Lafferty: Economic Development and the Response of Labor in Scandinavia (Oslo 1971), p. 43. The numbers on and after 1920 are from Kriser och Krispolitik (Uppsala 1974), Table I:4.

Table 2.2 The Occupational Distribution of the Population of Denmark, Sweden, and Norway (percentage)

actually developed heavy industry. However, Norwegian industry was highly capital intensive and did not demand a large workforce. Consequently, shipping, fishing, and forestry remained the most important occupations for the majority of the non-agrarian population during the inter-war period.

If we exclude consideration of social and popular movements and of the collective social protest as a sign of economic, social, and cultural struggles, the transition to a democratic political system in the three Nordic countries can be summed up by consideration of the events in Table 2.3.[4] In contrast to the pattern found in many other Western countries, voter turnout increased steadily throughout the period (although in an erratic pattern), as did the voter support for the Social

Events	Denmark	Sweden	Norway
In general universal suffrage for men	1849	1909	1898
Universal suffrage for men and women	1915	1920	1913
Democratization of the Upper House	1915	1920	--
Parliamentarism	1901	1917	1884
The foundation of the Social Democratic Party	1878	1889	1887
The first Parliamentary election with Social Democratic candidates	1879	1890	1894
The first election of a Social Democratic candidate to Parliament	1884	1896	1903
The first Social Democrats to take office in the Parliament	1916	1917	--
The first Social Democratic government	1924	1920	1935

Table 2.3 Events in the Transition to a Democratic Political System in Denmark, Sweden, and Norway

Democratic parties. Early on, the Danish Social Democratic party showed a steadily growing electoral support, followed by Norwegian and Swedish working-class parties. Around 1920, these parties were equal in size, with a backing of 32.6 percent in Denmark, 30.5 percent in Norway, and 36.1 percent in Sweden. Near the end of the period the Swedish Labor party had risen to 53.6 percent in 1936, followed by the Danish Social Dem-

ocratic party with 45.3 percent (in 1939) and the Norwegian Labor party
with 42.8 percent (in 1936).

So far, industrialization and its effect on the formation of the working
classes have been placed in a loose comparative historical perspective.
But for deeper insight into the relationship between industrialization,
workers' living conditions, societal position, and collective social protests,
we must search for more fundamental processes. Perhaps what ought
first to be considered is the process of proletarianization, that is, of
creating a class of people who do not control the means of production,
and who survive by selling their labor. Here, proletarianization will refer
to (a) the separation of workers from control of the means of production—expropriation—and (b) increasing dependence of workers on the
sale of their labor power—wagework.[5]

Charles Tilly considers proletarianization the most fundamental social
change in the Western world in the last few hundred years—more essential than related changes in income and social status. Proletarianization refers indirectly to an array of changes beginning in the agrarian
system of production and agrarian ownership of property, capital flow,
and new social and demographic structures, along with a characteristic
concentration of capital, which includes industrial production as well as
its spatial distribution. The historical version of this process addresses a
proletarianization that crystallized between the sixteenth century and
the middle of the nineteenth century in European rural villages and
rural areas, and that, during the nineteenth to twentieth centuries, would
be concentrated in the cities.

FROM PROLETARIANIZATION TO CLASS SOCIETY

Economic, demographic, and social changes in the agrarian society

Starting around 1730, proletarianization, population pressure, and
poverty characterized rural northwestern Europe from Norway to France
and from England to Schleswig-Holstein. At the end of the eighteenth
century and the beginning of the nineteenth century, the disorganization
of the estate system in Denmark caused the formation of a new social
class of independent peasants and an increase in the number of dependent crofters and landless day laborers. In Sweden and Norway a
similar and perhaps even more intense transformation took place. Between 1751 and 1850, the percentage of the male rural population that
was landless increased from 51 percent to 71 percent in Sweden. In
Norway, as the number of peasants went up by 27 percent, the proportion of crofters doubled and the number of landless tripled between
1801 and 1855.[6]

Between 1755 and 1850 this process resulted in the "emancipation" of the peasant, and class division within the rural society brought about a fall in real wages of landless laborers and peasants. These effects must be considered in relation to the enclosure movement, growing population pressure, and reorganization of the production and marketing systems. Several new case studies explain in detail the background of this transformation.

In Gørslev, a small, fairly typical Danish peasant village, the number of peasant households decreased from 20 to 18 between 1787 to 1880, while the group of landless farm workers and crofters rose from 38 households to 77.[7] The eighteenth century saw a unification of hitherto scattered farms around the estate (the main manor), as well as a standardization of the "copyhold" farms; that is, all the farms in the village were made fairly equal in size. This structural reorganization, implemented by the estate owner, would facilitate the later organization and common actions of the peasants. The growing population pressure intensified the antagonism between the landless and the property-holding peasants. In particular, the more fertile territory in East Jutland and the Islands (and of South Sweden and East Norway) would become the site of a widespread proletarianization of the agrarian population. Sale of labor power and exploitation of resources not utilized by the farmers often became the last possibility for the landless and smaller crofters to make a living.[8]

This growing class division spread to the peasant household. P. O. Christiansen writes that "although differences had long existed in the internal influence and prestige within the farm household as well as in the village, it was first in the period of growing 'farm capitalism' that the relation between the servant-group and the peasant family became crystallized in a clear 'them and us' relationship."[9] The peasant's participation in daily work changed: having once taken part in production on equal physical terms with the farm workers, he now took over a more administrative and controlling role. In a steadily growing market-oriented economy, the peasant learned to transform the rural "overpopulation" into his own profit in goods and money. Differences in work conditions, in standards of living, and in ways of life became more and more pronounced—dependence, exploitation, and exclusion followed this process of proletarianization.

One of the best and most thorough investigations of those conditions under which work itself was separated from the means of production is C. Winberg's microdemographic study of a district in the southwestern part of Sweden (Västergötland) between 1776 and 1883.[10] Winberg largely rejects the theory that the increase in the number of landless was due to high rates of reproduction—their birthrate was too low. Clearly, it was more closely related to widespread social mobility. In 1850, 40 percent of the heads of landless households were of peasant origin, while only 20 percent of all peasants were recruited from the landless rural population.

In some locations this reorganization gave rise as well to a new organization of work, the so-called statar-system, and with it a new group of settled, landless farm workers (the "statars," who were often paid in kind), that amounted to nearly 4.2 percent of the agrarian population. According to Ingrid Eriksson and John Rogers, "the statar-system, as part of the proletarianization process, was the result of a conscious effort on the part of the large estate owners to create a landless proletariat which would provide cheap and efficient labor and which could be easily controlled."[11] In some other areas, however, it was not so much the alteration of the agrarian system of production—accomplished through the manipulation of the market by estate owners and farmers—that created a new stratum of dependent farm laborers, but industrial concentration in the sawmill industry (and, to a lesser degree, mining), which, during the 1850s in many locations, took over the ownership of large timber-producing areas. In this way, these industries secured for themselves a continuous supply of raw material *and* a fixed stock of workers from those former freeholders already settled in the area.[12]

Between the middle of the eighteenth and the end of the nineteenth century, all three Nordic countries underwent a transformation that resulted in the creation of a large landless proletariat. The various microdemographic investigations call attention to downward social mobility as the most important cause of this transformation. Out of necessity, and under pressure, the peasants sold their farms and became wage earners. Proletarianization did not immediately lead to poverty, however. Until the end of the eighteenth century, the differences in standards of living between small freeholders, crofters, and day laborers were not great, but soon thereafter profits began to increase, and the peasants and freeholders consolidated their economic, social, and political position.[13]

It was proletarianization that in the long run resulted in dependence, poverty, and involuntary mobility. Included among those opportunities which, in principle, were open to landless laborers were:

—emigration
—the primary rural labor market
—the industrial-rural labor market
—the urban labor market, and
—the industrial-urban labor market.

Correctly or not, many historians today perceive overseas emigration as having been the safety valve that saved the Nordic countries from widespread poverty and social unrest. It is evident that the impact of this large-scale emigration on the native population was considerable. Between 1864 and 1914, Norway lost close to 40 percent of its natural increase, compared with Sweden's 25 percent and Denmark's 10 percent. In the 1840s and 1850s, it was overwhelmingly peasants with small holdings who emigrated in families; later, from about the 1860s, single emigrants began to dominate the emigrant path, and most of them came from proletarianized population groups. Some of them returned and managed to establish themselves as independent peasants by means of accumulated capital.[14]

Some of the proletarianized farm laborers, as well as their daughters and sons, remained farm workers throughout their lives. Some worked as day laborers, *statare*, or farm servants, while others combined specialized local activities with farming to carve out a precarious niche for themselves. For instance, some farm laborers settled down in coastal areas, where they made a living as primitive fishermen supported by smallholdings. Workers who subsisted through such specialized local activities and seasonal work should be classified as belonging to a so-called dual economy. The sector in which the dual economy dominated was characterized by hidden unemployment and under-employment, with a marginal product of labor lower than the traditional or conventional wage and wage rate determined by tradition, not by the competitive market mechanism.[15]

Both Sweden and Norway had an extensive industry situated in rural districts,[16] while in Denmark the industrial-rural sector was of far less importance. In 1872, 22 percent of the industrial labor force was located in rural areas, with the majority in brickyards and limestone quarries.[17] Thus, in the case of Sweden and Norway, there is reason to treat industrialization as a process distinct from urbanization and to distinguish between an industrial-rural labor market and an industrial-urban labor market, in addition to a separate non-industrial labor market, particularly in the larger cities.

The rural-industrial community

The localization of industry in Norway and Sweden was determined first of all by motive power, labor supply, the market, and means of transport. Industrial expansion from around 1870 did not fundamentally change the pattern of localization. There were still good opportunities for smaller production units, but now new industries arose alongside the old. In Norway, the electrometallurgy and electrochemical industry established a foothold, while more diversified Swedish industry began in the countryside. The absolute number of workers employed in rural areas rose from 17,309 in 1870 to 223,000 in 1930 (corresponding to

38 and 49 percent, respectively, of the total industrial labor force in Sweden [no such numbers exist for Norway]). Many were employed in the expanding mining, wood, and lumber industries, which produced mainly for the export market and therefore were located near the large waterways and the coast. As so-called mill towns (*brukssamhälle*) (mainly in the paper and glass industries, the sawmill industry, and mining), the large factories had attached to themselves old traditions in the rural village. Their somewhat isolated situation and hierarchical composition changed as new technology was introduced and the workforce expanded.

An increasing need for services, entertainment, and outdoor recreation in the mill community attracted diverse groups—businessmen, hawkers, artisans, innkeepers, political and religious agitators, casual laborers, and others—who took up residence near the mill communities in what O. Hellspong has called a "complementary community," signifying a step toward decentralization of economic and social functions in the homogeneous and patriarchal local community. Examples of this include Borlänge outside Domnarvet, Landviken outside Högbo, and Timraa outside Vivetavarv.[18] Many industries gave rise to larger rural communities and later regular urban settlements, just as some industries, among them the sawmill industry, were located close to towns or urban areas. This illustrates how complicated it became, over time, to distinguish between rural and urban industry and thus between workers in rural areas and workers in towns.

Recruitment of labor to rural industry has received but slight critical examination and has focused largely on the Swedish and Norwegian sawmill industry.[19] Our investigation shows a principal difference between enterprises with a long local tradition and more recent ones that came into existence and expanded strongly after 1850. The former were able to draw on a core of "natives" who were born and grew up in the area and who, at the outset, were familiar with the factory. Typically, one member of the family had worked at the mill, and often the son followed the father.

The fast-growing sawmill industry increasingly used internal recruitment, too, but in addition had to supplement local labor with seasonal workers and with immigrants. The seasonal workers[20] came from poor and overpopulated districts and from villages with little adjoining land. However, after 1900, the decline of the wood industry and the increase of alternative employment opportunities elsewhere strongly reduced the significance of labor migration to this discussion.

A closer look at the occupational origin of long-distance migrants shows that some previously had worked in the same industry. Others had been employed in different industries, but surprisingly few came directly from agricultural work. Many of the long-distance migrants lost daily contact with their original milieu; nevertheless, they managed to maintain some connection by keeping themselves informed through letters and with the help of migrants and seasonal workers. Some migrants came in groups from the same village or parish, and it was quite common for men and women from the same or a neighboring locality to marry.[21] In other words, the transition to employment in rural industry did not imply any psychological or social break, but represented a rational adjustment to a fluctuating labor market.

Industrialization and urbanization

The central place of urbanization in the study of social change has long been known among European and American historians, however, it is only in the last few years that Scandinavian social historians have undertaken a number of major projects addressing this question.[22] Urban history in Denmark focuses mainly on the physical aspects of towns and cities, that is, it emphasizes industrial environments: factory buildings and facilities, working-class dwellings, and industrial architecture.[23] Urbanization and industrialization were not parallel in Denmark, Sweden, and Norway. This is not to say that they were independent of each other, but urbanization in Denmark was already fairly advanced before industrialization had much impact.[24] From about 1870, heavy industrialization evolved with its center in Copenhagen, the national capital. The number of industrial workers doubled between 1873 and 1897, just as the provincial towns and the middle-sized market towns became more and more characterized by industry. The concentration of factories in the large old town or city can be explained by the home market character of Danish industry, based as it was on raw materials from abroad. Industry's need for easy access to a market, to raw materials, to a labor force, and to capital led many enterprises in the direction of the larger seaports which, besides Copenhagen, include Odense, Aarhus, Aalborg, Vejle, and Helsingor.

In spite of the different patterns in localization between Denmark on the one hand and Sweden and Norway on the other, they had in common the fact that industrialization intervened decisively in the processes of urbanization from the second half of the nineteenth century on and transformed the cities' trade and occupational structures, as well as their social and demographic patterns.

Comparing countries has some obvious advantages, but it also should be possible to add some assumptions about city size and the distribution of cities in a hierarchy of trade area functions. The capital cities of Copenhagen, Stockholm, and Christiania each differed from other cities by having a larger occupational diversity in handicraft and industry, as well as a considerable number of servants and casual laborers. The capitals and the larger cities were also the first to be divided functionally into residential and trade area districts, changes followed closely by social segregation and extensive class divisions. The middle-sized and smaller towns were less differentiated socially, and their development often depended on a few trades.

Industry's demand for labor (the industrial-urban labor market) was met by:

1. proletarianized artisans and journeymen;
2. the many casual laborers and servants in the city;
3. people previously occupied in agriculture;
4. workers from rural industry; and
5. second-generation industrial workers.

Incorporation of artisans' trade and the craftsmen in the industrial sector had to do with the dismantling of the guilds in the middle of the nineteenth century. Some occupations disappeared entirely, including needlemakers, chandlers, coopers, weavers, and shoemakers; others, such as brewery workers, tannery workers, joiners, and iron and metal workers, were replaced only partly by new industries. Some journeymen had to get unskilled jobs, but most of them managed to get into those factories that took over craft production.[25] The gradual transition from handicraft to industry made it possible for the artisans to practice their skills, but as mechanization proceeded and job requirements were reduced, they lost their professional independence. It should be added that a good many artisan shops carried on as subcontractors to the industry, and even expanded. However, none of these trades and professions was unaffected by economic concentration. Having more journeymen and unskilled workers at the same workplace increased the distance and the tensions between journeymen, semi-skilled, and unskilled laborers and the master artisan/employer, as was the case in the building trades.

Documentation for the remaining recruitment channels can be found in two studies on Sagene, a suburb of Christiania, and the smaller Swedish town of Oskarshamn. Jan E. Myrke attaches importance to the fact that the workers who were employed in the growing textile industry and mechanical workshops in Sagene around 1874 were not recruited from migrant male and female farm laborers or servants with a rural background, but, on the contrary, from skilled and unskilled workers from Christiania. More specifically, it seems that an informal network of family, neighbors, and friends played a very important part in setting up those channels by which newcomers were recruited to the industry.[26]

In Table 2.4 workers at the mechanical workshop in 1899 in Oskar-

Socioeconomic Group	Born before 1850	Born 1850 and after
Entrepreneur and tradesman	–	8
Artisan	7	47
Academician, civil servant	–	–
Public and local authority officials	5	21
Factory and handicraft worker	10	74
Peasant	37	23
Unknown	–	4
Total	59	177

Table 2.4 Workers at Oskarshamn in 1899 Classified by Birth Year and Father's Occupation

shamn have been classified according to the occupation of their father and as to whether they were born before or after 1850.[27] Handicraft, industry, and agriculture contributed the largest numbers. It is interesting, too, that workers born after 1850 mainly had artisan and industrial backgrounds. The increasing significance of internal recruitment is confirmed by similar research into Kockum's mechanical workshop in Malmö and Lindholm's mechanical workshop in Gothenburg. Of course, regional deviations might come into play, but the same tendency regarding larger internal recruitment shows up among 23,000 workshop laborers in Sweden[28] and in an investigation of social mobility in Aarhus,[29] both studies dealing with the period around the turn of the century.

The previous occupation of the workers from Oskarshamn's mechanical workshop in 1899 gives additional information on their social background.[30] (See Table 2.5.)

Trade	Number
Industry	87 (of whom 22 came from the mechanical workshop industry)
Handicraft	18
Commerce	46
Agriculture	41
Total	192

Table 2.5 Workers at Oskarshamn in 1899 Classified by Previous Occupation

The assumption that industry and, to a lesser extent, agriculture are the most essential bases for recruitment is to some extent supported by the above tabulation. Compared with the data on father's occupation, the downward tendency of artisans suggests that many sons of handicrafts-men were not able to succeed their fathers in their occupation, or to enter the artisanal trade at all. Instead, many of them might work for a while in commerce or in agriculture, employment that did not require great skills.

Most of the workers came from the surrounding areas of Oskarshamn but, unfortunately, we lack good information on individuals and cannot compare geographical origin with occupational origin. However, Bo Öhngren shows that the mechanical workshop industry recruited a num-ber of laborers from rural districts, but that many of these in fact had been working in rural industry. Those results correspond closely to the "stair-step" model, according to which the immigrating (and unskilled) labor force entered the poorest paying jobs (the urban labor market of casual laborers, day laborers, servants, handymen, and so on) while those already resident occupied the better jobs and advanced socially. In other words, the already established workers were continually being pushed up by the flow of newcomers. Recently migrated farm laborers not only had to cross a rural-urban barrier, as it has been claimed, but also a rural-industrial threshold. Farm laborers lacked resources and fared poorly in competition for the better jobs in the industrial-urban labor market.[31]

Between 1860 and the early 1890s, a considerable portion of industry in Stockholm used steam power and therefore produced in large units. From the early 1890s until 1910, many factories converted to electricity and thus to smaller units of production and increasing specialization. The number of women, semi-skilled, and skilled workers grew along with the level of qualification of the total labor force.[32]

The new class of industrial and factory workers, generally termed operatives, enjoyed a certain status, consisting of higher salary and regular work, which separated them from artisans and from casual laborers in regard to work conditions, workplace organization, and patterns of residence. In retrospect, the industrial working class differed from the pre-industrial working class by having a large number of employed young people, and nearly as many women as men, many of whom (especially women) were unmarried.[33]

The transformation of the system of production in rural areas by the estate owners, the peasants, and the sawmill industry in accordance with their demand for a casual, dependent labor force intensified migration among landless farm workers. Work migration took place in well-defined surroundings—in other words, it was frequent but short and localized. Industrialization in rural and urban areas, along with the growing economic significance of the cities, might not have changed the *intensity* of migration, but, on the other hand, it did change the *pattern*. Industrial districts and the cities became the destination for many families and single people. Migration and the search for employment were often supported by younger members of the family or by friends who had set out in advance to investigate job possibilities.

The urban and industrial-urban labor market attracted many people. Industrial districts had the largest number of immigrants and emigrants along with the largest surplus of migrants. From this Öhngren concludes that industrialized towns and cities received a considerable oversupply, and that the industrial demand for labor increased the urban population[34] in a rhythm that followed the economic fluctuations in Stockholm and Copenhagen until the turn of the century.[35]

Some of those migrants to the cities returned to their places of origin; others continued their search for work in other towns or surrounding industrialized rural districts, and still others took "the big jump" to America. Those who settled down permanently were assimilated into an urban structure undergoing rapid change after 1870. A minority succeeded in achieving social mobility,[36] but most people were absorbed into the group of day laborers, casual workers, and servants, or entered the building trade and factories as unskilled labor.

The migration to the cities, the population surplus, and the industrial expansion disrupted the older pre-industrial urban structure. Functional differentiation and social segregation occurred first in the larger cities. The doubling of the population of Copenhagen between 1840 and 1911, along with a tenfold rise in the number of industrial workers, changed the geographical limits of the city.[37] Between 1840 and 1870, industry had been localized in inner Copenhagen, but as production became centralized in larger, often heavily mechanized units, industry moved to the outskirts of the city. The inner city thus was left to light industry and turned partially into a service area. The changing distribution of economic activity resulted in a division of workplace and home and in growing class segregation. The upper class, as well as the affluent middle class, moved out of the city, whereas the better-situated part of the working class began to dominate the social composition in the newly developed peripheral urban areas. The residents were predominantly skilled workers, artisans, smaller self-employed craftsmen, and lower officials. Poor people and casual laborers continued to take up residence in inner Copenhagen, in the back buildings, lofts, and basements of the older working-class quarters. Since about 1910, an unbroken thinning of working-class quarters could be seen, while the suburbs in the western and southern parts of the city more and more were beginning to look like "regular" working-class residential areas.

In smaller towns, environmental and residential development is evident in the transition from the concentric to the radial town. The etymologist Peter Dragsbo maintains that the radial class divisions of most of the Danish towns, "north, south, east, and west became notions with a social context," whereas the formation of residential areas came into being in different ways. We find several examples of the rebuilding of older artisan quarters and the setting up of working-class building societies; still, it became more common to find a solution to the increasing problem of working-class housing through apartment houses for workers on the outskirts of the town.[38] Similar stages of development were manifested in Sweden.[39]

Until the turn of the century, the settlement of workers in segregated and socially homogeneous quarters was followed by other fundamental changes. Income became more regular, conditions of employment became more secure, circulation among workplaces decreased, and housing and living conditions gradually improved. Moreover, U. Gustafson observed among working-class people of Stockholm a decline in mortality, a rising rate of marriage, a lower age of marriage, decreasing nativity, and an increasing geographical stability—social phenomena that contributed to the stabilization of the nuclear family. Other changes included economic levelling caused by increasing demand for the unskilled labor force, plus changes in the social organization of work (indicating growing work discipline, larger units of production, and uniformity of work processes), by which the social distance diminished between skilled and unskilled, and indeed among groups of skilled workers. It might indicate that industrialization and, as a concomitant, urbanization, not only led to a demographic, economic, and social stabilization of urban society, but also gave rise to a homogeneous working-class population.

FROM SOCIAL PROTEST TO CLASS CONFLICT: SHAPING A DEMOCRACY
Hunger riots and crowds—strikes and demonstrations

The wage earning, the working, and the poor part of the common people is called on to gather at the end of Slottsbacken on the 20th of August at eleven o'clock at night to destroy the below-mentioned blood-suckers, who with high rates cause general times of high prices.... Bring with you iron bars and axes: The hungry soldier may also be present.[40]

This call for a riot to be staged in Stockholm on August 20, 1798, distributed to "manifold gateways and staircases, and no less than all of our basements, coffeehouses, and other public rallying grounds," did not trigger any popular uprising. On the other hand, we hear of several people gathered in Malmö from December 8 to December 10, 1799, about which the historian Rolf Karlbom writes:

Around six o'clock a lot of people gathered in the streets and passages under noise and squalls. Soon everybody pushed forward to the Slottsplatsen. Both hussars and soldiers were immediately ordered out. The mass was not willing to disperse. They complained bitterly of the high price of rye and bread. They threatened the grain dealers, whom they accused of being the cause of higher prices and of the difficulties of getting certain goods.... [According to a contemporary observer, the crowd was made up of] a lot of vagrants staying in town as casual laborers, factory workers, soldiers on leave, and others, men as well as women and children.

Alarmed by the crowd, the authorities and the bourgeoisie of Malmö called in a company of soldiers from the nearest garrison, which subsequently restored "law and order." Still, in 1855, high prices of provisions could lead to protest, but the form of action had changed:

On the 10th of July the carpenters marched through the streets of Malmö. It took place in a silent and calm way, and without any unlawful acts. On the 12th of July the carpenters handed over a letter to the master carpenters signed by the "Altgeschälle."... They called attention to the fact that the prices of all necessities had doubled. They had as many work hours as the bricklayers. Their own implements were thirtyfold as expensive. Each of them demanded to be paid the same as the bricklayers "in accordance with his work ability," or they would all send in their resignation, and seek to earn [their] scanty demand in other places and in other trades.

The strike that followed ended with a victory for the journeymen. The difference between the reactions in 1798 and 1855 is dramatic and reflects incipient changes in the forms of production and the composition of the participants. No longer was it a partially unorganized, mixed group of proletarians who protested against the authorities and the grain dealers, but an organized, homogeneous occupational group that demonstrated and stopped work in order to carry through demands for "fair pay and a fair price"—for wages corresponding to their work effort.

It is possible to follow closely the changes in the forms of protest of the Swedish lower classes in Rolf Karlbom's *Hunger Riots and Strikes, 1793–1869.* In order to get a chronological description of changing forms of collective action, I have classified Karlbom's protest descriptions as shown in Table 2.6.

Karlbom's careful study in the records, where he explicitly omits so-called political protests, certainly does not include all collective actions that occurred during the period. Nevertheless, it should be possible from this study to draw some conclusions about the form of actions, the social composition, the source of inspiration, and the different motives of the protestors.

The great number of conflicts classified under "other forms of protest" includes apparently unorganized demonstrations, and confiscation riots (that is, confrontations between customs officials, smugglers, and sympathizing groups of commoners). It was dependent groups of proletarians and journeymen who directed their discontent toward the authorities and, in the case of hunger riots, also toward the bourgeoisie—first and foremost to the merchants who dealt in buying, selling, and transporting basic provisions. Real hunger riots occurred in times of fast-rising prices, whereas strikes must be seen as a reaction to high prices and, as well, to new work rules often combined with employers' cuts in wages.

Nearly all protests show evidence of informal organization, preparation, and communication initiated by some active and leading persons from the ranks of the local working-class population. Very likely, the protests were "local" in form and content, but often the inspiration came from persons outside the community, such as seasonal workers, traveling journeymen, seamen, and dockers. That most conflicts took place in seaside towns and near other important arterial roads is first of all explained by the confrontation among poor people, grain dealers, and authorities in connection with transport and shipping of grain. But they may also be explained by sources of inspiration that the common people could pick up from other cities in the country, and from international revolutionary movements and events, as has been documented by proclamations during demonstrations (committed to writing by the police) and distributed handbills, in addition to press coverage.

Year	Hunger Riots	Strikes	Other Forms of Protest	Total
1795–99	3	2	6	11
1800–04	1		8	9
1805–09			2	2
1810–14		1	2	3
1815–19				–
1820–24		1	1	2
1825–29		1	5	6
1830–34			2	2
1835–39			3	3
1840–44			4	4
1845–49		1	6	7
1850–54	1	3	1	5
1855	10	5	8	23
1856–60		4	2	6
		6	2	8
	5	2	2	9

Table 2.6 Kinds of Protest, 1795–99 to 1866–67

According to Karlbom, the "protest tradition of humble people" and the emergence of the working-class movement originated from a knowledge of conflicting interests, a striving to resolve obvious difficulties, and a willingness to request and appeal before violence. "In this respect the working-class movement already had found its melody one hundred years ago, composed in the midst of bitter distress and thirst for brandy, broken illusions, and a feeling of brotherhood."[41]

Inspired by George Rudé and Georges Lefebvre, Karlbom has written the only profound study of pre-industrial collective actions in Scandinavia. In addition, there exist a few minor studies covering both Denmark[42] and Norway.[43] They complement the results of Karlbom, but they do not give additional knowledge of the variety and extent of collective protests. What can be proven with certainty is that more organized and socialist-inspired protest and strike activities began to manifest themselves in Denmark and Norway from around 1848, brought about by political agitators, Danish and German journeymen with news and inspiration from a disturbed Europe.

The most thorough attempt to deliver a comparative historical analysis of "protest behavior" and the development of the working-class movement in Denmark, Sweden, and Norway was done in 1922 by the Norwegian historian Edv Bull, Sr., since followed up by Walter Galenson,[44] who managed to maintain Bull's theses concerning industrial growth as being a disintegrating, frustrating, and therefore radicalizing factor. Later, Seymour Martin Lipset used Galenson's work in his description of political development in Scandinavia,[45] and recently the Norwegian-American social scientist W. M. Lafferty has tried to test the Bull-Galenson hypothesis concerning the ideological response of the working-class and labor movement to the process of industrialization, on the "total-system level."[46]

None of the writers who has addressed the question of "protest behavior" has been convincing in his arguments, and after a fruitless attempt to test the anomic theory put forward by Emile Durkheim, Lafferty joins Val R. Lorwin, who emphasizes "non-economic variables" such as politics, religion, cultural patterns, class conflict, historical events, and the role of personalities in his analysis of national differences in the response of labor to industrial development.

In this chapter, I have used neither the Bull-Galenson hypothesis nor Lorwin's interpretation, but the political process theory of mobilization and collective action.[47] This theory explains how capitalism and state-building restructured and created the basis for the variations and the direction in three fundamental components of collective actions: those interests about which people will organize and act; their capacity to act according to those interests; and the possibility to do so collectively.

I have tried to argue tentatively that the class of estate owners, the group of peasants with large- and middle-sized holdings, the export industry, grain dealers, and middlemen, in agreement with the state, consciously forced through a transformation of the system of production and effectuated an economic policy that proletarianized a large part of the peasant population and of the craft population. However, continuing market expansion, industrialization, proletarianization, mass migration, and eventually urbanization, changed the internal organization of the working class in a direction that, in the second half of the nineteenth century, made it possible for the following elements to be transformed into a strategy that defended and advanced the interests of the working class:

—accumulated experiences with formal and, especially, informal organization, and different forms of conflict (as described by Karlbom)

—experiences with former and contemporary popular movements

—artisan traditions

—external sources of inspiration, and

—experience with intra- and extra-mural repression.

The working-class movement between class and state

The early labor movement

The first socialist working-class organizations in Scandinavia came into existence during the early 1870s, but not until the mid-1880s did workers in large numbers begin to rally around them. From the 1890s on, unskilled and female workers were mobilized (farm laborers first joined the labor movement during the inter-war period). Around the turn of the century, no fewer than 50 percent of the urban working-class population in Denmark belonged to some labor union, whereas the proportion was lower in Sweden and lowest in Norway.[48]

As mentioned above, the early phase of the organized labor movement was dominated by skilled workers, but for that reason recruitment was not socially uniform. Support for these organizations by workers varied according to locality, the size of the workplace, occupation and occupational status, trade traditions, income, age, marital status, social background, place of birth, agitation, and communication. The "typical" worker who joined a labor union was young (between 20 and 30 years of age), well-paid, and male, employed as a skilled worker in a smaller urban industrial plant.[49]

Neither the peasant movements, the liberal·cultural labor associations, the self-help societies, nor, for that matter, the section of the First International, influenced the organizational possibilities of the workers to an appreciable degree.[50] On the other hand, one must recognize the importance of "popular" movements, including religious and temperance movements; in Steven Koblik's words, "the political awareness and participation stimulated by the industrialization process after 1870 built upon these already established popular movements."[51] This hypothesis finds support in his recently completed project on "The Functions of Class Society: The Popular Movements." The intention of that project was not only to describe the development of the different movements, but also to examine the relationship between popular movements and the early labor movement (see Figure 2.1).

Sven Lundqvist has pointed out that the temperance movement, in particular, represented a relevant form of organization for a large segment of artisans, journeymen, and industrial workers.[52] Many workers were members of the temperance movement, and some here received their first training in organizational techniques, abilities they later used to profit in their building up of the labor unions.[53]

The fundamental vehicle behind the formation of the labor movement is to be found neither in the world of ideas, in ideology, or in popular movements, but rather in artisanal traditions. These should be understood as informal networks of occupational consciousness, status consciousness, guild traditions, the traveling of journeymen and, more formally, journeymen's associations. The importance of the consequences of the intra-European work migration for the developing early labor movement is paramount.

As early as 1943, the Danish historian G. Nørregaard was investigating the dimensions of journeymen's migration.[54] Though this migration fell toward the end of the nineteenth century, Harold Bruun realized the importance of the phenomenon when he said, "It gives particular rise to reflection that exactly those occupations which in [Denmark] formed the shock troops of the labor movement—printers, cigar makers, construction workers—actually belonged to those with the most wanderlust."[55] Danish journeymen in Germany, but also journeymen from abroad—especially Germany—helped to spread the organizational thinking of socialism in Denmark. In Norway A. Zachariassen has observed a very similar pattern: "On the whole, the labor movement in Norway had a strong influx of foreign laborers, especially Danish and, to a lesser degree, Swedish handworkers."[56]

The inter-Nordic and international network of contacts shortly after 1870 was taken over by the labor unions. As an example, unions in Copenhagen took the initiative to organize and to raise the wages of cork cutters, tobacco workers, and glovers in Malmö, not owing to any ideological motives, but to prevent Danish employers from importing workers from Malmö who were willing to accept lower wages.[57] Put in a more general way, one which displays the basic premises of the unions, John Logue said in his *Toward a Theory of Trade Union Internationalism* that "provided trade unions are democratic, autonomous organizations, they will pursue the short-term economic interest of their members."[58] In agreement with this we find that, as the working-class movement was growing in size and organizational strength, part of the reason for international solidarity and contacts disappeared. The international journeyman tradition declined as a result of changes in national economies; also, as the labor movement was "integrated" into the state apparatus,

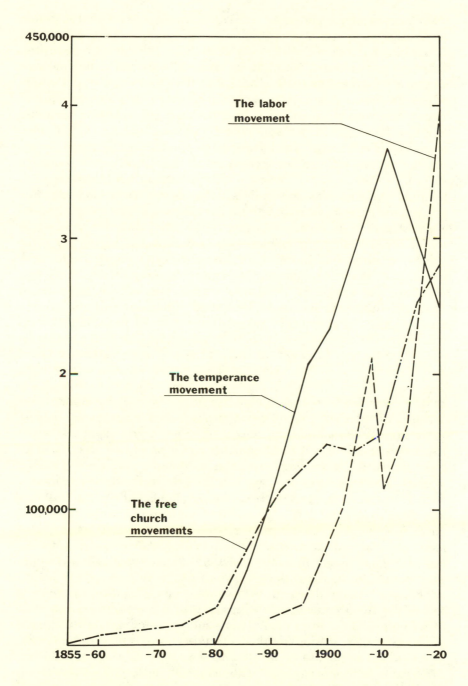

Figure 2.1 Total Number of Members of the Free Church Movements, the Temperance
Movement, and the Labor Movement, 1855-1920

their international exchange had to go through some setbacks and restructuring.

Before 1870 labor conflicts were a relatively rare but far from unknown phenomenon in Scandinavia. Figure 2.2 shows a strong increase during the period from 1870 to 1900, especially from the mid-1880s, when the trade unions (in Sweden the journeymen's associations) strengthened their position considerably. It is also evident that the number of strikes and the foundation of working-class organizations followed the business cycle closely in both Denmark and Sweden (before the turn of the century we have only sparse quantitative information on working-class organizations and strike activity in Norway), and that strike activity in absolute and relative numbers was higher in Denmark than in Sweden. During the first phase of mobilizing the working class, it was the organized skilled workers who most frequently went on strike and led the way in the planning of strikes: in setting up strike meetings, the election of strike leaders, establishing strike funds, garnering support from colleagues at home and abroad, and spearheading sanctions against strikebreakers. Moreover, as the unions were getting stronger, it became clear that they tried to prevent "unpremeditated" strikes, and they introduced special strike rules to strengthen the influence of the organizational committee.

In Jane Cederqvist's detailed study of strikes in Stockholm between 1850 and 1900, it is evident that strikes of unskilled workers differed from those of the skilled.[59] Until the mid-1890s, strikes of the unskilled seldom included more than one workplace, were short, and had many participants; the workers did not set up strike funds or choose a strike committee; and the strike demands were limited to defensive salary questions. It was only with the emergence of unions for the unskilled that their strike forms began to alter; they became longer, had fewer participants, were more offensive in their demands and, above all, were more successful. In other words, strikes among skilled and unskilled were becoming more alike toward the turn of the century. According to Cederqvist, the growing number of strikes and the changes in the nature of the strike among unskilled laborers were consequences of a socioeconomic and demographic stability that offered a fundamental basis for the formation of organizations. The organizational efforts and high strike activity during the 1880s and 1890s among artisans and skilled workers is evaluated as a response to industrialization.

In the Nordic countries, the path to equal and universal suffrage and parliamentarism was prepared by the peasant movement—the combat between lords and peasants—and, to a lesser degree, by the liberal, bourgeois, urban movements. The outcome of this conflict was the "modern" political party system.

The working-class Social Democratic parties in Denmark, Sweden, and

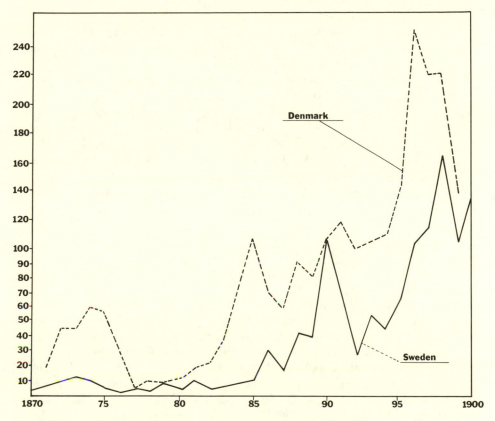

Figure 2.2 Total Number of Strikes in Denmark and Sweden, 1870-1900

Norway all were based on the labor movement. In Denmark and Sweden, the Social Democratic parties made progress in coalition with the liberal parties (representing peasants and the urban middle class) facing the class of estate owners and the urban upper class. In Denmark the labor organizations succeeded relatively easily in mobilizing the working class for the Social Democratic party in competition with the conservative right-wing urban party ("Højre"). In Sweden, it was only after the turn of the century that political mobilization began to speed up after the popular movements had split into a liberal and a socialist movement. In Norway the competition with the liberals for the organization of the working class meant that the Norwegian Socialist party, founded in 1887, took a longer time to win seats in parliament. Around the turn of the century, the organizational and political party mobilization of the working class had progressed furthest in Denmark; for a time, higher rates of organization, higher strike activity, better-planned strikes, and stronger party affiliation gave the Danish labor movement the leading position in Scandinavia.

Class conflict and democracy

Until 1890 the attempt of workers to maintain their own freedom at the workplace was suppressed.[60] To neutralize labor conflicts the employers used unorganized strikebreakers, who were easily available, and, when necessary, police and military forces. "Troublesome" workers were silenced through blacklisting, lay-offs, or job transfers. With the emergence of the socialist labor movement, the employers slowly lost some of their control over the supply of labor. Furthermore, in order to strengthen their position against the employers, the labor movement centralized professional and technical activities in nationwide federations of labor: Denmark and Sweden in 1898, followed by Norway in 1899. However, the support for trade union membership was much greater in Denmark and Sweden than in Norway. The adoption of the principle of industrial unionism became generally accepted in Sweden after 1912, and in Norway during the inter-war period, but it has never been adopted in Denmark. Industrial organizations made possible extensive conflicts across occupational borderlines and the formation of joint strike funds. In Denmark, the industrial structure (small industrial units and strongly differentiated production) and the interests of skilled and artisanal workers successfully opposed this form of organization. Throughout the whole period the strength of the working class continued to rise in all three countries, interrupted only by a slight decline in union membership caused by economic depression and lost strikes.

The growing intra- and extra-mural strength of the workers was to be faced quickly with the counter-mobilization of the employers, who established their own nationwide associations: by 1896 in Denmark, by 1900 in Norway, and by 1902 in Sweden.[61] The first three decades of the new century witnessed an industrial-political fight, where the workers and the employers alternately made use of strikes or demonstrations and the lockout in an attempt to subdue the rival party.[62] Extensive changes in the structure of the labor market and the economic-political system followed these conflicts.

I have chosen the statistics of strikes and lockouts as the best conflict indicator; they describe quite well the trend, the rhythm, and the intensity of the confrontation.[63] The similarity in labor conflict between the three countries is due in part to the business cycle and in part to international political events. In each case the strategy of the parties was influenced by (a) external events, (b) the expected and actual responses of the opposite party, (c) internal control over its own members, and (d) the relations with the surroundings; in short, potential and actual voters and coalition partners.

Most of the smaller strikes concerned wages, while larger conflicts commonly confronted more directly the question of control over the workplace and national political rights. The big lockout of 1899 in Denmark, the lockout in the iron and metal industry in 1911 in Norway, the conflicts in 1903 and 1905, and the "big conflict" of 1909 in Sweden all had to do with "the right to direct and distribute work." By this time the first steps had been taken to involve the central organizations in labor conflicts via negotiations and collective bargaining (see Figure 2.3).

The political aspects of the conflicts were obvious, and particularly manifest in Sweden around 1902, in 1909, and at the end of World War I.[64] Pressure from part of the labor movement resulted in almost complete manhood suffrage. In 1917, parliamentarism as a principle was confirmed, and in 1920 both men and women obtained universal suffrage. The sharp antagonism between classes in Scandinavia shows up in other ways, too, and thus, the inter-war period became not only the time for large and centralized labor conflicts, but also the period with the largest variation and intensity in the pattern of the conflict.

The increasing power of the working-class movement may be explained by the ongoing proletarianization of part of the population and the growing membership of political organizations (most notably in Sweden). Besides these, there also was established a whole series of socialist sub-organizations—youth leagues, women's organizations, educational and cultural associations, and cooperative movements.[65]

The effort of the labor movement to use the parliamentary system as a vehicle for its interests is reflected in its almost constant progress in general elections until the outbreak of World War II. Some scattered findings from a small Danish town near the end of the nineteenth century suggest that "industrialization, by which is meant the alteration of the

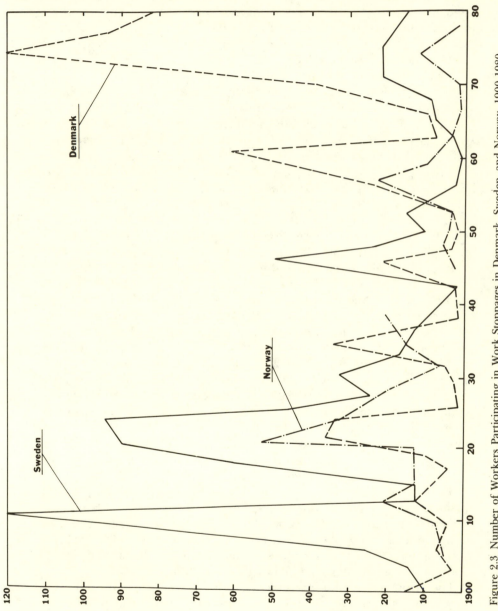

Figure 2.3 Number of Workers Participating in Work Stoppages in Denmark, Sweden, and Norway, 1900-1980

occupational structure, implied that a substantial part of the population was permanently reduced to manual work."[66] In this town an increase in manual workers stood out as the most important factor behind the voter support for the Social Democratic party. In regard to socioeconomic variables, the largest support is to be found among unskilled workers, followed by skilled workers, artisan masters, shopkeepers, and lower-level officials. After 1910, the proportion of voters supporting the Swedish and Danish Social Democratic parties stayed nearly at the same level. The support was slightly lower for the Norwegian Labor party, which had to wait longer for representation in parliament and for participation in the government. The reason for this Norwegian political lag might be the country's decentralized structure, the "center-periphery" problem or, as others might call it, the political consequences of a "dual economy," unfortunately still a largely unexplored phenomenon.

World War I, the conflicts in the early 1920s, the crisis interference and regulations during the depression of the 1930s, and the threat from fascist movements increased the influence of the labor market organizations and led to greater and more permanent government participation and a further takeover of offices by the local Social Democratic parties. We might conclude that during the first part of the twentieth century the Scandinavian labor movements managed to formulate a political strategy that Walter Korpi has called "an economic growth strategy of class conflict," which also can be seen as a "welfare strategy."[67] According to this theory, the working-class movement aimed at applying its resources to the gaining of control of the apparatus of the state. State powers, it was thought, would be able to limit the power of capital and to mitigate the social consequences of a partially free market for commodities and labor, regarded as a necessity for efficiency of production. Following this argument, the strike and the demonstration as power manifestations would give way to political alternatives such as social politics, labor market politics, and economic politics, and in that way alter the resource distribution of the society. By such means the fundamental conflicts were removed from the industrial to the political sector.

This strategy succeeded insofar as the Danish and Swedish labor movements during the 1930s, and the Norwegian labor movement in the late 1940s, gained voter support and, for a significant period, took governmental power and carried out a number of sweeping reforms resulting in a more equal distribution of total production, which in the long run changed the power structure of the society.

NOTES

I wish to thank the people at the Center for Research on Social Organization (CRSO) of the University of Michigan, Ann Arbor, and the CASH-group (Collective Action Social History) who met weekly at the house of Charles and Louise Tilly, for their inspiration and constructive criticism. Also thanks to Nancy Bartlett who corrected my syntax and grammar. My stay at CRSO during the 1981–82 academic year, as well as this article, was made possible by a grant from the Danish Research Council for the Humanities.

1. For Nordic bibliography with references to historic-statistical material (vital statistics, social statistics, economic statistics, and political statistics), see B. Schiller and B. Oden, *Statistik för historiker* (Stockholm, 1970). For quantitative historical literature published after 1970, see the following notes.

2. The economic development of Denmark, Sweden, and Norway is documented in the following works: Lennart Jörberg, "The Nordic Countries 1850–1914," in *The Fontana Economic History of Europe*, 4:2 (London, 1973); and L. Jörberg and Olle Krantz, "Scandinavia 1914–1970," in *The Fontana Economic History of Europe*, 6:2 (Glasgow, 1976), both edited by Carlo M. Cipolla; W. R. Mead, *An Historical Geography of Scandinavia* (New York, 1981), and *Kriser och krispolitik i Norden under mellankrigstiden*, Nordisk historikermötet i Uppsala 1974. Mötesrapport (Uppsala, 1974).

The problem of economic development or growth has received special attention; see Svend Aage Hansen, *Okonomisk vaekst i Danmark*, vol. 1, 1720–1914 (Kbh., 1972), and vol. 2, 1914–1970 (Kbh., 1974). See also S. Aage Hansen, *Early Industrialization in Denmark* (Kbh., 1970); S. Lieberman, *The Industrialization of Norway 1800–1920* (Oslo, 1970); Fritz Hodne, *An Economic History of Norway 1815–1970* (Bergen, 1975); L. Jörberg, *Growth and Fluctuations of Swedish Industry 1869–1912* (Lund, 1961); and the still useful work by Dorothy S. Thomas, *Social and Economic Aspects of Swedish Population Movements 1750–1933* (New York, 1941).

3. An overall description of the emigration from the Nordic countries to America is to be found in *Emigrationen fra Norden indril l. verdenskrig*, Det Nordiske Historikemøde i Københaven, 1971.

4. This outline by and large follows Nils Elvander's section on "the process of democratization" in Scandinavia, taken from his *Skandinavisk arbetarrörelse* (Stockh., 1980), the basic work on the development of the Social Democratic parties in Denmark, Sweden, and Norway from the time of their foundation to 1980. See also Stein Kuhnle, *Patterns of Social and Political Mobilization: A Historical Analysis of the Nordic Countries* (Beverly Hills, California, 1975).

5. Charles Tilly, "Proletarianization: Theory and Research," Center for Research on Social Organization Working Paper, No. 202, University of Michigan, 1979, p. 1; and Tilly, "Demographic Origins of the European Proletariat," CRSO Working Paper No. 207, Univ. of Mich., 1979.

6. The stage of development has been described by Øyvind Østerud, *Agrarian Structure and Peasant Politics in Scandinavia* (Oslo, 1978); and D. G. Grigg, *Population Growth and Agrarian Change* (Cambridge, England, 1980), chap. 15. Annette Vasström, "Etnologien og studiet af lokal kultur," in *Nye strømninger i dansk lokalhistorie* (Historia 1, Aarhus, 1981).

7. Palle Ove Christiansen, "The Household in the Local Setting: A Study of Peasant Stratification," in *Chance and Change: Social and Economic Studies in Historical Demography in the Baltic Area*, ed. S. Akerman a.o. (Odense, 1978).

8. Orvar Löfgren, "The Potato People: Household Economy and Family

Patterns among the Rural Proletariat in Nineteenth Century Sweden," in *Chance and Change*.

9. P. O. Christiansen, "The Household in the Local Setting," p. 57.

10. C. Winberg, *Folkökning och proletarisering. Kring den sociala strukturomvandling pa Sveriges landsbygd under den agrara revolutionen* (Göteborg, 1975); in English also by Winberg, "Population Growth and Proletarianization," in *Chance and Change*.

11. Ingrid Eriksson and John Rogers, *Rural Labor and Population Change: Social and Demographic Developments in East-Central Sweden during the Nineteenth Century* (Uppsala, 1978), p. 242.

12. Mats Rolen, *Skogsbygd i omvandling. Studier kring befolk-ningsutveckling, omflytning och social rörlighet i Revsunds tingslag 1820–1977* (Uppsala, 1972).

13. About poverty in Sweden, see Olle Lundsjö, *Fattigdomen pa den svenska landsbygden under 1800–tallet* (Stockh., 1975).

14. For Denmark see Kristian Hvidt, *Flight to America: The Social Background of 300,000 Danish Emigrants* (Lond., 1975). Sweden is discussed by H. Runblom and H. Norman, eds., *From Sweden to America* (Minneapolis, 1976), and "Norway," in *Vandringer*, Fetschrift for Ingrid Semmingen (Oslo, 1980).

15. See F. Hodne, *An Economic History of Norway*, pp. 9–15.

16. D. S. Thomas, *Social and Economic Aspects*, chap. 3: "Industrialization"; and Michael Drake, *Population and Society in Norway 1735–1865* (Camb., 1969), pp. 80–82.

17. R. Willerslev, *Studier i dansk industrihistorie 1850–1880* (Kbh., 1952), tables in supplement 3.

18. O. Hellspong and S. Löfgren, *Land och stad. Svenska samhällstyper och industrisamhällen*. For the genesis of "complementary communities," see O. Hellspong, *Borlänge-studie av ett brukssamhälle* (Falun, 1973).

19. For Sweden, in addition to O. Hellspong and S. Löfgren, *Land och stad*, see Bo Gustavsson, *Den Norrländska sagverksindustrins arbetare 1890–1913* (Uppsala, 1965); Björn Rendahl, *Emigration, folkomflytning och saesonarbete i ett sagverksdistrikt i Södra Hälsingland 1867–1910* (Uppsala, 1972); Anders Norberg, *Sagernas Ö. Almö och industrialiseringen 1860–1910* (Uppsala, 1980). For Norway, see Edv. Bull, *Arbeidermiljø under det industrielle gennombrudd* (Oslo, 1958), still the most thorough study on workers in the wood industry.

20. For seasonal workers in Sweden, see Göran Rosander, *Herrarbete, Dalfolkets saesonvisa arbetsvandringer i jämförande belysning* (Uppsala, 1967).

21. Norberg, *Sagernas Ö. Almö*, pp. 79–80.

22. Urban history and urban monographs in Denmark, Sweden, and Norway are discussed in John Westergaard, *Scandinavian Urbanism: A Survey of Trends and Themes in Urban Social Research in Sweden, Norway and Denmark* (Kbh., 1966).

23. See the following publications: Ole Degn, *Urbanisering og industrialisering* (Kbh., 1978), chap. 5; Henrik Fangel, "Forskning i byhistorie," in *Nye strømninger i dansk lokalhistorie*; Per Boje, *Det industrielle miljø 1840–1940. Kilder og litteratur* (Kbh., 1976); Gunnar Viby Mogensen, a.o., *Socialhistorie. Kilder og studieomrader vedrørende dansk socialhistorie efter 1890* (Kbh., 1975); and Ole Hyldtoft, "Industrial Buildings and Dwellings—The Industrial Environment in Denmark 1840–1940," in *Industrial Buildings and Dwellings*, No. 2 (1978).

24. See Bo Öhngren, "The City and Environs: Voluntary Associations and

Urbanization in a Comparative Perspective 1890–1975," and Thomas Hall, "Swedish Urban Environment," both in *Industrial Buildings and Dwellings*, No. 2 (1978). Also see Jane Cederqvist, Uno Gustafson, and Sven Sperlings, "Industriarbetarklassens uppkomst: Stockholms arbetare 1850–1914," in *Historisk Tidsskrift*, No. 4 (1972). For the project on the popular movements in Sweden, see Sven Lundqvist, *Folkrörelserne i det svenska samhället 1850–1920* (Stockh., 1977), especially the bibliography p. 31, notes 1 and 2; the "migration project" is referred to in Runblom and Norman, *From Sweden to America*, and in B. Kronborg and T. Nilsson, *Stadsflyttere* (Uppsala, 1975); Sivert Langholm, "On the Scope of Micro-History," in *Scandinavian Journal of History*, 1 (1976); and Jan E. Myhre, "The Christiania Study," in *Industrial Buildings and Dwellings*, No. 2 (1978). Grethe A. Blom, ed., *Urbaniseringsprocessen i Norden*, vol. 3: *Industrialiseringens første fase*. Also see Flemming Mikkelsen, *Arbejderkultur. Skitse til en hverdagslivets socialhistorie* (Aarhus, 1981), on the conditions of life of the working class in Denmark, Sweden, and Norway from 1870 to 1930.

25. Some handicraft trades' transition to factory production, as far as Denmark is concerned, is covered in G. Nørregaard, *Arbejdsforhold indenfor dansk håndvaerk og industri 1857–1899* (Kbh., 1943), and F. Mikkelsen, "Industrielle foretagere i Odense omkring 1870," in *Erhvervshistorisk Aarbog*, 1980; for Sweden see Bo Öhngren, *Folk i rörelse* (Uppsala, 1974).

26. Jan E. Mykre, *Sagene—en arbeiderforstad befolkes 1801–1875* (Oslo, 1978).

27. David Papp and Bo Öhngren, *Arbetarna vid Oskarshamns varv kring sekelskiftet* (Rapport 3 fra Sjöhistoriska Museet, 1973), p. 23.

28. B. Öhngren, "Mikrohistoria pa makroniveau. Den svenske verkstadsindustriarbetaren i riksperspektiv kring sekelskiftet," in *Historieforskning pa nya vägar*. Festskrift till Sten Carlsson 1977, ed. Lars-Göran Tedebrand.

29. Th. Geiger, "Soziale Umschichtungen in einer däischen Mittelstadt," in *Acta Jutlandica*, 1951.

30. Papp and Öhngren, *Arbetarna vid Oskarshamns*, p. 29.

31. B. Öhngren, "Urbaniseringen i Sverige 1840–1920," in *Urbaniseringsprocessen i Norden*, vol. 3; and Tom Rishøj, "Udviklingen i den sociale mobilitet i det storkøbenhavnske omrade i perioden 1850–1950," in *Sociologiske Meddelelser*, 13 serie 1969.

32. Uno Gustafson, *Industrialismens storstad. Studier rörande Stockholms socials, ekonomiska och demografiska struktur 1860–1910* (Stockh., 1976).

33. J. E. Myhre, *Sagene*, chap. 16.

34. B. Öhngren, "Urbaniseringen i Sverige 1840–1920," pp. 295–300.

35. U. Gustafson, *Industrialismens storstad*, pp. 40–46; see also Per Boje and Ole Hyldtoft, "Økonomiske, geografiske og demografiske aspekter," in *Urbaniserings-processen i Norden*, vol. 3.

36. For the link between geographical and social mobility, see B. Kronborg and T. Nilsson, "Social Mobility, Migration and Family Building in Urban Environments," in *Chance and Change*.

37. On Copenhagen, see especially P. Boje and O. Hyldtoft, "Økonomiske, geografiske og demografiske aspekter."

38. Peter Dragsbo, *Mennesker og huse i Aabenraa* (Esbjerg, 1978).

39. T. Hall, "Swedish Urban Environment", and O. Hellspong/Löfgren, *Land och stad*.

40. The examples have been taken from Rolf Karlbom, *Hungerupplopp och strejker 1793–1869* (Lund, 1967), pp. 42, 57, 155.

41. Ibid., p. 264.

42. F. Mikkelsen, *Arbejderkultur*, chap. 4.

43. *Tidsskrift for Arbeiderbevegelsens Historie*, No. 1 (1981), with a special theme on hunger riots and strikes.

44. W. Galenson, "Scandinavia," in *Comparative Labor Movements*, ed. W. Galenson (New York, 1952), and note 65 below.

45. Seymour Martin Lipset, *Political Man* (New York, 1963).

46. W. M. Lafferty, *Economic Development and the Response of Labor in Scandinavia* (Oslo, 1971); and Lafferty, *Industrialization, Community Structure, and Socialism: An Ecological Analysis of Norway, 1875–1924* (Oslo, 1974). In both works, Lafferty is making use of the "anomy" argument within the framework that Lipset and Stein Rokkan have called "the sequence of thresholds which lie in the path of any movement pressing forward a new set of demands within a political system." These thresholds are presented as legitimation, incorporation, representation, and executive (majority) power—purely descriptive terms, in reality often overlapping and relating to the exclusion of political rights. The same approach has been used by Ø. Østerud in *Agrarian Structure*.

47. For the most comprehensive elaboration of this theory, see Charles Tilly, *From Mobilization to Revolution* (Reading, Mass., 1978).

48. For a Nordic bibliography on the labor movements in Denmark, Sweden, Norway, and Finland, see S. Hentilä and H. Saarinen, eds., *Forskningsläget inom arbetarröelsens historia i Norden* (Helsingfors, 1974). For an English-language outline of the labor movements in Denmark and Sweden, see *Scandinavian Journal of History* 3:4 (1978).

49. B. Öhngren, "Mikrohistoria pa makroniveau."

50. On these movements, see Ø. Østerud, *Agrarian Structure*, and the special issue of *Scandinavian Journal of History*, 5 (1980).

51. Steven Koblik, ed., *Sweden's Development from Poverty to Affluence 1750–1970* (Minneapolis 1975), p. 177.

52. Sven Lundqvist, *Folkrörelserne i det svenska samhället 1850–1920* (Stockh., 1977).

53. Ibid., pp. 120–121.

54. G. Nørregaard, *Arbejdsforhold indenfor*, chap. 9.

55. H. Bruun, *Den faglige arbejderbevaegelse i Danmark indtil aar 1900* (Kbh., 1938), p. 136.

56. A. Zachariassen, *Fra Marcus Thrane til Martin Tranmäl* (Oslo, 1962), pp. 78–79.

57. B. Blomkvist, *International i miniatyr. Studier i skansk arbetarrörelse före 1880 och dens internationelle kontakter* (Lund, 1979).

58. John Logue, *Toward a Theory of Trade Union Internationalism* (Univ. of Gothenburg, Research Section Post-war History, Pub. 7, 1979), as part of a larger project on the internationalism of the labor movement.

59. Jane Cederqvist, *Arbetare i strejk. Studier rörande arbetarnas politiska mobilisering under industrialismens genombrott. Stockholm 1850–1900* (Stockh., 1980).

60. For a comparative approach to the Scandinavian labor movement, see N. Elvander, *Skandinavisk arbetarrörelse*, and the relevant sections in *Kriser och krispolitik*.

61. Industrial relations in Norway and Denmark have been the subject for W. Galenson in *Labor in Norway* (Camb., Mass., 1949), and Galenson, *The Danish System of Labor Relations* (Camb., Mass., 1952).

62. See G. K. Ingham, *Strikes and Industrial Conflict* (Lond., 1974).

63. For references to labor conflicts in Sweden and Denmark, see *Arbog for Arbejderbevaegelsens Historie*, 1979; for Norway, see *Tidsskrift for Arbeiderbevegelsens Historie*, 1 (1977).

64. Bernt Schiller, "Years of Crises, 1906–1914," and Carl-Göran Andrae, "The Swedish Labor Movement and the 1917–1918 Revolution," both in S. Koblik, *Sweden's Development*.

65. See N. Elvander, *Skandinavisk arbeterrörelse*, pp. 186–187.

66. See S. Kuhnle, *Patterns of Social and Political Mobilization*; Niels Thomsen, "Urbaniseringen og den politiske adfaerd," in *Urbaniseringsprocessen i Norden*, vol. 3; and N. Elvander, *Skandinavisk arbetarrörelse*, chap. 3.

67. Walter Korpi, *The Working Class in Welfare Capitalism: Work, Unions and Politics in Sweden* (London, 1978), chap. 4.

3

The Persistence of Precapitalist Relations of Production in a Tropical Export Economy: The Amazon Rubber Trade, 1850–1920

Barbara Weinstein

Industrial growth during the nineteenth century may have been confined primarily to Europe and the United States, but the process of industrialization had a significant impact on the populations of many pre-industrial nations. Even though no Latin American country could boast of a genuine industrial sector until the early twentieth century, the economic revolution overseas led to new investments and new forms of labor recruitment throughout Latin America, particularly in the exporting regions. To be sure, Spanish and Portuguese colonies had been producing minerals and foodstuffs for European markets since the sixteenth century, but rapid industrialization and urbanization in the seats of empire in the nineteenth century combined to cause considerable expansion in export-oriented production. New consumption habits and expanded urban demand overseas led to increased production of coffee, beef, sugar, and cotton, while the needs of foreign industry and agriculture led to booms in guano, nitrate, copper, and rubber production.[1]

With slavery on the wane and colonial systems of forced Indian labor extinct, investors in the new export-oriented enterprises were forced to seek other means of recruiting laborers in a region where capital was scarce and where much of the indigenous population retained some access to the means of subsistence. Not surprisingly, there was a great deal of variation in the methods developed to resolve this situation, variations of which depended upon several factors: the nature of the export enterprise; the availability of capital (whether foreign or domestic); the strength and orientation toward the state; and the capacity of the potential labor pool to resist exploitation. Only in a few cases did a rapid transition occur from forced to free (i.e., wage) labor—the experience of coffee-producing São Paulo, where government-subsidized immigration from southern Europe facilitated a speedy change from slave to wage labor, was exceptional.[2] Elsewhere, more openly coercive methods were the rule. To meet the needs of the Cuban sugar plantations and the Peruvian guano fields, planters imported Chinese coolies whose work contracts were so restrictive that their condition amounted to indentured servitude. Other countries, such as Guatemala, eventually invoked vagrancy laws that forced peasant farmers into at least seasonal employment. The mining zones of northern Chile and highland Peru, meanwhile, developed a system of *enganche* whereby seasonal workers were recruited through advances in cash or in kind (the latter usually tools and foodstuffs). Finally, in parts of Bolivia, Peru, Ecuador, and Central America, peasants were forced into export-related production by the expansion (through fair means or foul) of the large estates, which made some sort of labor-exchange relationship unavoidable, even while the capital-poor landlords continued to allow their workers some access to the means of subsistence.[3]

In a number of cases, such as the Cuban sugar industry or the mining zones of Peru and northern Chile, these various forms of coercion proved to be transitional. As the availability of local and foreign capital grew, as new technology made a trained, full-time labor force more desirable, and as rural society itself was transformed by the impact of the export enterprises, relations of production in these areas became increasingly capitalistic, with wages emerging as the main basis for recruitment. There were, however, areas where export production became an important segment of the local economy but that did not experience a transition to more capitalistic forms of labor recruitment. In some of these areas, the procurement of laborers continued to depend upon some extra-economic form of compulsion. In addition, there were a few cases where the worker (or more accurately, the petty producer) managed to maintain some control over the means of production even as the level of exports rose.[4]

A leading example of the latter was the Amazon rubber economy. For a period of some 70 years, approximately from 1850 to 1920, the rubber trade dominated the economic life of the Amazon basin. Still, in most parts of the region the *seringueiros* (tappers) who produced the rubber, though exploited in a variety of ways and often vulnerable to violence and coercion, were able to resist proletarianization. That is, the average *seringueiro* managed to retain some control over his work rhythms, as well as some discretion over the disposal of his product. Thus the American rubber boom, unlike export booms elsewhere in Latin America or in the industrial economies of Europe and the United States, did not generate a transition to a mode of production in which the producers were completely separated from productive resources or compensated by wages. How and why the Amazonian tappers were able to avoid the fate of workers throughout the world in the late nineteenth and early twentieth centuries should provide us with insight, not only into the Amazonian case itself, but also into the general process of proletarianization.

To understand the issue of labor recruitment during the rubber boom, it is necessary first to consider the history of the Amazon prior to the rubber era. Without question, the series of events which had the most dramatic impact on the structure of Amazonian society was the European conquest and colonization of the valley. Throughout the seventeenth and eighteenth centuries, epidemics of European diseases (to which the indigenous peoples had no immunity), slaving expeditions, and constant warfare combined to cause a drastic decline in the size of the Amazonian population, as well as radical changes in its composition and distribution. By the mid-eighteenth century, many of the survivors of this demographic holocaust had seen their traditional tribal cultures shattered, and either had relocated to one of the region's numerous missions or had been forced into working for the Portuguese colonists.[5] Even with an extensive missionary network and a well-staffed administrative system, however, the Portuguese crown was unable to control the entire population of the valley. One consequence of this was the emergence of a *caboclo* population—an Amazonian peasantry composed of detribalized Indians and persons of mixed ancestry who engaged in subsistence farming and gathering. While this was a far more precarious life than the one afforded them by the traditional tribal communities, which had engaged in highly complex patterns of agriculture, hunting, fishing, and gathering, it certainly allowed the *caboclos* a far more autonomous lifestyle than would the Portuguese-run plantations or collecting expeditions.[6]

Autonomy did not mean complete separation from the market economy, however. Many of the *caboclos* supplemented the output of their subsistence plots by gathering substances such as cacao beans, palm oil, and Brazil nuts, which grow wild in the Amazonian forest. These marketable commodities could then be traded to an itinerant peddler or delivered to a nearby trading post in exchange for tools, firearms, and nonessential foodstuffs that the *caboclo* family could not produce on its own. In the course of the transaction, the *caboclo* was likely to be "swindled" by the local merchant, who usually had a monopoly of trade in a particular area, allowing him to set the prices for goods being bought and sold. However, the relationship between gatherer and trader was not necessarily coercive in any obvious sense. Similarly, many of the *caboclos* who began gathering rubber in the early nineteenth century did so, at least initially, on a voluntary basis.[7]

Along with the various nuts and spices, Amazonian natives had been collecting the grayish, milky latex of the *Hevea brasiliensis* (the most common rubber-producing tree) for centuries. They knew that, once coagulated, the sap of the *hevea* became an elastic and impermeable substance which could be easily fashioned into bottles, balls, and ceremonial syringes. By the end of the colonial era (Brazil gained its independence from Portugal in 1822), European interest in this unique substance had been piqued, and small quantities of rubber were being exported from the Amazon. Yet demand for rubber remained relatively cool during the first few decades of the nineteenth century, largely because of the material's distressing sensitivity to changes in temperature. This made it wholly unsuitable for use in machinery, and even of limited value for certain consumer goods. It was only after Charles Goodyear perfected the vulcanization process in 1839, making rubber impervious to both heat and cold, that demand for the Amazonian gum began to rise dramatically.

Accustomed to occasional gathering activities, the *caboclos* easily could be induced by the new rubber merchants to spend part of their time tapping wild *heveas* and coagulating the latex—especially if the *aviadores* (literally, suppliers) were willing to offer larger quantities of tools and food in exchange for the rubber. Indeed, rubber tapping must have seemed quite attractive to the Amazonian "peasant" since it could be combined with other economic activities (such as hunting, fishing, and small-scale cultivation), and it ensured the gatherer of an annual six-month break, since latex cannot be tapped during the rainy season. It is nonetheless true that, even during the earliest years of commercialized rubber production, there already were reports of *seringueiros* being cheated and abused by itinerant *aviadores*. What often began as a voluntary association between tapper and trader could eventually deteriorate into a coercive relationship, with the tapper spending more and more time in the rubber fields at the behest of his merchant *patrão* (boss). Nevertheless, in the years prior to the actual boom in rubber production, the relationship between tapper and trader seems to have been a relatively flexible one.[8]

Ironically, the main source of resistance to the initial expansion of the rubber trade in the Amazon was the traditional elite—planters and ranchers who viewed the gathering economy as pernicious economically or as a threat to their dwindling labor supply. Moreover, events of the late 1830s further strengthened the resolve of the "agrarian class" to oppose the spread of rubber extraction. Between 1835 and 1838 a wide-ranging social and political upheaval known as the *Cabanagem* (so named because of the guerilla-like bands of *cabanos* responsible for much of the combat) wracked the Amazon Valley. The cost of the revolt was severe: it is estimated that as many as 30,000 people out of a population of a few hundred thousand lost their lives as a result of the fighting or the subsequent epidemics.[9] Travelers' accounts from the period also attest to the extensive destruction of sugar mills, cattle herds, and other rural property. But perhaps most distressing to the surviving coterie of planters and ranchers was the widespread disorganization of the rural labor force as a result of the uprising. Many enslaved Africans and quasi-enslaved Indians joined the guerrilla bands which roamed the region during these years, while others simply took advantage of the turbulence to escape their bondage.[10]

The dispatching of imperial troops from Rio to help crush the rebellion only resolved the most immediate problem facing the local authorities. In the aftermath of the *Cabanagem*, the agrarian elite and its political representatives continued to complain of widespread banditry, cattle-rustling, and criminal vagrancy. Indeed, under pressure from local property holders, the president of the province of Pará (which at this point encompassed the entire Brazilian Amazon) resurrected a colonial institution known as the Corpo de Trabalhadores, literally, the Labor Corps. This pseudo-military forced-labor brigade was to function as a source of workers both for private enterprises and public works. Those targeted for impressment into the brigade included all non-white males who could not prove either substantial ownership of property or gainful employment.[11]

The official rationale for the Corpo de Trabalhadores was, of course, to restore order and to reduce criminality. The objectives of the program, however, clearly went beyond combating banditry, as demonstrated by the stated policy of drafting rubber tappers into the brigade. Speaking seven years after the end of the *Cabanagem*, one provincial vice-president explained: "There are many criminal types, and some of these are escaped prisoners, deserters, runaway slaves and other individuals who, even though occupied, as they say, in rubber collecting, nevertheless live in complete independence."[12] In short, unemployment and vagrancy were not the only criteria for impressment into the Corpo since the rubber tappers were not, strictly speaking, either unemployed or vagrant. But many of them did "live in complete independence," or else their *patrão* was a recent immigrant from Portugal or the Levant, rather than a scion of a traditional landed family. Had the Corpo achieved its objectives, it would have channeled back such autonomous producers into the agrarian or transport sectors, where they would have labored for the benefit of the provincial elite, rather than for themselves or for a group of upstart merchants.[13]

The scheme soon proved a failure, however, for a variety of reasons. First of all, the provincial government simply did not have enough troops to patrol a region as immense as the Amazon and to combat widespread resistance to the new measures. Of course, the administration did score a few successes; when a band of alleged *cabanos* turned rubber tappers invaded an island owned by Pará's leading slaveholder, the provincial president dispatched a gunboat that managed to dislodge the intruders.[14]

But this was a fairly unusual case, and one that involved an already claimed piece of territory situated relatively close to the capital city of Belém. By contrast, most of the *seringueiros* were tapping *heveas* in far more remote areas where much of the land was still officially vacant or unclaimed.

Secondly, and equally important, there was a current of opinion emerging within political and commercial circles by mid-century that was much more favorable to the expansion of rubber extraction. By the 1850s, rubber had established its position as the Amazon's leading export—and as the provincial government's principal source of revenue.[15] This made it increasingly unwise to implement policies designed to disrupt rubber production, and by the 1860s the Corpo de Trabalhadores had been summarily abolished. Complaints about the growth of the extractive economy and its allegedly deleterious effects on regional agriculture continued to be voiced in the provincial assembly and regional newspapers, but active government opposition to rubber production virtually had ceased.

The picture of the rubber economy at mid-century that emerges from the land records, official reports, and other accounts of the period is a far cry from the popular image of Amazonian society during the rubber era. The more vivid and colorful accounts of the rubber years have tended to portray the Amazon as a series of vast rubber estates owned by ruthless entrepreneurs and worked by miserable debt-peons permanently shackled to their *hevea* trails.[16] Judging from the comments of both critics and supporters of the rubber trade, however, it seems that the vast majority of the rubber tappers as late as the 1870s were squatting on vacant lands and freely moving on to new areas as soon as the output of the rubber trees began to decline. Even the registers of land claims and purchases reveal very few estates that would be considered large by Amazonian standards. Conversely, there are a large number of entries in the registers for claims that include only a few trails of rubber trees, most likely worked by the family of the claimant. Moreover, the fact that many of these *posseiros* (squatters) lacked regular family names and declared themselves illiterate confirms that they came from "humble" backgrounds.[17]

As for the tappers being debt-peons, it is true that many of them were indebted to a local trader or a wealthier neighbor who would advance them goods on credit at the onset of the tapping season.[18] From there it was not difficult for the *patrão* to keep the *seringueiro* in debt, especially since the *aviador* usually had a free hand in setting the price of goods supplied to the tapper. Yet there is little indication that these debts typically served as a form of enserfment; rather, they seem to have been the customary means for building up a clientele. This is not to say that the client could operate without restriction; if a tapper who was indebted to one *aviador* started selling his rubber to another, he ran the risk of retaliation from his original *patrão*. But in a region as vast as the Amazon, escape to another zone of rubber extractions, particularly during the early years of the rubber era, seems to have been relatively easy, thereby limiting the effectiveness of debt as a means of control.

Generally speaking, the spatial characteristics of the rubber economy were heavily responsible for the way in which Amazonian society evolved during the nineteenth century. It is vital to emphasize that at no time during the rubber era did the Amazon produce a significant quantity of plantation rubber; virtually all the rubber exported by the region came from trees that grew wild throughout the valley. And like most other plants native to the Amazon, the *Hevea brasiliensis* grows in a highly scattered pattern, meaning that one can find only one or two rubber trees per acre even in areas of fairly dense concentration. If the average *seringueiro* tapped some 300 trees on a regular basis, that meant that he would have to cover a stretch of thickly forested territory encompassing approximately 150 acres. Consequently, the tappers themselves were highly dispersed and isolated, and came into contact with large numbers of fellow gatherers only when they delivered their rubber to market— usually no more than once a week, and often as rarely as once a month. Indeed, any tapper who could manage it fled the rubber fields during the rainy season to help mitigate the severe sense of isolation.[19]

This dispersion of the tapper force had a number of significant ramifications. Obviously, the large distances involved in the rubber trade made it very difficult for a *patrão* to maintain any regular surveillance over his clients. This meant not only that he could not easily prevent them from moving to other areas, but also that he could not hope to control the tappers' work rhythms. Thus the isolation, though psychologically painful, did aid the tapper in retaining some autonomy in the realm of production. Meanwhile, there were ways in which the isolation worked to the trader's advantage. It facilitated the *aviador*'s efforts to monopolize commerce in a particular area: without access to other sources of goods and services, the *seringueiros* became highly dependent upon the *patrão* to market their rubber and to supply them with tools, food, and medicine. Finally, the scattered patterns in which the *seringueiros* (and their families) lived and worked made any form of mutual assistance or cooperation extremely problematic. While the tappers might congregate on weekends or during the rainy season, their most frequent human contact outside the family (or one other tapper who shared the hut) was likely to be the *patrão*. As a result, there were very few cases of collective resistance during the 70–year period in which rubber production dominated the Amazonian economy.[20] When rebellion did occur, it was usually on an individual basis.

By the 1870s, the rubber trade had already transformed certain aspects of life in the Amazon valley. In 1867, the imperial government of Brazil opened the great river to foreign ships, and steam transport quickly became a regular feature of regional commerce. Encouraged by the growing demand for rubber in the United States and Europe, foreign firms began sending agents to the Amazon to finance the activities of the local middlemen and to establish control over the actual export transactions.[21] At the same time, the number of "*aviador* houses," responsible for the distribution of goods to the tappers and the transfer of rubber to the foreign exporters, was multiplying rapidly. Nevertheless, the rubber market during the mid-1870s could hardly be called booming. Prices tended to fluctuate, and few new applications for the Amazonian product were being developed in the industrialized nations. Moreover, even during those periods when demand soared, the ongoing shortage of labor in the Amazon and the nature of the mode of production and exchange made it difficult for the regional economy to respond.

Ironically, it was a climatic disaster of unprecedented proportions elsewhere in Brazil that resolved the most pressing problems facing the Amazon rubber traders. The northeast of Brazil, and especially the province of Ceará, had long been accustomed to droughts that temporarily turned the region's backlands into uninhabitable desert, forcing its residents to migrate to coastal cities or scattered oases. But the *seca* of 1877 was unusually severe, and the resultant emigration was unusually heavy. Small farmers, ranchers, and laborers fleeing the parched hinterland swelled the slums of Fortaleza, capital of Ceará, only to find that the impoverished coastal city offered them little relief. There was, however, one other alternative for the desperate refugees: by the late 1870s, the price of rubber was once again on the upswing, prompting agents of Amazonian firms to begin recruiting tappers in the drought-stricken northeast. With prospects at home so poor, thousands of Cearenses accepted the agents' offers of tools, food, and passage to the Amazon— on credit. The rubber fields of Pará and Amazonas may have been utterly foreign to the northeasterners, but they offered a means of survival and perhaps a way of saving some money to rebuild their modest properties once the drought had passed.[22]

The combined impact of the sudden price rise and the influx of new laborers is evident in the export statistics of that period. Whereas the amount of rubber passing through the port of Belém climbed only slightly between 1865 and 1875, thereafter the volume of rubber exports rose almost constantly. In addition, the extraction of rubber spread far beyond the original centers of production, with tappers moving into virgin upriver *hevea* fields in the western province of Amazonas, and even as far upriver as the Peruvian and Bolivian Amazon. And this process of expansion wrought more than just a change in the scale or dimensions of the rubber trade. With the onset of the genuine boom period in rubber production, the political and financial power of those operating the trade rose accordingly, putting the thousands of northeasterners who entered the *hevea* fields each year in a markedly different position from their predecessors.

In almost every way, rubber tapping proved considerably more oppressive for the greenhorn Cearense than for the native *caboclo*. Unaccustomed to gathering as a way of life, the northeasterner would find the trek through dense forest over barely discernible trails particularly exhausting. One also can imagine how enervating the traditional method of rubber coagulation—which required slow rotation of a latex-covered paddle over a stream of oily smoke—must have been for someone unaccustomed to the steamy Amazonian climate. Even more important, the average Cearense tapper was unlikely to enjoy the same freedom of movement as the early *seringueiros*. Indeed, from the very start the Cearense's position was somewhat different. Whereas the *caboclo* tapper usually entered the rubber economy by staking out a couple of trails in an area with which he was familiar, the Cearense was normally sent to a specific district by the rubber-trading firm that had recruited him, to work trails that the firm considered (formally or informally) its exclusive domain. Thus, the Cearenses had less of an opportunity to become *posseiros*. By the same token, the Cearenses tended to be channeled into new and more remote zones of rubber production, which placed them further away from alternative sources of goods and services and made them even more dependent upon the *patrão*. Likewise, the remoteness of the location could make "escape" more dangerous and difficult, especially since the Cearense was unfamiliar with the Amazonian terrain.[23]

The typical upriver *patrão* was also likely to be a more formidable foe than his downriver counterpart. Landholding and commercial records indicate that, in the older districts, it was unusual for a single firm or individual to dominate an entire area. Therefore, a beleaguered tapper in need of protection often could switch his allegiance to a new *patrão* who was eager for additional clients. During the early decades of the rubber era, the rubber traders also exercised relatively little political power, and this limited the extent of their control over the *seringueiros*. By contrast, the *aviador* houses that conducted the trade in the upriver districts boasted more extensive financial and political resources and frequently established commercial hegemony over vast domains.[24] For example, the house of F. M. Marques reported in 1899 that it had established a virtual monopoly over trade on the Javary and Curuca—rivers that flowed through rich rubber-producing areas near the Brazil-Peru border.[25] Obviously, a tapper working along those rivers who was dissatisfied with (or frightened of) his *patrão* had little recourse.

In some areas, ambitious rubber traders resorted to unspeakable depredations and atrocities to recruit laborers. During the last decade of the boom (1900 to 1910), *aviador* firms eager to take advantage of the soaring prices pushed into isolated areas of the Peruvian Amazon and began enlisting the services of tribal Indians. Those tribes which proved uncooperative became the targets of massacres and other forms of wholesale violence until they agreed to work as rubber gatherers. In some areas, the treatment of these tribal communities was so brutal that it amounted to genocide. When a British parliamentary commission investigated the activities of a Peruvian company (that had several British stockholders) in the Putumayo area, the revelations shocked even those investigators hardened by years of experience with colonial wars and strategies of imperial domination.[26]

While events in the Putumayo were genuinely horrifying, the international sensation that these revelations generated has tended to distort perceptions of the rubber economy elsewhere in the Amazon. Fortunately, the methods used in the Peruvian districts were not the norm for the rubber trade as a whole; very specific factors account for the particularly brutal exploitation that occurred in that area. Owing to the extreme isolation of the Putumayo, the Araño family was able to establish its domain without interference from any other commercial firm or any government body. Unlike the rubber districts of the Brazilian Amazon, there simply were no countervailing influences or competing powers in the area. Perhaps even more important, the rubber being extracted in the Putumayo was *caucho*, which comes from the *Castilloa elastica*—a tree that normally is destroyed by the tapping process, in contrast to the *hevea*, which can be tapped for as many as 50 years. This meant that the Arañas had no economic incentive to create long-term relationships of patronage and clientele with the Indian tribes.

In light of the horrible fates suffered by the Huitoto and other tribes in the Peruvian and Colombian Amazon, it is interesting to note the degree to which the impact of rubber production varied from area to area. One might expect the Mundurucú of the Tapajóz River in Pará to experience the same brutalization as the Huitoto, especially since the Tapajoz rubber districts lay within the domain of Raymundo Pereira Brazil, a merchant and *seringalista* (estate owner) known to have been ruthless and autocratic. Yet a 1912 survey of land claims in the Tapajoz area includes an entry for the Cadiriry River, a tributary, which is described as "the exclusive domain of 400 tame [*sic*] Mundurucú Indians" engaged in rubber tapping and manioc cultivation.[27] Moreover, anthropological studies of the Mundurucu reveal that the tribe was coaxed into the rubber trade and frequently cheated by local traders, but that it was not coerced. Participation in the trade did eventually destroy much of the tribal culture, but this was due largely to the corrosive effects of the merchandise the Mundurucú received in exchange for their rubber. Increasingly dependent on commodities that they themselves could not produce, members of the tribe spent more and more time on the rubber trails, thereby impeding the maintenance of traditional agriculture and hunting cycles.[28]

In general, it is necessary to emphasize that the greater restrictions imposed upon the Cearenses and other upriver tappers were never absolutely effective. Despite the more oppressive conditions, many *seringueiros* in the western Amazon managed to maintain some autonomy and physical mobility. We know, for example, that Cearense tappers in the Acre—an area that originally belonged to Bolivia—rose up by the thousands in the 1890s, not to seek revenge against their *patrãos*, but to follow the latter in an attempt to claim the Acre for Brazil. Once the conflict was over, the armed *seringueiros* returned to their trails and only showed further signs of rebellion when in 1907 Brazil's federal government attempted to "regularize" land titles in the area.[29] It seems that many of the Acreano tappers were *posseiros* like their downriver counterparts, and feared that registration of titles would cost them money at best, or their land at worst. Such evidence suggests that the tappers in this important upriver rubber district had not been reduced to helpless debt-peons. Indeed, two Bolivian officials writing about conditions in the remote Beni district (which borders on the Acre) seem to confirm this impression. Clearly speaking from the rubber trader's point of view, the two authors maintained that the *aviadores* in the area were unable to pressure the *seringueiros* into producing more rubber and were not even successful in keeping the tappers in the rubber fields during the rainy season. The latter meant a constant loss of clients through truancy or competition. So serious did the authors believe the problem to be that they recommended the importation of Chinese coolies, claiming that the traders could double the output of the rubber fields with immigrant labor.[30]

Far from being alone in their opinions, the Bolivian officials were echoing the sentiments of many other politicians, journalists, and businessmen in the Amazon. By the 1890s, a crescendo of criticism was being directed at the *aviador* system and the entire structure of the rubber trade. Only in rare cases did such criticism stem from humanitarian considerations; for most of the commentators the main concern was the inefficiency and limited productivity of the existing system. For example, the journalist Cezar Chauvin attacked the *aviadores* in the pages of Pará's leading newspaper, claiming that their commercial practices were responsible for the *seringueiros'* "slovenly" work habits. Treating the subject allegorically, Chauvin spun a tale of two tappers—Simão Preto and Pedro Caboclo—who shared a hut on a rubber estate in Pará. Simão, a Brazilian of African descent, diligently tapped his trees and coagulated his rubber daily, while Pedro, a native of the region, did only desultory tapping and preferred to collect the latex in flasks rather than perform the

arduous task of defumigation. At the end of the week, both *seringueiros*
delivered the fruits of their labor to the trading post owned by the local
patrão and promptly learned that the price of manioc flour had doubled
since their last visit. As a result, Simão, despite all his efforts, failed to
make even the slightest profit from his rubber. Pedro, on the other hand,
felt no disappointment since he never expected to earn enough for his
subsistence from rubber tapping, and simply resolved to devote more
of his time to hunting and fishing. Eventually, the author concludes,
Simao will become so discouraged by the *aviador*'s manipulations that he
will adopt the ways of the indigenous population and cease to be an
industrious, productive worker.[31]

This particular attack came from a local source, but the most serious
and energetic criticisms of the *aviador* system came from the foreign
business community. By the late 1890s, rubber had become an extremely
strategic raw material for the industrial economies of Europe and the
United States. The bicycle craze in those countries had given rise to the
pneumatic tire industry and had greatly increased the demand for raw
rubber. Thus, even with the contribution of various rubber producing
colonies in Africa (whose product was usually vine rubber and inferior
to the Amazonian gum), the price of the material was rising rapidly, and
shortages were a constant concern. Increasingly, foreign rubber buyers
expressed the fear that the Amazonian economy, with its lack of regi-
mentation and its elaborate network of middlemen, would prove incap-
able of meeting world demand. Furthermore, these foreigners complained
that the tappers' independent work routine led to such practices as the
adulteration of rubber.[32] There seems to have been some justification
for this claim; many *seringueiros*, perhaps prompted by the constantly
rising prices of basic goods, resorted to inserting stones, sand, and manioc flour into the balls of rubber. This allowed them to increase their
"productivity" without additional labor, and since the rubber would not
be inspected until it reached Belém or Manaus, the adulteration would
be almost impossible to trace to a specific tapper.

Having assessed the Amazonian system of production and finding it
sloppy, inefficient, and wasteful, it is not surprising that foreign trade
journals like *India Rubber World* began to encourage interested parties
in the United States and Europe to invest directly in rubber production.[33]
In part because of the skyrocketing rubber prices and soaring demand
of the late 1890s, their advice did not fall on deaf ears. By the turn of
the century, such corporations as the Comptoir Colonial Français, the
Amazon Rubber Estates, Ltd., and the Rubber Estates of Pará, Ltd., had
been incorporated with the expressed purpose of participating in the
production end of the wild rubber economy and of reorganizing that
economy so as to put the tappers on a wage basis and to eliminate the
middlemen. As the exultant editor of *India Rubber World* put it: "Not the

least important feature of the coming development is likely to be the placing of the rubber lands under private control and a more intelligent, systematic and economical supervision of rubber gathering, with the result of rendering supplies more certain and regular, and prices somewhat lower and less liable to fluctuation."[34] Similarly, a local critic of the traditional production methods noted that these new corporations, having spent huge sums (at least by Amazonian standards) to purchase large stretches of rubber-producing territory, had a much greater incentive to protect the rubber trees and make real improvements in their holdings, than the old-line *aviadores* and their clients.[35] In short, these observers viewed the arrival of the foreign rubber corporations as heralding a new era of economic development in the Amazon—and one that would occur on a decidedly capitalist basis.

From the outset, the foreign companies encountered a number of unforeseen difficulties. For example, the Rubber Estates of Pará had to scrap its plan to conduct its labor operations entirely on a cash basis, since the *seringueiros* on the land it had purchased refused to gather rubber without the customary advance of goods and tools. The Comptoir Colonial, meanwhile, found that dispensing with the middleman was no easy matter. According to its managers, the company never received the exact merchandise it had ordered—that is, when the goods arrived at all. And they admitted that their inexperience in the region left them vulnerable to various sorts of swindles. Moreover, it was these companies' misfortune to have initiated their Amazonian operations at a time when rubber prices were entering into a brief but sharp decline.[36]

Although such problems were serious, they need not have proved fatal. Yet every one of the foreign corporations that had invested in Amazonian rubber production at the turn of the century managed to go bankrupt within a few years' time. Indeed, as early as 1902, an article in *India Rubber World* (which had recommended Amazonian investments enthusiastically only a short while before) warned its readers that there seemed to be "certain conditions existing in the vast and sparsely settled and loosely governed districts in which the rubber trees grow which, for the time at least, are most unfavorable to foreigners investing their money there."[37] Although this last statement is rather vague as to the particulars of the situation, a few of the foreigners with personal experience in the rubber fields left far more detailed accounts of their adventures which can help us to understand what, from their point of view, went wrong.

In exploring the reasons for these ignominious failures, it has to be kept in mind that the foreign corporations had aspirations that went beyond simply substituting themselves for the traditional *aviadores*. As noted earlier, these companies, which had strong ties to manufacturing interests, hoped to revolutionize rubber production with "modern business methods" that would routinize the work of the tappers and dispense with the middlemen. They saw the *aviador* system as lacking any effective mechanisms for increasing the output of the *seringueiros*, and contended that the large number of intermediaries merely served to drive up prices. Thus their common strategy was to conduct all commercial transactions on their own and to pay the tappers in cash at flat rates—unlike the *aviadores*, who "purchased" the rubber from the tappers and usually made payment in the form of overpriced goods and tools.

On paper, this may have seemed like a very clever strategy, but the companies failed to take into account the wishes of the tappers themselves, and this proved to be the real sticking point. In virtually every case, the tappers quietly refused to deliver their rubber (or the large majority of it) to the new corporate *patrão*. Thus, the Brazilian Rubber Trust "received" only 60 tons of rubber from a property that had been producing over four times as much under the previous regime. According to Ashmore Russan, the former manager of this enterprise, there probably was no decline in the actual *amount* of rubber being produced, but the *seringueiros* had simply decided to sell it to other buyers. "In the rubber regions of Brazil," Russan concluded, "the produce does *not* belong to the owner of the estate. It belongs to the collector—the rubber cutter."[38]

Even though we have no personal accounts from the tappers themselves, it is easy to imagine why they proved so uncooperative. Accustomed to determining their own work pace and to considering the rubber they tapped their own personal property, the *seringueiros* must have balked at the demands of the foreign estate owners, which clearly threatened to erode what little autonomy the Amazonians maintained. Moreover, the foreigners had greatly overestimated the attractions of payment in cash. Given how isolated the tappers were, cash wages only meant that additional effort would have to be expended to purchase necessary goods. The new set-up also made it hard for the tappers to resist selling their rubber to interloping traders, since the latter frequently offered the tappers goods that otherwise would be difficult to come by. Indeed, the *aviadores* may have inflated prices and supplied *seringueiros* with inferior merchandise, but their willingness to take special orders for food, clothing, or medicine made a significant difference to the tapper working in a remote rubber district.

Of course, the foreigners were not alone in having to contend with the interloping traders, or "river pirates," as they came to be known. Russan explained that the local *aviadores* had developed methods for dealing with trespassing traders and wayward tappers, but such methods could only be used by those who "have lost all respect for the sixth commandment," and he sternly advised foreigners against resorting to violence. Lest such advice be interpreted as indicating softheartedness or superior morality, it should be mentioned that Russan's motives in the matter were purely practical. He warned other foreigners that the use of violence could land them in jail or worse, unlike the *aviadores*, who could commit occasional acts of violence with impunity. Why the distinction? Stated simply, the foreigners were by no means welcomed by all members of the local elite. Many of the political bosses in the interior were *aviadores*—precisely the middlemen which these corporations wished to eliminate—and who therefore suspected that the presence of these outsiders threatened their livelihood. Consequently, not only could the foreigners not expect the same sort of leeway or "protection" afforded other participants in the rubber trade, but they even were subject to various forms of harassment.[39] The result was a situation in which the tapper could resist the demands of the corporate *patrão* without running the risk of reprisals, and it was to this turn of events that Russan attributed his company's failure. To strengthen his argument, he pointed out that corporate efforts had been much more successful in the Belgian Congo, where the "most barbaric methods" had been condoned by the authorities.

What remedy could be applied to this situation? According to the former manager of the Brazilian Rubber Trust: "There is none so far as the foreign company is concerned, except foreign labor. . . . Chinamen or Japanese who will work for a wage at anything they are set to do, seem to me essential to the success of the foreign company working rubber properties in Brazil." But his disillusionment with the Amazonian rubber gatherer was mild in comparison to a disgruntled American investigator who wrote to *India Rubber World* with a "Suggestion for Pará"; with tongue firmly in cheek, he announced his discovery of the "ideal solution" to the Amazon's labor problems—a workforce of trained monkeys.[40]

This was hardly the first time that disappointed capitalists had rationalized a financial debacle by citing the inherent "laziness" or intractability of a particular ethnic group or laboring class. What is interesting about these foreigners' assessment of the rubber tappers is how sharply it contrasts with the standard image of the *seringueiros* at the height of the boom, an image which portrayed them as enserfed, dehumanized, and helpless. Of course, the tappers' position vis-a-vis the foreigners was strengthened by the complicity of local officials, but the *seringueiros'* response to "modern business methods" indicates that they were accustomed to a certain amount of autonomy in their work routine and viewed themselves as independent producers, not wage laborers. In addition, it was not just the foreigners' lack of political clout that allowed this situation to persist, since even the powerful *aviadores* who dominated local politics rarely established complete control over their clients.

Different levels of political power were not all that distinguished the traditional *patrão* from the corporate *seringalista*. Whereas the foreigners identified with the interests of the overseas manufacturers who wanted increased production and lower prices, the *aviadores* did not necessarily share these objectives. As long as prices were rising (and it could be assumed that prices would continue to rise if rubber remained scarce), the *aviador* did not need to increase his clients' output to increase his profits. What he wanted was not to revolutionize rubber production, but to gain as much control over the trade within the existing economic framework as possible—whether through monopolization of marketing, use of violence, or occasional displays of paternalism. Thus, unlike the foreign investor, the *aviador* did not strive to proletarianize the tappers.

The *aviador* was also in a position to appreciate just how difficult this would be to accomplish. Throughout the boom, Amazonian rubber continued to be gathered almost exclusively from wild trees, so that the tapper population remained highly dispersed. With both the extraction and the processing of latex occurring on a highly decentralized basis, the *patrão* could not hope to create the mechanisms for constant surveillance which we associate with mines, plantations, and, of course, factories. This meant not only that the *seringueiros* often had ample opportunity to escape from an especially abusive or exploitative *patrão*, but that they also retained a great deal of discretion over their work patterns. Therefore, *aviadores* might have discouraged their clients from devoting their time to subsistence activities but could rarely prevent a tapper from going hunting or fishing.[41] Certainly the *seringueiros* were often intimidated by the *patrão*'s threats of reprisal, but in a situation where the demand for new clients almost always outran the supply, it made little sense for an *aviador* to be unduly severe with a tapper who was not sufficiently productive. Moreover, since the *aviador* invested almost no capital except for the cost of the goods that he advanced to the tapper, he did not suffer any serious losses if a *seringueiro*'s output failed to grow.

Developments subsequent to the collapse of the wild rubber market (1910–1912) underscore how little the export boom had disrupted traditional Amazonian patterns of production and exchange. As plantation rubber from Asia entered the market in greater and greater quantities, the price of rubber dropped precipitously, going from a high of about three dollars a pound to a low of well below a dollar in less than a decade. The majority of the large *aviador* firms went bankrupt in the aftermath of the crash, and many local observers warned that prices were falling so low that it would soon become unremunerative to tap wild rubber. Yet the export statistics for the years from 1910 to 1920 do not reveal a dramatic decline in production. Indeed, the total output for the Amazon in 1917 was slightly higher than the figure for 1911. Rubber production did finally drop markedly in the 1920s, but this was due to the rising price of Brazil nuts—a product which temporarily replaced rubber as the Amazon's leading "extractive" commodity.

The relatively mild repercussions of plummeting prices demonstrates both the extent and the limits of the Amazonian population's involvement in the market economy. While thousands of *seringueiros*, discouraged by the lower prices or the bankruptcy of their *patrão*, poured into the urban centers or migrated away from the region altogether, the vast majority continued to participate in the extractive sector.[42] They did so for a number of reasons; after years of combining production for the market and production for subsistence, few Amazonians (whether *caboclos* or Cearenses) were in a position to become totally self-sufficient. Undoubtedly they had become accustomed to using such goods as firearms and metal fishhooks, not to mention certain foodstuffs that they could not produce for themselves. True, their rubber could no longer "purchase" as much merchandise as previously, but that simply meant that they had to expand their subsistence activities accordingly. Furthermore, in some areas the *patrão* had become powerful enough to establish either formal or informal control over access to land. Usually lacking the capital and labor to develop the land agriculturally, the *patrão* would allow the local inhabitants to cultivate subsistence plots if they agreed to spend some portion of their time tapping rubber.[43]

It is evident from the post-boom export statistics that Amazonian society had gone beyond the point where a crash in the market for a particular extractive commodity could generate a wholesale return to strict subsistence production. However, the ability of the rubber tappers (and Brazil-nut gatherers) to survive when confronted by a severe price drop demonstrates the continuing viability of the subsistence sector. Clearly, even those Amazonians who were permanently tied into commodity relations had not been completely separated from the means of production. Moreover, the ability of the gathering population to combine rubber and Brazil-nut collecting implies ongoing autonomy and physical mobility.

The continuing appeal of the gathering economy is confirmed by a series of events that occurred in the 1930s. In the late 1920s, the Ford Motor Company bought up some large stretches of land along the Tapajóz River, intending to plant thousands of *heveas* in the hope of imitating British successes in Asia. From the outset, the venture known as Fordlandia found itself bedeviled by environmental problems and regional political disputes, any one of which could have proved fatal to the enterprise. Judging from the Brazilian government's reports on the project, however, the most serious problem facing the company was labor recruitment. Despite the fact that Ford was offering what most observers agreed were reasonable wages and accommodations by Amazonian standards, the company found it difficult to retain its labor force. When asked to explain this difficulty, its managers claimed that they had been unable to compete with the attractions of the extractive economy.[44]

As far back as the 1840s and 1850s, earlier visitors to the Amazon had commented upon the indigenous population's peculiar "addiction" to gathering activities and concomitant distaste for routinized labor. Typically, the British naturalist Alfred Wallace contended that only European or American colonization could make commercial agriculture flourish in the Amazon, since "rubber-making and gathering cacao and Brazil-nuts are better liked [by the natives] than the regular cultivation of the soil."[45] Not surprisingly, many of these statements by Europeans and North Americans were racist in tone; apparently, these travelers viewed the "indolent disposition of the people" as either cultural or genetic. Yet, interestingly enough, the much larger *caboclo* population of the post-boom period, which included descendants of African slaves and Cearense migrants, as well as detribalized Indians, exhibited a similar preference for collecting activities over routinized labor. Indeed, small producers all over the globe have shared the Amazonian's distaste for regimented and routinized labor and have avoided it as long as alternatives to such labor existed. Of course, for the inhabitants of the industrialized nations, the alternatives rapidly disappeared. But for the Amazonians, other options continued to exist—at least until recent decades. Because of the sheer size of the region, its huge stretches of unclaimed or undeveloped territory, and the limited resources of its regional elite, for many years after the boom the typical rural inhabitant of the Amazon retained sufficient access to the valley's economic resources to survive without being reduced to wage labor.

NOTES

1. For contrasting historical treatments of the export economies, see Roberto Cortés Conde, *The First Stages of Modernization in Spanish America* (New York, 1974); Jonathan V. Levin, *The Export Economies* (Cambridge, Mass., 1960); Andre Gunder Frank, *Capitalism and Underdevelopment in Latin America: Historical Studies of Chile and Brazil* (New York, 1967).

2. On the transition from slave to free labor in São Paulo, see Michael M. Hall, "The Origins of Mass Immigration in Brazil," Ph.D. dissertation, Columbia University, 1969; Warren Dean, *Rio Claro: A Brazilian Plantation System, 1820–1920* (Stanford, Calif., 1976), pp. 156–193.

3. Denise Helly, *Idéologie et ethnicité. Les Chinois Macao à Cuba: 1847–1886* (Montréal, 1979); Levin, *The Export Economies*, pp. 27–123 (on the guano trade); Heraclio Bonilla, *Guano y burguesía en el Perú* (Lima, 1974); Florencia E. Mallon, *Defense of Community in Peru's Central Highlands* (Princeton, 1983); Michael Montéon, "The *Enganche* in the Chilean Nitrate Sector, 1880–1930," *Latin American Perspectives*, 6:3 (Summer 1979), pp. 66–79; David McCreery, "Forced Wage Labor in Rural Guatemala, 1876–1945," paper presented at the meeting of the Social Science History Association, Oct. 23–25, 1981; Arnold J. Bauer, "Rural

Workers in Spanish America: Problems of Peonage and Rural Oppression," *Hispanic American Historical Review* 59:1 (Feb. 1979), pp. 34–63.

4. The particular "staple" involved clearly was not the deciding factor. In Colombia, small producers played a major role in the coffee economy, whereas forced and free labor were used in Guatemala and Brazil. Charles W. Bergquist, *Coffee and Conflict in Colombia, 1886–1910* (Durham, N.C., 1978), pp. 21–27; McCreery, "Forced Wage Labor"; Dean, *Rio Claro*, pp. 88–193.

5. The best study of the years following the conquest is David Graham Sweet, "A Rich Realm of Nature Destroyed: The Middle Amazon Valley, 1640–1750," Ph.D. dissertation, University of Wisconsin, 1974. See also John Hemming, *Red Gold* (Cambridge, Mass., 1978), esp. chaps. 9, 11, 18, and 19.

6. For a brief but excellent discussion of the formation of the *caboclo* population, see Eric B. Ross, "The Evolution of the Amazon Peasantry," *Journal of Latin American Studies*, 10:2 (Nov. 1978), pp. 200–210.

7. For a more extensive discussion of the early tapper-trader relationship, see Barbara Weinstein, *The Amazon Rubber Boom, 1850–1920*, (Stanford, Calif., 1983) esp. chaps. 1 and 2.

8. One of the more reliable accounts of the early rubber trade accuses the *aviadores* of taking undue advantage of the tapper's isolation and of committing some serious abuses, but sees such problems as confined to the more remote rubber districts. A. C. Tavares Bastos, *O vale do Amazonas*, 3rd ed. (São Paulo, 1975), pp. 200–207.

9. This would reduce the population of the Brazilian Amazon to approximately 130,000. See Robin L. Anderson, "Following Curupira: Colonization and Migration in Pará, 1758–1930," Ph.D. dissertation, University of California-Davis, 1976, p. 250.

10. Roger Bastide, "The Other Quilombos," in Richard Price, ed., *Maroon Societies* (Garden City, N.Y., 1973), pp. 195–197; Weinstein, *The Amazon Rubber Boom*, chap. 2.

11. Marechal Francisco Jose de Souza ao dr. Bernardo de Souza Franco, *Espozição do estado e andamento dos negocios da provincia do Pará*, April 8, 1839. The "Bodies of Laborers" are also mentioned in William Lewis Herndon, *Exploration of the Valley of the Amazon* (Washington, D.C., 1853), pp. 256–258. During the colonial period, the Corpo de Trabalhadores was composed of subjugated Indians who were used as rowers in river convoys or as laborers in the construction of Portuguese settlements. See Colin M. MacLachlan, "The Indian Labor Structure in the Portuguese Amazon, 1700–1800," in Dauril Alden, ed., *The Colonial Roots of Modern Brazil* (Berkeley, Calif., 1973), pp. 224–225.

12. João Maria de Moraes, *Discurso pelo vice-presidente do Pará*, Aug. 15, 1846, pp. 4–5.

13. The hostility of the traditional elite toward the rubber trade was exacerbated by the large number of Sephardic Jews who participated in the trade. William H. Edwards, *A Voyage up the River Amazon* (Philadelphia, 1847), p. 36.

14. Sebastião do Rêgo Barros, Presidente do Pará, *Falla à assemblêa legislativa do Pará*, Aug. 15, 1854, p. 4.

15. The influential 1866 report by A. C. Tavares Bastos (*O vale do Amazonas*), for instance, counseled expansion of the rubber trade.

16. See, for example, Richard Collier, *The River That God Forgot* (New York,

1968); Howard Wolf and Ralph Wolf, *Rubber: A Story of Glory and Greed* (New York, 1936); Jose Maria Ferreira de Castro, *The Jungle: A Tale of the Amazon Rubber Tappers* (New York, 1935).

17. Instituto de Terras do Pará (ITERPA), *Registro de posse*, municipio de Breves (1855–1859).

18. According to one observer of the rubber economy, "The Amazon is the land of credit. There is no capital. The *seringueiro* owes the '*patrão*,' the '*patrão*' owes the '*aviador* house,' the '*aviador* house' owes the foreigner, and so it goes." Mário Guedes, *Os seringaes* (Rio de Janeiro, 1920), p. 128.

19. A provincial official who attempted to gauge the population of a municipal seat in the "islands" rubber district of Pará found his task an impossible one due to the sharp seasonal fluctuations in the number of inhabitants. Domingos Soares Ferreira Penna, *Obras completas*, vol. 1 (Belém, 1971), p. 117.

20. One of Belém's daily papers did report a case in which a group of irate *seringueiros* murdered their *patrão*. This was, however, an unusual incident. *Folha do Norte*, Jan. 14, 1914.

21. For accounts of American experiences in the early rubber trade, see "The Early American Rubber Trade in Pará," *India Rubber World* (New York), Nov. 15, 1893, p. 41; and "The Pará Rubber Trade 40 Years Ago," *India Rubber World*, Dec. 15, 1982, pp. 66–67.

22. On the northeastern droughts and their impact on the rubber trade, see Roberto Santos, *História econômica da Amazônia, 1800–1920* (São Paulo, 1980), pp. 97–107. One recent study of the rubber trade contends that migration from the northeast to the Amazon persisted even once the drought had passed. João Pacheco de Oliveira Filho, "O caboclo e o brabo: notas sobre duas modalidades de force-de-trabalho na expansão da fronteira amazônica," *Encontros com a Civilização Brasileira*, 11 (May 1979), pp. 101–140.

23. On the upper reaches of the Xingu River, for example, there was a well-patrolled spot known as "Paga-Contas" (Pay the Bills). Any tapper caught going downriver who could not prove that he had paid his debts would be returned to his *patrão* or sent to a worse fate. Interview with Anfrísio Nunes Filho, Belém, January 1978.

24. José Porphírio de Miranda, ruler of the Xingú, married the niece of Pará's political boss at the height of the boom, and such potentates as Raymundo Pereira Brazil and José Júlio de Andrade had themselves "elected" intendent of their *municípios*. Weinstein, *The Amazon Rubber Boom*, chap. 4.

25. Ashmore Russan, "Working Rubber Estates on the Amazon," *India Rubber World*, Oct. 1, 1902, pp. 5–6.

26. For accounts of the Putumayo tragedy, see W. E. Hardenburg, *The Putumayo, the Devil's Paradise* (London, 1912); Wolf and Wolf, *Rubber*, pp. 84–101; Collier, *The River That God Forgot*.

27. Raymundo Pereira Brazil, *O rio Tapajóz* (Belém, 1914), p. 33.

28. Robert F. Murphy, "The Rubber Trade and the Mundurucú Village," Ph.D. dissertation, Columbia University, 1954.

29. In 1907, Governor Bueno de Andrade of the Acre wrote President Afonso Pensa urging him to postpone implementation of the land law in the federal territory (Acre), explaining that the Acreanos "feared" property regulations and might revolt. Arquivo Nacional (Rio), *Coleção Afonso Pena* (1907), Document

1.2.49. For a general account of the Acre conflict, see Lewis A. Tambs, "Rubber, Rebels and Rio Branco: The Contest for the Acre," *Hispanic American Historical Review*, 46:3 (Aug. 1966), pp. 254–273.

30. Manuel V. Ballivián and Gasto F. Pinilla, *Monografía de la industria de la goma elástica* (Bolivia, 1912), pp. 110–112.

31. *A Província do Pará* (Belém), Jan. 5, 1900. This article is also interesting for its use of racial stereotypes peculiar to the Amazon. The industrious tapper described in the article is a black ex-slave, while the lazy but clever tapper is a native Amazonian.

32. "Cheaper Rubber from the Amazon," *India Rubber World*, Feb. 1, 1901, p. 161; Henry C. Pearson, *The Rubber Country of The Amazon* (New York, 1911), pp. 38–40.

33. See, for example, "A Brilliant Enterprise," *India Rubber World*, Apr. 15, 1892, pp. 209–210; "A Rubber Farm for Sale," *India Rubber World*, Dec. 1, 1901, p. 77. Consular reports also encouraged Americans and Europeans to invest in rubber production. "Consular Report on Rubber Exports, Acre Situation, and Pará and Manaus Markets," in *Dispatches from the United States Consuls in Pará*, Record Group 59 (Roll 8, Vol. 10), Jan. 24, 1900; Great Britain (Foreign Office), *Diplomatic and Consular Reports*, Miscellaneous Series, "Report on the State of Amazonas" (no. 530), June 1900.

34. "Growth of Manaos as a Rubber Center," *India Rubber World*, Apr. 1, 1901, p. 196.

35. *A Provincia do Pará*, Sept. 26, 1898. The Rubber Estates of Pará was reported as paying £350,000 for its property in Anajas.

36. For a detailed account of these enterprises, see Weinstein, *The Amazon Rubber Boom*, chap. 6.

37. "Some Rubber Trading Experiments," *India Rubber World*, June 1, 1902, p. 275.

38. Russan, "Working Rubber Estates," pp. 5–6.

39. In one widely publicized incident, two British estate managers were beaten up by local ruffians employed by the municipal political boss. Although the identities of the perpetrators were well known, they went completely unpunished. Information on this episode can be found in the archive of the Brazilian Ministry of Foreign Relations (Itamaraty), *Avisos do estado do Pará*, July 4, 1899, and in *Folha do Norte*, July 3, 1899.

40. "A Suggestion for Pará," *India Rubber World*, Oct. 1, 1902, p. 4.

41. Joseph Woodroffe, *The Rubber Industry of the Amazon* (London, 1915), pp. 53–57.

42. For a discussion of the short- and long-term effects of the decline, see Weinsten, *The Amazon Rubber Boom*, chap. 8. Both the impressionistic accounts and the statistical data from the decline years strongly contradict Celso Furtado's contention that the Amazon "regressed to the most primitive form of subsistence economy" after the collapse of the wild rubber market. *The Economic Growth of Brazil* (Berkeley, Calif., 1971), pp. 147–148.

43. A good account of the rubber trade in the post-boom period can be found in Charles Wagley, *Amazon Town: A Study of Man in the Tropics* (New York, 1953), pp. 64–101.

44. Discussions of the labor problems on the Ford rubber plantations can be

found in the Arquivo Nacional (Rio), Conselho Federal do Comércio Exterior, PR 83/Processos 1061, 1061 (vol. 2), 1063/1940, "Medidadas de emergencia em amparo a borracha e castanha"; "Atividades da Cia. Ford Industrial do Brasil, no Rio Tapajóz"; and "Transporte de trabalhadores nacionais para a região amazônica." For a general account of the Ford ventures in the Amazon, see John Galey, "Industrialist in the Wilderness: Henry Ford's Amazon Venture," *Journal of Inter-American Studies*, 21:2 (May 1979), pp. 264–289.

45. Alfred H. Wallace, *A Narrative of Travels on the Amazon and Rio Negro* (London, 1853), pp. 79–80. Of course, the vast majority of the Amazonian population was engaged in manioc cultivation at the time of Wallace's visit, but he apparently did not regard such subsistence farming as the "regular cultivation of the soil."

4

Agriculture and Industry in the Nineteenth-Century Stéphanois: Household Employment Patterns and the Rise of a Permanent Proletariat

Michael Hanagan

Increasingly, proletarianization, the process by which an industrial work-force is formed, has dominated the thinking of labor historians. At present, many historians of the nineteenth-century working class are searching for the point at which pre-industrial workers first confronted factory life. According to these historians, the shock of the new industrial order was a key factor in the formation of modern working-class consciousness. Also, historians are inquiring into the background of the militant proletariat that developed in nineteenth-century cities in order to understand the impact of class formation on the culture and political consciousness of a mature working class.

This concern for proletarianization has come from scholars with very different historical perspectives. Marxists like E. P. Thompson have emphasized how past political experiences were assimilated into the enduring culture of the working classes. Other Marxists like E. J. Hobsbawm have focused on the gradual accumulation of experiences which over the course of a generation collectively formed the "rules of the game" of social conflict between workers and employers. Peter Stearns has depicted nineteenth-century worker revolts as part of a difficult process of adjustment during which workers confronted a new and unfamiliar industrial world. And a Parsonian sociologist like Neil Smelser has stressed how the loss of family solidarity at the workplace provoked great protest.[1]

While these historians and sociologists have reemphasized the importance of class formation, they have typically taken for granted one important aspect of the process. Almost all these formulations assume the existence of a permanent proletariat; they assume there existed a working class that expected to spend its entire life in industrial employment. In the following discussion, the term "permanent proletariat" will be used to denote a working class that anticipated spending the whole of its economically active life in an industrial occupation.

But historians know very little about the process by which a permanent proletariat was formed. Of course, everyone knows that industrialization spread across Europe at an uneven pace and that different regions of Europe developed their own special mix of industrial occupations, but how closely tied are industrialization and occupation to permanent proletarianization? More systematic research needs to be done concerning the factors that created the permanent proletariat and how these factors varied over time and place among industrializing regions. Does the formation of a permanent proletariat typically coincide with some definite stage in the spread of factory industry? Can regional factors be identified that are likely to produce different rates of permanent proletarianization, and can differences in the rate of permanent proletarianization help explain the uneven character of working-class protest in pre-industrial Europe? Finally, how did the timing and the circumstances of proletarianization affect the ability of workers to protest and the kinds of struggles in which they became engaged?

The Stéphanois region of France provides an interesting vantage point from which to observe the different stages in the formation of a permanent proletariat because this region, centered around the city of Saint-Etienne in the southeast of France, was one of the earliest industrializing regions on the European continent; it has been called the "cradle of the Industrial Revolution in France." Between 1800 and 1870 it was probably the fastest urbanizing region of France. In a country that witnessed relatively slow but steady industrial growth, the Stéphanois region was a pace-setter. Before the onset of French industrial transformation, it was a center of pre-industrial production, especially silkweaving and hardware. In the years between 1815 and 1840, mechanized textiles and milling developed there. Coal production increased during the entire period, but most rapidly after 1840, and heavy metalworking also developed after 1840. The pattern of regional economic development is a familiar one: first, the gradual growth of pre-industrial textiles, followed by industrial transformation in textiles and the introduction of water-powered mills, and finally, the development of heavy industry based on metalworking and coalmining.[2]

This chapter focuses on the Stéphanois region of France during the principal stages of its industrial development: domestic industry, the rise of the factory system, and the growth of heavy industry. It will show that the extent to which a permanent proletariat developed was not simply a product of technology which was roughly identical in all industrializing regions; rather, the growth of a permanent proletariat was the product of the interaction of technology and local levels of capital accumulation with the local forces of agricultural supply. Regional agricultural patterns and industrial conditions, themselves the results of geography and antecedent economic forces, played an important role in determining the rate of formation of a permanent proletariat during the period of the Industrial Revolution, and this rate may have varied from region to region as levels of capital accumulation and agricultural circumstances varied.

Differences in the pace of the formation of a permanent proletariat had considerable impact on the location and direction of social protest. As long as the countryside remained the home or the ultimate destination of the majority of industrial workers, their protests were often carried out in rural areas where their neighbors were agriculturalists, and the issues they fought for reflected their isolation from the larger industrial world and their need to appeal to their neighbors for support. Permanent proletarianization changed the location and the demands of worker protest. Of course, this new group of workers marched and struck within an urban environment. More important, the issues raised in strikes and demonstrations reflected the precarious circumstances of their new condition. Workers frequently had to fight to maintain the wages and benefits that were the basis for their position as permanent workers; workers also fought to gain control over the industrial institutions on which their position as permanent proletarians depended.

Throughout the whole period between 1770 and 1870 substantial numbers of unskilled and semi-skilled industrial workers had inhabited the Stéphanois region of France. Periodically these industrial workers had been involved in the periphery of local politics. They had participated in the club movement during the Terror, demonstrated in 1848, and rioted in 1871.[3] Yet the socialist movement that began to develop among industrial workers in the 1870s, a movement to which the modern Stéphanois working-class movement traces its roots, was essentially a new phenomenon. What continuity there was between the urban political movements among industrial workers of the first three quarters of the nineteenth century and that of the last quarter was roundabout. It was a tradition communicated to late nineteenth-century industrial workers by means of radical artisanal workers or by the rural communities that sent the industrial workers to the city.[4] This chapter suggests that structural factors connected with the formation of a permanent proletariat can help explain the timing of the appearance of an enduring industrial worker political movement in the Stéphanois, and also the political outlook that migrants from the countryside brought with them to the city.

The key factors that determined the kind of proletariat that emerged in the region between 1780 and 1880 were the supply of labor available in local agriculture and the kind of workers demanded by local industry. The basic determinants of the agricultural supply of labor were the manpower requirements of local agriculture, the system of land tenure prevalent in the countryside, and the size of the agricultural population. If the local agricultural supply of labor proved insufficient, the main alternative was long-distance labor recruitment. Labor recruitment was a costly and time-consuming process exceeding the financial capacities of many early industrialists. The basic factors in industrial demand had to do with the kind of workers industry wanted, and whether local industry had the money to pay for the kind of workers it preferred.[5]

The most simple and straightforward consequence of the interaction of agricultural supply and industrial demand for labor occurred when peasants left the land to become lifetime proletarians in urban industry. Initially, however, this one-way trip from the land to the factory was infrequent; for most of the period under discussion, industrial work was only an interlude in a basically agricultural career. In the stage of domestic industry, industry remained in the countryside and continued as a side-line of agriculture. In the second stage, the rise of the factory system, an urban workforce developed, but most workers labored in urban industry on a temporary basis, as part of an early phase in a life-cycle pattern of employment. Only in the final stage of industrial evolution, with the growth of heavy industry, did a permanent proletariat begin to develop. Of course, not every industry exhibited all phases of this evolution. Some industries, such as Stéphanois textiles, did not develop a substantial permanent proletariat at any point during the century; rather, the successive stages describe tendencies within important industries that developed successively during the period of industrial transformation in the Stéphanois. In chronological order, the different stages of Stéphanois industrial evolution will be examined so as to isolate the factors that shaped the development of a local workforce.[6]

At the turn of the eighteenth century, domestic industry, the first stage of industrial development, flourished in the Stéphanois. Local conditions such as climatic factors and the pre-existing forms of land tenure played a vital role in influencing the number of workers in agriculture who could be diverted to industry. Climatic conditions in the region affected agriculturalists' participation in industry. For several reasons, the rugged character of the highlands that surround the Stéphanois valleys on three sides provided a reservoir of seasonal labor for Stéphanois industry. First, the long winters that reign in all these plateau areas ensure that little outdoor work can be performed for half the year. In the Haute-Loire, snow falls about half the year and stays on the ground for three months of the year. Second, the highlands are also subject to violent fluctuations in temperature and rainfall, which make it even more difficult for mountaineers to plan their year around agriculture. Summer may come suddenly, and rainfall is uneven; the clay soil receives too much rain one year and none the next.[7] Third, agricultural labor requirements, themselves a function of climatic conditions, fluctuate greatly. Both sowing and harvesting must be done quickly. And in summer and fall, agricultural work is bunched together into a few short periods of intense work when all available hands are desperately needed, followed by periods of relative inactivity. In short, the normal preoccupations and concerns of agriculturalists are intensified and magnified in the Stéphanois.

Land tenure also influenced the supply of agricultural labor to industry; many local agriculturalists possessed small holdings. That most rural households owned some property made a difference in the formation of the workforce. The presence of a large agricultural proletariat in the region might have facilitated the recruitment of an urban proletariat. Agricultural proletarians were a particularly mobile group, and they might have provided a casual urban workforce, moving into the cities when released from seasonal agricultural work. Unfortunately for local industrialists, the only substantial agricultural proletariat to develop in the region arose in the Forezien plain to the north of the Stéphanois. The plain was a humid, marshy area with high mortality rates; the area constantly needed to recruit workers from outside to maintain its workforce, and it provided few recruits to local industry.[8] Similarly, a proletarianized rural industrial workforce would have also speeded the formation of a permanent urban proletariat. Some proletarianized areas of rural industry did emerge, but for the most part Stéphanois rural artisanal households succeeded in retaining ties to the soil.

By and large, Stéphanois entrepreneurs had to make do with an agricultural population composed of smallholders or of tenants with long-term leases. Peasants predominated in the mountainous areas surrounding Saint-Etienne where smallholdings restricted the mobility of the agricultural population.[9] Not that peasants were immobile. In other areas of France, male peasants migrated to Paris to find work after the harvest was completed, but even in Paris these workers were a seasonal or temporary workforce. Even in such areas as the Creuse and Haute-Vienne, wives and young children remained behind to tend the hearth.[10] Yet, however far they might wander, farm and family served as powerful magnets to draw migrant workers back to their rural homes.

Though their long-term participation in industry was unlikely, smallholder households frequently possessed a labor surplus; many agricultural households had extra members whose labor could not be productively employed on the small parcel of land the household controlled. If entrepreneurs were willing to engage workers in domestic industry in the countryside, they could obtain a cheap, reliable workforce. No matter how low wages in domestic industry might be, they only increased the number of families who could survive in the countryside. And times of depression only made rural workers all the more dependent on farming and fastened them more firmly to the land. When good times returned an employer could count on most of his workforce being where he had left it. In 1826 a military observer commented:

The commerce of Saint-Etienne provides activity and perpetual motion to the entire population. In each village one manufactures, and cottages are transformed into workshops whose products supplement those of Saint-Etienne. The different branches of industry practiced there occupy in all more than 20,000 workers scattered over town and countryside. The latter are at the same time agriculturalists and artisans, they pass from one labor to another and return very quickly to their fields in times of commercial stagnation.[11]

Having looked at agricultural supply factors in the emergence of industry, let us now look at industrial demand. The requirements of technology determined the kind of labor industry was looking for, but the technological demands of early industry were sufficiently flexible that they could be adjusted to the conditions of local agricultural supply. Early Stéphanois industrial technology required little in the way of skill from its workers, it did not need substantial physical strength, and it did not insist on urban residence. Expanding local industry built upon the types of skills which most peasants possessed. Most peasant women knew how to spin and to weave. After 1750, automatic silk looms *à la basse lisse* required far fewer skills than did the looms *à la haute lisse* that were the monopoly of urban silkweavers.[12] And most peasant men had a rudimentary knowledge of smithing. The forging of simple metal products needed little more ability than the average adult male peasant possessed.

Cottage industry was also well suited to the financial capacity and the capitalization of local entrepreneurs. Perhaps the best way to characterize the pre-industrial economy of the late-eighteenth and early-nineteenth centuries in the Stéphanois region is to note the low level of capital accumulation. Eighteenth-century entrepreneurs in the region kept their capital fluid and balked at too great an investment in any one enterprise.[13] In industries that demanded less skill or in more mechanized industries, the number of workers laboring for a single employer grew, but the work was usually "put out" throughout the countryside or distributed to workers who owned their own machinery. In this way, employers both avoided investing in fixed assets like factories and benefited from cheap rural labor. Undoubtedly eighteenth-century employers would have preferred to supervise and to discipline their workforce, but in most cases the economic costs of pre-industrial factories were too high. Not for the Stéphanois entrepreneurs was the costly strategy of a Peter Stubbs of Warrington as described by T. S. Ashton. Stubbs was an eighteenth-century English file-maker who moved many of his former outworkers into a factory where they could be supervised.[14]

In the earliest stages of its industrial development, the characteristics of the industrial workforce were formed in the small space left unoccupied by agriculture; Stéphanois industry remained dominated by agriculture. For example, the timing of industrial activity was regulated by the timing of the harvest and the sowing. Rural textile and garment production was easily integrated into the routine of agricultural life on a seasonal basis. Gilbert Garrier has discovered the records of four brothers, velvetmakers of the Monts du Lyonnais on the edge of the Stéphanois, who noted the number of days they worked in velvetmaking each month. The record for each of the years, such as the year 1839 shown in Table 4.1, gives an insight into the alternating agricultural and seasonal rhythms of industrial worker life, as well as the workings of a family economy.[15]

The brothers' calendar reflects local agricultural conditions well. March and April were still months of industrial activity because the harsh summer months made a spring planting inadvisable. Agriculture picked up in May and June as the land was prepared for plowing. July to October was a frenzied period of activity as last year's fallow was plowed and planted with rye, while at the end of the period the rye planted the preceding year was harvested.

Metalworking was another industry whose workers sought industrial employment when they were deprived of agricultural opportunity. Already by the late eighteenth century observers marveled that, following the season, the Stéphanois population made a smooth transition from agricultural to industrial work.[16] One late-eighteenth-century visitor estimated that 30,000 persons were employed in cottage industry within 35 kilometers (7 leagues) of Saint-Etienne; the men were typically involved in metalworking, the women in silkmaking.[17]

More evidence of the agricultural domination of regional employment can be seen in the age and sex composition of the industrial workforce; participation in industry was determined by the priorities of agriculture. The adult males who could perform the heaviest physical labor were almost always allocated to agriculture during the season. Women and children were the most frequent participants in the cottage labor force. Silkmaking, either spinning or weaving, was the largest single employer in cottage industry, and it was usually performed by women and children.[18] And silkmaking was the closest that cottage industry came to year-round activity. Men and young males were engaged in seasonal forging, and entire families were employed in cutlery, but it too was a highly seasonal industry.[19]

Early industry had to follow the rhythm of agriculture because industry did not provide a wage sufficient to support the individual worker. In Stéphanois industry, capitalist productive relations dominated. Profit and loss were the sole criteria for employment; cheap labor was de-

	Jan.	Feb.	Mar.	Apr.	May	Jun.	Jul.	Aug.	Sept.	Oct.	Nov.	Dec.	Total
1.	21	8	--	--	--	--	--	--	--	--	10	15	54
2.	24	16	4	4	--	--	--	--	--	--	8	4	60
3.	24	20	14	12	6	8	--	--	--	--	8	24	116
4.	28	25	21	12	10	6	4	--	--	--	27	25	158

Table 4.1 Days of Work of Four Velvetmakers of Soucieu, 1889

manded and unnecessary labor fired. In a plentiful labor market, capitalism tended to reduce the price of labor below a minimum subsistence level. In the short run this made sense, but it could be self-defeating. By reducing wages to low levels, competitive capitalism made the worker dependent on the peasant economy, and in the long run often lost him and his family to the agricultural sector. But in an age when employers did not require any particular types of skilled workers, the transient character of the workforce was less important than the size of the pool; for every worker who dropped out a replacement was usually available.

The real foundation of capitalist expansion founded in cheap labor was the regime of domestic production in agriculture. As the Russian economist A. V. Chayanov noted long ago, farmers did not fire their sons and daughters when their contribution to total revenue fell below marginal cost.[20] In general, no single individual could afford to work for wages that fell below minimum survival standards, but family members might well work for such wages; at least they would be contributing something to the family economy.

Wages in cottage industry were uniformly lower than those minimally necessary for the survival of the individual worker. A government survey in 1848 demonstrated that most silkmakers and semi-skilled ribbonmakers in the labor force did not receive sufficient wages for their own survival, and that no seasonal worker received wages sufficient to support a family. The 1848 survey throws a valuable light on economic conditions within the region. Not only did the survey collect information on wages, but local officials were also asked to calculate a survival wage for a single worker and a family of four. In every rural canton, women and children silkworkers, laboring 12 hours a day, received less than a survival wage even if their salaries are calculated on the basis of year-round employment, not taking into account the frequently mentioned fluctuating conditions of the silk trade. One report estimated that rural silkworkers could not find work one-third of the time.[21]

The same failure to provide a family susbsistence minimum prevailed in metalworking. Rural hardware makers' typical family wages were almost adequate for the minimum family budget, but fell dramatically below it when the seasonal nature of the work is taken into account. Because all but the very youngest family members were expected to work, the fund necessary for worker replacement and that necessary for family survival almost coincide for hardware workers. Nailmaking still depended on water-powered mills, and these mills were inactive for three months of the year because of a lack of water.[22] A mid-nineteenth-century observer noted that "as little as they are, the resources which come from industrial wages add something to those [resources], as modest as they are, found cultivating the earth, either as sharecroppers or as laborers."[23]

The logic of industrial workers' protest in the early-nineteenth-century Stéphanois flowed from their location in the countryside and the precarious nature of their existence. The rural location of the industrial workforce meant that villages and small towns were the center of their struggles. The marginal nature of their circumstances focused their concern on the price of bread; the bread riot was their characteristic form of protest. During the French Revolution Stéphanois cottage workers who were dependent on the purchase of grain or bread in the market were a particularly active group. The first outbreak of open social conflict in the Stéphanois occurred in May and June 1790, when the population of several small towns engaged in domestic industry rioted against grain hoarders. In Chazelles-sur-Lyon, a small center of hat production, and in Saint-Bonnet-le-Château, a capital of ribbonweaving and lockmaking, crowds rioted against bakers who were accused of stockpiling grain; the stores uncovered by the crowd were auctioned and sold at a price set by the crowd. At Saint-Bonnet the crowd also broke into an Ursuline convent and auctioned off its grain stores. While some full-time workers inhabited these towns, they were centers of outworking for the nearby countryside. In Saint-Bonnet and its region, most women were involved in ribbonweaving *à la basse lisse* and most men were engaged in arms manufacture and lockmaking, occupations subject to a very extensive division of labor.[24] Doubtless many domestic workers from the surrounding countryside joined the urban population in these riots. The concern of these domestic workers with the rising price of grain and their consequent demand for the establishment of a "just price" gave domestic workers a common political objective with their artisanal brothers in the large city. During the revolution, in the regional center of Saint-Etienne, some 25 kilometers away, skilled artisans dominated the popular movement.[25]

The examples of Saint-Bonnet, Chazelles-sur-Lyon, and Saint-Etienne show that historians of the revolution who look for a militant industrial proletariat in the large city are looking in the wrong place. In the large city the artisan dominated, both in numbers and in capacity to protest. Most of the permanent working class in the large eighteenth-century city consisted of artisans. The greater income of artisans gave them the leisure time to participate in political discussions and the resources to join popular clubs. In order to find the semi-skilled or unskilled industrial worker playing a leading role in protest, it is necessary to look to the countryside and to the rural community.

In the early nineteenth-century Stéphanois, the next phase of regional economic development, the emergence of the factory system, brought rapid change. Urban development accelerated rapidly, and mechanization made its appearance in the region. Despite the seemingly revolutionary nature of these changes, the rise of the factory system did not entail a sharp break in the fabric of popular life, either among agriculturists or among workers in factory industry. In the era of the early factory system, agricultural conditions continued to determine the rhythm of industrial development. Not only did local conditions in agriculture still exert great importance within the industrial sector; most important of all, the industrial workforce remained temporary, and its composition was still determined by the forces of agricultural supply.

The task of Stéphanois industrialists was enormously facilitated because in the stage of factory industry, as in the preceding stage of domestic industry, the supply of agricultural labor grew in rough synchronization with the industrial demand for labor. When the nearby supply of labor began to slacken, industrialists simply expanded their area of industrial recruitment to more distant, untapped areas. The labor market in agriculture still offered an irresistible attraction to local businessmen.

The opportunities for industrial expansion in the rural labor market flowed from the pre-existing patterns of local landowning. Since at least the eighteenth century, the rural areas affected by industrial change had been predominantly inhabited by peasants, although sharecroppers and tenants had constituted a large minority, and a prosperous middle peasantry had flourished. Industrial income supplemented farm earnings and thus accentuated the pattern of small-scale holdings by promoting the consolidation of independent farming; sharecropping and tenantry became rarer. Owners of large and middle-sized farms in all the areas affected by industrialization bemoaned the scarcity of part-time agricultural labor. From the beginning of the eighteenth century onward, large owners in the Plateau de Livradois had lamented the seasonal migration of sawyers because of its effect on farm laborers' wages.[26] Domestic industry in the Haut-Vivarais also seems to have raised workers' wages.[27] In 1843 an observer who noted the sorry state of agriculture in the valley of the Gier listed the "dearness of labor" as one of the principal factors.[28]

At first, industrial demand only increased the local population's attachment to peasant agriculture. Aided by industrial wages, peasant families strengthened their position in the Stéphanois highland areas. The poor quality of land in the highlands, combined with the high wages demanded by agricultural workers, encouraged wealthier landlords to invest elsewhere. The small savings acquired through industrial work enabled some families to buy parcels of the newly available land. Between 1770 and 1870, the highland areas of the Stéphanois shook free of tenancy and sharecropping. At the same time, almost everywhere in the mountain areas, average farm size declined as large or medium plots gave way to small holdings.[29]

Besides the conditions of local land tenure, traditional regional patterns of crop selection also encouraged the growth of peasant agriculture. Outside observers often noted that dairy farming and cattle raising would have been the most productive use of local land, yet movement in this direction was difficult.[30] Most land was sown with grain; rye outdistanced wheat in all but one canton of the arrondissement of Saint-Etienne throughout the whole period. The winter hardiness of rye, combined with its tolerance for moisture and its ability to grow in acidic soils, made it the natural crop of the mountain regions. Yet rye was a crop that did not facilitate capital accumulation. It responded poorly to scientific farming methods and increased inputs of labor. While rye supported the local farming economy, it did not encourage the kind of saving that would have enabled local farmers to buy expensive cattle herds. Rye cultivation made it difficult for local farmers to break out of the circle of rural poverty.[31]

Local industrialists were able to hire workers fresh from the countryside and put them to work directly. Textiles and metalworking, the typical industries involved in the factory system, did not demand substantial numbers of skilled workers. Thus, the industrial demand for labor in the early years of the factory system in the Stéphanois encouraged local entrepreneurs to draw on agricultural reserves.

The braidmakers of Saint-Chamond provide an example of the typical unskilled worker of the early industrial revolution. From its origins in the Stéphanois in 1816, braidmaking was unskilled work performed by female workers. Like much of the technology of early nineteenth-century textiles, braidmaking seems to have required very little initiative or skill on the part of individual workers.[32] In 1840 Armand Audiganne noted: "Ingenious machines do all the painstaking work leaving the women the less tiring tasks, whether of the eye or of the hand." The comparatively simple machines of the early period were also relatively inexpensive, and within a short period there were over 20 braidmaking firms in Saint-Chamond; few firms employed more than 200 workers.[33]

For technological reasons, the work schedule of local industry meshed with that of local agriculture and greatly facilitated the use of rural workers in factory industry. Local climatic conditions were an important factor in the application of early technology, and climate affected the industrial demand for labor as well as its supply. In this period, both in textiles and in metalworking, much mill work involved waterpowered machinery, and this type of employment was highly seasonal. Part-time employment in milling hardly originated with the industrial revolution; Stéphanois laments about the erratic nature of mill work date back to the eighteenth century. But water-powered milling expanded in this period, as did the size of the mills.[34] Whatever their size, the mills came to a complete stop for between three and six months every year; generally mills stopped in the summertime when falling water levels made mill operation impossible and during winter when the streams froze. As shown by the example of the velvetmakers of Soucieu, mentioned earlier, summer closing coincided with the most intense period of farm activity. At the time when work was most needed, milling released its hands to the agricultural economy. In 1848, the canton of Le Chambon-Feugerolles reported 3,000 metalworkers subject to seasonal unemployment due to reduced water power.[35]

Judged by its effect on the daily life of the workforce, the geographic location of industry was the most important difference between the era of domestic industry and that of the factory system. The factory was a powerful urbanizing force. Some rural dwellers could walk to the factory on a daily basis, but most workers had to move away from rural homes and live in the city. Although performed in a different physical environment, factory work still remained temporary work. Just as peasants had moved back and forth between industry and agriculture in the stage of domestic industry, so they continued to move between industry and agriculture under the factory system. But in the period of the Industrial Revolution such movements meant migration.

Here again, braidmakers provide a characteristic example of work in the early factory system. Braidmaking occupied one stage in the life cycle of most workers; when they left braidmaking they abandoned industrial work and usually left the city to return to the countryside. Most of the workers were young women between 15 and 25, women who "generally leave the workshop between ages 20 and 30 in order to marry."[36] Most of these female workers came from the surrounding countryside. Individual companies maintained dormitories for them in the city.

Yet, while female braidworkers remained in the city and worked for their dowry, they were still very much part of farm families. Companies organized transportation to take them back to their relatives in the country on Sunday; often workers returned with provisions that enabled them to supplement their meager urban diet.[37] According to one author, night work was limited in Saint-Chamonnais textiles because rural parents protested their daughters' participation in nighttime activities.[38]

Other Stéphanois industries such as coalmining also employed a component of seasonal male workers. As Stéphanois mining expanded and the mining pits deepened, the demand for timbering in the mines greatly increased, and many montagnards went to work as lumberjacks.[39] Construction also produced the seasonal migration of sawyers from the Puy-de-Dôme to the Stéphanois, sawyers whose grandsons and granddaughters would one day become permanent residents of the valley towns.[40]

Capital requirements in early factory industry were higher than in domestic industry but not sufficiently high to free the early nineteenth-century entrepreneurs from their parasitic relationship to the rural economy. For early employers, the temporary migration of workers to the

city was not a choice but a necessity. Although factory work that concentrated workers in the city increased wages, it did not raise them
sufficiently to support proletarian families. Even fiercely competitive
capitalist enterprises had to pay wages sufficiently high to support industrial workers in the city. The factory system in no way lessened the
capitalists' search for a cheap and docile labor force, but it imposed the
additional constraint that the labor force had to be physically located
near a common workplace. Urban living meant that the cost of bed and
board had to be paid by the capitalist, since it could no longer be automatically imposed upon a farm family. While wages might be high
enough to enable a worker to put something aside if he or she was willing
to sacrifice, individual wages were insufficient to support workers' families.

For factory workers, the countryside remained an indispensable source
of support and their ultimate destination. Although they were living in
the city, claims on farms stayed crucial for skilled and semi-skilled industrial workers. Wages in braidmaking have been labeled "trivial"; female braidmakers received less than one franc a day for 12 hours' work.[41]
Braid employers built dormitories and furnished soup stock for meals
so that these workers could survive in the city at all. In 1838 male mill
workers received a salary just approaching minimal family survival levels,
but these salaries did not provide the possibility of saving to tide a worker
through unemployment or a brief sickness.[42] Sawyers also received low
daily wages; employment in sawyering was so erratic that it makes no
sense at all to calculate a yearly income.[43]

All temporary workers received less than did the semi-skilled permanent workforce of coalminers and metalworkers that was just beginning to develop in the Stéphanois at this time. There is no need to
exaggerate the income of these permanent workers. As numerous accounts attest, the wages of these permanent proletarians were barely
sufficient for family formation. Still, wage differentials between temporary workers and the average coalminer were considerable; more than
three to one for braidmakers, more than three to two for mill workers
and sawyers.[44] Thus, family-minded temporary workers in the city continued seeking their fortune in agriculture; temporary migration was
not imposed on such workers by the circumstances of their employment.

The new conditions of much early industrial work, temporary but
urban-based, had an important impact on industrial worker political
activity. Most of the political militancy of industrial workers during the
first half of the nineteenth century revolved around responses to economic crises such as those of 1847 and 1848. During times of industrial
crisis, semi-skilled and unskilled workers were turned out of their temporary jobs in large urban centers; these returning workers often brought
with them to the countryside political programs and strategies that were
influenced by their experiences in the larger industrial world. The town

of Saint-Bonnet-le-Château, which played a leading role in local protest in 1790, also played a key role in the Stéphanois countryside in 1848. But much had changed in Saint-Bonnet since 1790. Domestic industry was in decline. According to census figures, the population of the town reached its height in 1846. The road between Saint-Bonnet and Firminy that opened up in 1847 enabled outworkers in Saint-Bonnet to buy cheap coal in the Stéphanois, but it also made it easier for local workers to leave for the bigger industrial cities; the 1851 census revealed a population decline, and this falling trend continued for much of the rest of the century. The working class that had grown up in and around Saint-Bonnet during the early decades of the nineteenth century was increasingly being forced to orient itself to the larger Stéphanois labor market. Already between 1845 and 1848, migrants from Saint-Bonnet and surrounding communities show up in the marriage records of Saint-Etienne in far larger proportions than in the eighteenth century.[45]

The participation of local workers in the larger working-class world can be seen in the events of 1848 in the region. The issues raised by protestors in 1848 focused not so much on the price of grain but on employment. The economic crisis provoked by the revolution hit with special severity in Saint-Bonnet because it hit not only local industries but also sons and daughters employed outside the area who returned to swell the unemployment rolls. Returning migrants not only swelled the ranks of the hungry; they also brought with them new slogans and demands learned in cities like Saint-Etienne and Lyon. On May 12, 1848, when the city council announced that it could no longer employ all the jobless on road repairs, a riot broke out in Saint-Bonnet. In actions that foreshadowed the June days in Paris, local workers demanded that all the dismissed workers be restored to their positions. The city council responded by calling in troops.[46]

While the summoning of the troops stilled workers' demands for municipal aid, it also helped to turn popular protest in another direction. On May 31, 1848, the city council of Saint-Bonnet again requested the dispatch of troops to the troubled city; this time it requested the presence of a permanent garrison. The city council complained that with municipal aid now completely abolished, 400 unemployed workers were roaming the area; many of these jobless were entering into nearby forest land during the night and stealing wood. The council added that "respect for property is forgotten." The commanding general in Lyon regretfully refused the council's request because the growth of class tension all across the country made it imperative for the army to concentrate its troops for action, not to disperse them through the countryside.[47]

If records existed giving us the identity of the protestors in the streets of Saint-Bonnet, we would probably find some workers whose last employment had been in Saint-Etienne or Lyon or Rive-de-Gier rather than in Saint-Bonnet. While these temporary proletarians were relatively absent from the ranks of the protestors in these cities, still they likely played a big role in the small town. Interestingly, native Stéphanois coalminers made use of the departure of migrants to put forward demands that migration be limited and recruitment in coalmining be restricted to native young men. The miners felt that such restriction would also benefit agricultural production, which they believed was suffering because too many rural dwellers were swarming into the mining communities. Migrants dazzled by city ways (Rive-de-Gier had a population of almost 12,000 in 1846) and unaccustomed to mining ways soon "wished that they had never set foot in the mines."[48]

During slack times the temporary proletarians created by the early industrial revolution returned to the countryside to demand their rights in the communities to which they felt they truly belonged. The change in the forms of protest which occurred in Saint-Bonnet in the last two weeks of 1848 is also revealing of the nature of this working class. A demand for government aid to the unemployed is typically classified as a characteristic of industrial worker protest, while taking wood from nearby forests is characteristic of peasant protest. The easy transition in Saint-Bonnet from one action to the other shows the half-way nature of this group of domestic workers and peasants who existed in an intermediate zone between agriculture and industry.

In the next stage of local development, the stage in which heavy industry emerged, local industry freed itself from its dependence on agriculture. In fact, local agriculture found itself becoming subject to the industrial economy. The growth of a large urban market created new opportunities for local agriculture. James Lehning has described this process in considerable detail in the case of one commune on the southern edge of the Stéphanois region.[49] The proximity of an urban market made it possible for owners of only a few cows to produce dairy products for the market; an expanding local urban economy lowered the costs of entry into the dairy business.

By transforming local agriculture, emerging heavy industry destroyed the basis for the old rural economy of temporary labor surplus, which had underpinned the earlier industrial economies. Unlike earlier agriculture pursuits, dairy production was not only fairly profitable but provided year-round work for family members regardless of sex or age; as dairy production expanded, seasonal employment disappeared. Those rural dwellers too poor to buy cattle were the most likely candidates for permanent migration to the city. Increasingly after mid-century, the rural supply of temporary labor, either seasonal or life-cycle, began to diminish. More and more, rural migration to the city was confined to the ranks of the permanently dispossessed and displaced, who became permanent workers in the city.

The reorientation of local agriculture produced by dairying had a number of important consequences for industrial worker political action. First, of course, it meant that the industrial city became the exclusive scene of industrial worker militancy. But it also meant the disappearance of an important social group that linked worker militancy with rural revolt. In 1790 and again in 1848, industrial workers had served as catalysts for protest in at least some areas of the Stéphanois countryside. When the rural population became almost exclusively agricultural, the tempo of rural discontent lost an important means for harmonizing itself with urban protest. Finally, with the drying up of the rural reservoirs of industrial labor, it became more difficult for migrants from the country to assimilate into the industrial working class. Lacking any familiarity with industrial workers in the countryside and possessing little contact with industrial working-class culture, the peasants employed in urban industry must have found it more difficult to participate in urban industrial life than had their ancestors.

Outside capital was the driving force in the emergence of the third stage of industrial evolution to the Stéphanois; the initial form of heavy industry to develop in the region was coalmining. The increased market for coal in the expanding national economy had forced small coal producers to dig deeply, but for lack of capital the master miners and the owners of the mineral rights were unable to properly shore up the new pits or to drain them. The result was a series of cave-ins and floods that threatened the whole basin. The inability of small producers to finance deep mining enabled large capitalists, men from outside the Stéphanois, from Lyon and Paris, to enter. The pioneer in the field was the Compagnie des mines de Roche-la Molière et de Firminy, founded in 1820. The vast funds possessed by the company enabled it to widen and to mechanize the pits and then to link them together into a coordinated system.[50]

The large resources controlled by a substantial corporation unleashed new forces in the Stéphanois; the new industry created by capital investment required a new type of worker. For routinized production, employers needed a disciplined, regular workforce. Collective work groups that had previously existed were dissolved; task rates were abolished, and trained engineers took over much work formerly performed by the master miners. And although the skills required for mining diminished, they did not disappear; one estimate gives four months as the time necessary to train an average below-surface miner.[51] Mining was tough physical labor, and while children were sometimes used on the surface to sort out rock from the coal and underground to maintain vents, only adult men were used at the coalface.[52] The task before the coal company was to find a large number of adult males and to maintain some percentage of them in coalmining as the core of a permanent workforce. This was no easy matter since, as we have seen, male participation in mining on a semi-skilled basis had long been only a temporary stage in masculine employment, and the manpower needs of the mining companies were expanding rapidly.

What was crucial for the development of a permanent proletariat in the Stéphanois was that a large company operating in the region possessed sufficient resources to make progress toward this goal. By the beginning of the 1840s sufficient levels of capital accumulation had been reached in some key Stéphanois industries to support the creation of a permanent proletariat. In 1846 the Compagnie des mines de la Loire had been formed; it united most of the mining companies of the Loire into one centralized company employing nearly 4,000 workers in the Loire and was one of the largest and most powerful concerns in France at that time. This company could certainly afford to pay for such a workforce. The Compagnie was not a generous employer, and it used its monopoly power on several occasions to reduce workers' wages. But in 1848, when many local concerns simply shut down to wait for better times, the Compagnie de la Loire made use of its financial strength to preserve its workforce *in situ*. In 1850 the prefect of the Loire wrote: "The *Compagnie de la Loire* amassed mountains of coal while industry demanded only the smallest quantities.... It had powerfully seconded my efforts during the bad times."[53] Table 4.2 shows the evolution of yearly miners' salaries and the regularity of work in three French mines during one of the most turbulent periods of French history. The power of a large corporation to maintain production against the efforts of smaller companies is impressive. If these figures are accurate, it suggests that during this period the Stéphanois may have had the largest permanent proletariat of any mining basin in France.

What was necessary for the creation of a permanent proletariat? In order to recruit a permanent labor force, it was necessary to provide wages sufficient to support a family. But what was a family subsistence wage? First, of course, the wage had to be high enough to feed and clothe the worker and also his wife and child during the time when they could not earn money to support themselves. Family subsistence wages, then, varied with the local opportunities for female and child labor. But wages sufficient for daily survival were inadequate for the creation of a stable workforce. Provision had to be made so that the worker could support himself through seasonal changes in industrial production, and so that he could offset the routine interruptions in work time caused by sickness and injury. As long as routine emergencies meant that workers and their families had to depend on ties to relatives and friends in the country, workers would be very hesitant to establish themselves and their families permanently in industry. The longer the miner remained away

Evolution of Yearly Salary	1847	1848	1849	1850	1851	1852	1853	1854
Loire	796	705	790	755	776	740	822	861
Gard	756	765	101	92	690	627	615	1,320
Nord	531	510	515	536	535	531	566	613

Average Number of Days Worked Per Year	1847	1848	1849	1850	1851	1852	1853	1854
Loire	300	245	278	290	271	271	286	285
Gard	306	288	44	40	333	288	284	444
Nord	276	257	266	255	271	273	286	308

Source: Pierre Guillaume, La compagnie des mines de la Loire 1846-1854: essai sur l'apparition de la grande industrie en France (Paris: Presses universitaires de France, 1966), p. 141.

Table 4.2 Miners' Salaries and Regularity of Work in Three French Mines

from the country, the less likely he would be to call upon them for aid with any confidence.

In the very early period, when the first employers introduced new technologies into metalworking, the presence of a stable group of skilled workers from England was secured by long-term contracts and high wages. The wages of these foreign metalworkers were very high, partly because the employers had to lure them from their native land, and also because they had to permit them sufficient savings to provide themselves individually against the dangers of accident, illness, and unemployment.[54] In order to create a really large workforce, a cheaper solution had to be found. In fact, as soon as the size of the workforce began to grow, companies turned to the creation of company insurance programs, which provided some protection against accident and illness. Company programs could accomplish these ends at reduced costs. After all while accidents were quite frequent in newly emerging heavy industry, the majority of workers did not suffer serious injury. It was far cheaper to establish a fund for that minority that did suffer accidents than to have to provide compensation for each worker in the form of individual wages. Early nineteenth-century French laws required that mining companies had to establish a fund to provide for accidents, but the regulations governing such funds were so vague as to be meaningless. It was only with the formation of the Compagnie des mines that a serious fund to aid injured or disabled workers and their families was established.

But the administration of these programs soon became one of the first and most frequent targets of worker protest. In the Stéphanois all the early nineteenth-century company insurance programs on which evidence is available demanded joint contributions from workers and employers.[55] Yet almost all the decisions regarding the administration of such funds were made solely by the company, and this was a major working-class grievance. Workers were suspicious of the company's administration of such programs; they had good reason for their suspicion. Companies did manipulate the size of the funds in order to emphasize their own generosity. Companies generally claimed that the fund was on the verge of bankruptcy, supported only by company donations, while workers tended to argue that the funds were composed largely of their own contributions and owed little to company good will. The size of this fund was important because it was the most convenient means for determining the extent of the benefits offered the workers. The larger the fund, the more workers could argue for improved medical care or larger compensation. As long as the company controlled the size of the fund and all information concerning its source, it set the terms of this important debate.

As important, companies never used the programs they developed to provide for workers' security against sickness and injury solely for these purposes. Companies were unable to resist the temptation to use these programs to discipline the workforce. The disciplinary uses of such programs were manifold, but several such uses were the source of particularly bitter grievance. First of all, although workers had subscribed their own wages to such funds, they lost all right to insurance programs if they left the firm or were fired. Also, company programs were often insufficient to take care of workers during long illnesses, and they were always insufficient to adequately provide for the care of families in the event of the worker's death. Companies supplemented the aid to which all workers were entitled by contributions on an individual case basis. In such cases, aid went only to those whom the company felt to be "deserving." Since injured workers or their families often had to make decisions about whether to take the company to court or to settle out of court, the discretionary aid provided by the company could be used as a tool of intimidation to force workers to settle out of court.

The issue of company control of insurance programs was prominent in miners' protests from the beginnings of the formation of a large coalmining workforce. In 1848, workers demanded representation in company insurance programs. Over the years such demands were widely voiced among the coalmining population, and the issue of creating a regional pension fund that would allow workers to move from one mine to another without losing their rights arose periodically in coalminers' struggles.[56] In the major strike of 1869, which attracted attention all over France, demands concerning the administration of company insurance were among several central demands. Moreover, workers sought to establish their own insurance programs to provide for supplemental aid in case of illness or accident. These private working-class societies became a training ground for leaders of the working-class movement. In the 1869 miners' strike, almost the entire leadership of the workers' independent insurance association was drafted into the leadership of the strike movement.[57]

Labor historians rarely show interest in workers' struggles over social insurance issues. This neglect is unfortunate, as the nature of these struggles in the period of the formation of a permanent proletariat must be viewed in a special context. In no sense of the term can they be described as concerning "fringe benefits"; nothing was more central to workers' struggles than these battles to secure a solid base for their continued existence as a permanent social class. Over the last several decades, much work in labor history has been concerned with issues of workers' control over their work. The discussion of workers' control has usually been focused on the battles of artisanal workers who fought to retain their traditional rights within the workplace. Yet the battles of miners, fighting over pension rights, can also be considered a kind of battle for workers' control. It was not a battle for workers' control in the traditional sense, but it was a battle in which workers fought to establish their right to exist on a basis that would free them from dependence on the arbitrary whims of employers.

These struggles over the control and provisions of company pension programs marked the beginning of the formation of a permanent proletariat; it would be decades before it was actually completed. Not everyone who benefitted from the wage increases and company programs designed to attract adult male workers became a permanent proletarian. As late as the 1870s, the chamber of commerce of Saint-Chamond noted that "as a rule workers are scarce during the summer, a period when nomadic workers return to their mountains to find work in the fields."[58] Many workers continued to labor under the same circumstances as before; perhaps some returned to their farms even more quickly than formerly because workers accumulated savings required to maintain a farm at an earlier date than previously.[59] Increased wages also probably lengthened commuting distances of workers within industry. As the role of temporary workers declined and wages in industry rose, the geographic region in which permanent workers resided also likely expanded. Adult males from farming families found industry economically attractive and shifted responsibility for the farm to other family members. What was important about this new phase of industrial development was that for the first time it was feasible for large numbers of industrial workers to form families in the city. The payment of wages sufficient to support working-class families made it *possible* for workers to break their ties with agriculture, but it did not *require* such a break.

Having established some of the more important factors in the creation of a permanent proletariat in the region, it is now time to inquire whether the case of the Stéphanois can tell us anything about the general process of class formation. First of all, it should be noted that the beginning of a continuous tradition of industrial working-class militancy from the 1880s on occurred years after the beginning of a permanent proletariat—after a good portion of the Stéphanois industrial working class was composed of permanent proletarians. If our argument is correct, serious industrial worker political movements in the city will rarely be found before the formation of a large permanent proletariat. Before the growth of a permanent industrial proletariat, it is necessary to look to the countryside to find militant semi-skilled or unskilled industrial workers. The location of protest will also affect the goals of the protestors; as shown by the example of Saint-Bonnet, rural industrial protestors are more likely to demand access to woodlands than urban industrial workers. For a much longer time, the bread riot is more likely to prevail in the countryside than in the town. Our argument suggests that due to the importance of local factors, the rate of growth of a permanent proletariat may vary widely over time and place, and the differences in growth rates may help explain the uneven spread of industrial worker political movements in the different industrial regions of France.

A look at the Stéphanois region sheds light on some key stages in the development of a permanent proletariat. The focus of our attention has been on the variable forces in industrial development. Of course, coal or iron ore was crucial to the emergence of heavy industry everywhere in the nineteenth century. All industrial regions were uncommonly well endowed with mineral resources; without minerals, no permanent proletariat could develop. But successful industrializing regions in different parts of Europe might vary in some important respects, and these variations might have important consequences for the growth of a permanent proletariat. The case of the Stéphanois shows that each phase of local industrial development was shaped not simply by the demands of technology but also by local conditions such as the climate, land tenure and cultivation patterns, and the capitalization of industry.

A different local environment might have produced variations on the rate of formation of a permanent proletariat. In the early phases of industrial evolution, because of the local climate, the seasonal rhythm of Stéphanois industry developed its own distinctive pattern. A more stable climate would have enabled local farmers to plan their production more effectively and would have made them less dependent on participation in industry to make up for their frequent crop losses. Also, had rainfall been more evenly distributed throughout the year, water-powered mill work would have been more continuous. In many areas of France water-powered mill employment is likely to have been more reliable than in the Stéphanois, with its dry Mediterranean summers. A stable climate would have made the development of a temporary proletariat in the agricultural countryside more difficult, while abundant rainfall would have made it less necessary. Local climate thus affected the emergence of a permanent proletariat, and in this roundabout manner, wind velocity and rainfall levels affected the growth of the workers' movement.

But patterns of land tenure in the region were probably more critical in the formation of a lifetime proletariat. Impoverished peasants were the raw material out of which a Stéphanois working class was fashioned. Had the Stéphanois peasantry been more prosperous, industrialists might have had to look outside the region for a proletariat and resort to long-distance recruitment. Long-distance recruitment was a costly process that could only have slowed the growth of a permanent proletariat, but this is not the only way in which it would have affected the growth of the regional worker movement. Employer-controlled recruitment would have given capitalists a powerful tool for selecting and controlling their workforce. Elsewhere recruitment was frequently channeled through conservative churchmen or directed toward foreign countries, like Italy or

Spain, which had workers who would accept lower wages than the French. Employer-controlled recruitment would have constituted a powerful obstacle to labor organization even after a permanent proletariat had taken root.[60]

Not only impoverishment but the peasant status of Stéphanois agriculture also affected the formation of an industrial working class. Stéphanois peasants became involved in industry because of the inadequacy of their agricultural income; industrial activity itself indicated an approaching crisis in local agriculture. Time and again the actions of protesting rural workers can be seen as a composite of agricultural and industrial demands. While industrial workers may not have played much of a role within the industrial city, they played an important role in coordinating urban and rural militancy. Ironically, it was the proximity of a growing industrial economy that created new barriers between city and country. First, the growth of a large urban area in the Stéphanois meant new agricultural opportunities; truck farming and dairying became the basis for a newly prosperous rural economy. Also, wages earned in industrial labor in the city enabled rural families to set themselves up in the new non-industrial rural economy. Thus, the conditions that were creating a permanent proletariat in the city also fostered a new prosperity and created the basis for a new social peace in the countryside. And the growing participation of industrial workers in an urban-centered working-class culture went hand in hand with the drying up of the rural industrial worker culture that had preceded it.

The effect of the proletarianization process on industrial worker social conflict was direct. In the early stages of proletarianization, when workers labored in domestic industry in the countryside, the demands of protesting workers were strongly influenced by the rural world in which they lived. In part this was because the workers themselves were involved in agriculture and shared the concerns of their peasant fellows. In part this was also because the kind of work in which they were engaged lacked many of the properties of modern industrial labor. There was no factory, the employer was not easily accessible, and their co-workers were distributed widely over the countryside. Under these circumstances, protesting domestic workers joined with others in the countryside to participate in grain riots or to assert their rights of access to local forest land. In 1848, under the influence of migrants from the city, domestic workers in Saint-Bonnet-le-Château also demanded the maintenance of municipal subsidies to the unemployed.

But the influence of the proletarianization process on industrial worker protest did not end when the worker had begun to establish himself permanently in the city. Demands for insurance and pension programs were a key aspect of early industrial worker protest. Workers fought to secure their permanent existence by battling for autonomy of the insurance programs that were essential to the industrial workers' existence. They also fought to secure some measure of industrial independence, to keep pension programs from being tools used by employers in disciplining the emerging working class. In the context of the creation of a permanent working class these worker demands take on a special significance.

Finally, the example of the Stéphanois tells us something not only about the forces that created a permanent proletariat but about their timing. Most accounts of the formation of the industrial working class stress the extent of the transformation that resulted from the initial contact of workers with an industrial economy. They emphasize the trauma of the work-floor experience or of the first contact with urban life. Our account suggests that the most dramatic change in the lives of industrial workers may have occurred long after their initial contact with factory or tenement; dramatic changes occurred when industrial work ceased to be a waystation and became a final destination. The origin of industrial work and the industrial working class are separate questions. The realization that they were condemned to life in the urban factory and the bitter protest and desperate appeals that resulted hit hardest long after the onset of industrialization; they hit at the point where a permanent proletariat began to be formed.

NOTES

Many people have offered helpful comments. I would like to thank particularly Miriam Cohen, Gay Gullickson, Steve Hochstadt, Chris Johnson, Lynn Lees, Leslie Moch, Peter Stearns, Charles Tilly, and Louise Tilly.

1. E. P. Thompson, *The Making of the English Working Class* (New York, 1966); E. J. Hobsbawm, "Custom, Wages, and Work Load in Nineteenth-Century Industry," in *Labouring Men*, ed. E. J. Hobsbawm (New York, 1964), pp. 405–435; Peter N. Stearns, *Lives of Labor: Work in a Maturing Industrial Society* (New York, 1975); and Neil J. Smelser, *Social Change in the Industrial Revolution* (Chicago, 1959).

2. On the course of industrialization in the Stéphanois, see Pierre Cayez, *Métiers jacquards et hauts fourneaux* (Lyon, 1978); Yves Lequin, *Les ouvriers de la région lyonnaise*, 2 vols. (Lyon, 1977); Maxime Perrin, *Saint-Etienne et sa région économique* (Tours, 1937); and Jacques Schnetzler, *Les industries et les hommes dans la région stéphanoise* (Saint-Etienne, 1975).

3. Information concerning the social composition of participants in Stéphanois protest can be found in Colin Lucas, *The Structure of the Terror: The Example of Javogues and the Loire* (Oxford, 1973); Maurice Durousset, "La vie ouvrière dans la région stéphanoise sous la monarchie de juillet et la seconde république" (DES, Université de Lyon, 1960); and Jean-Francois Vidal, "Le commune de 1871 à Saint-Etienne," (unpublished dissertation, Université de Saint-Etienne, 1970).

4. Michael Hanagan, *The Logic of Solidarity: Artisans and Industrial Workers in Three French Towns, 1871–1914* (Urbana, 1980).

5. In order to understand the process of class formation, it is necessary to analyze not only the processes of production but the processes of "reproduction." The issue of reproduction of the industrial working class is posed most clearly in the stages of petty-commodity production such as the phase of "protoindus-trialization" and during the period of temporary migration that preceded the creation of a permanent proletariat. On the question of protoindustrialization, see Franklin F. Mendels, "Proto-Industrialization: The First Phase of Industrial-ization," *Journal of Economic History*, 32:1 (March 1972), pp. 241–261; and on the geography of protoindustrialization, N.J.G. Pounds, *An Historical Geography of Europe 1500–1800* (Cambridge, England, 1979), particularly pp. 155–157 and 221–226. See also Peter Kriedte et al., *Industrialization before Industrialization: Rural Industry in the Genesis of Capitalism* (Cambridge, England, 1977).

The importance of pre-industrial proletarianization and the growth of a "tem-porary" labor force have been emphasized by Franklin F. Mendels, "Seasons and Regions in Agriculture and Industry during the Process of Industrialization," in *Region und Industrialisierung, Studien zur Rolle der Region in der Wirtschaftge-schichte der letzten zwei Jahr hunderte*, ed. Sidney Pallard (Gottingen, 1980); E. L. Jones, *Seasons and Prices: The Role of the Weather in English Agricultural History* (London, 1964); and Catherina Lis and Hugo Soly, *Poverty and Capitalism in Pre-Industrial Europe* (Atlantic Highlands, N.J., 1979). On the behavior of temporary migrants, see Michael J. Piore, *Birds of Passage: Migrant Labor and Industrial Societies* (Cambridge, England, 1979); and Leslie Page Moch and Louise A. Tilly, "Immigrant Women in the City: Comparative Perspectives," Working Paper No. 205 of the Center for Research on Social Organization, University of Michigan, 1979.

On the need to look at both the means of production and the means of reproduction, see Claude Meillassoux, *Femmes greniers et capitaux* (Paris, 1979), and Jane Humphries, "Class Struggle: The Case of Nineteenth Century British History," *Review of Radical Political Economics*, 9:3 (1977), pp. 25–41.

6. For some suggestive theorizing about stages of industrialization and work-ing-class development, see Herman Freudenberger and Fritz Redlich, "The In-dustrial Development of Europe: Reality, Symbols, Images," *Kyklos*, 17 (1964), pp. 372–401; Bruce Laurie and Mark Schmitz, "Manufacturing and Productiv-ity: The Making of an Industrial Base," in *Philadelphia: Work, Space, Family and Group Experience in the Nineteenth Century*, ed. Theodore Hershberg (Oxford, 1981), pp. 43–92; Stephen A. Marglin, "What Do Bosses Do? The Origins and Functions of Hierarchy in Capitalist Production," *Review of Radical Political Econ-omy* (Summer 1974), pp. 60–112; and Michelle Perrot, "The Three Ages of Industrial Discipline in Nineteenth-Century France," in *Consciousness and Class Experience in Nineteenth-Century Europe*, ed. John M. Merriman (New York, 1980).

7. On the local climate, see Gilbert Garrier, *Paysans de Beaujolais et du Lyonnais*, 2 vols. (Grenoble, 1973), 1:29–34; Jean Merley, *La Haute-Loire de la fin de l'ancien Régime aux débuts de la troisième République: 1776–1886* (Le Puy, 1974), pp. 20–27.

The military reports on terrain and climate available at the Archives Admin-istrative de la Guerre, Service Historique de l'Armée, Vincennes, hereafter cited as (AG), all reinforce this description of the climate. An 1837 report notes: "The city of Saint-Etienne is subject to great temperature variation; north winds and south winds blow there a good part of the year; that of the north which arrives after having passed over the highlands, is always cold and biting; that of the south on the contrary, warm and humid, because it has passed over the torrid zones and a vast expanse of sea." AG/MR 1266, December 31, 1837.

8. For help in defining a Stéphanois "region," I have relied on Jacques Schnetzler. Although Schnetzler is really interested in the period after 1820, he provides a useful description of the nineteenth-century rural areas that responded very closely to changes in the economy of the Stéphanois industrial center. This region can be roughly defined to include the arrondissements of Saint-Etienne and Montbrison in the department of the Loire and the arrondissement of Yssingeaux in the Haute-Loire. See Schnetzler, *Les industries et les hommes*, pp. 80–9. The best studies of local agriculture all are on the Haute-Loire; the outstanding work here is that of Merley, *La Haute-Loire*. For the Forezien plain see François Tomas, "Quelques traits de l'histoire agraire de la plaine du Forez," *Revue de Géographie de Lyon*, 38:2 (1963), 131–161.

9. Most of the mountainous areas from which disproportionate numbers of Stéphanois migrants came were predominantly areas of smallholdings already in the late eighteenth century; see M. and Mme. Tomas on the Monts du Forez, "Géographie social du Forez en 1788, *Bulletin de la Diana*, 34:3 (1965), pp. 80–117, and 109 on the arrondissement of Yssingeaux; Merley, *La Haute-Loire*, vol. 1, pp. 96–97; on the Monts du Lyonnais, see Garrier, *Paysans du Beaujolais et du Lyonnais*, pp. 134–135.

10. On migration of seasonal workers in France and on practically every other kind of migration pattern, see Abel Chatelain, *Les migrants temporaires en France de 1800 à 1914* (Lille, 1976).

11. "Mémoire militaire—sur le lever à vue de Saint-Etienne à la Loire, 1826," AG/MR 1266.

12. Philippe Hedde, *Revue industrielle de l'arrondissement de Saint-Etienne* (Saint-Etienne, 1836), p. 33.

13. On local capitalists in the eighteenth century, see Pierre Cayez, *Métiers jacquard et hauts fourneaux*, pp. 60–68; and Pierre Léon, *La naissance de La grande industrie en Dauphine* (Paris, 1954).

14. T. S. Ashton, *An Eighteenth-Century Industrialist, Peter Stubbs of Warrington 1756–1806* (Manchester, 1939).

15. Garrier, *Paysans du Beaujolais et du Lyonnais* 2:60.

16. E. Brossard, *Histoire du département de la Loire pendant la révolution française 1789–1799*, vol. 1, (Saint-Etienne, 1905), p. 284. On the division of labor in lockmaking, see Jean-Marie Roland de la Platière, *Lettres écrites de Suisse, d'Italie, de Sicile et de Malte, en 1776, 1777, et 1778*, vol. 6 (Amsterdam, 1780), pp. 450–451.

17. M. Messance, *Nouvelles recherches sur la population de la France* (Lyon, 1788), p. 122.

18. Roland de la Platière, *Lettres écrites*, vol. 6, pp. 450–451.

19. Messance, *Nouvelles recherches*, p. 118.

20. A. V. Chayanov, *The Theory of Peasant Economy*, ed. Daniel Thorner, Basile Kerblay, and R.E.F. Smith (Homewood, Ill., 1966), esp. pp. 90–117.

21. Archives nationales, Paris, hereafter cited as (AN), "Enquête de 1848—Loire," AN-C956.

22. See M. Devon, "L'utilisation des rivières du Pilat par l'industrie," *Revue de geographie alpine*, 32 (fasc. 2, 1944), pp. 241–305.

23. Louis Reybaud, *Etude sur le régime des manufactures* (Paris, 1859), pp. 219–220.

24. Alphonse Peyret, *Statistique industrielle du département de la Loire* (Saint-Etienne, 1835), p. 94; and Brossard, *Histoire du département de la Loire*, vol. 1, pp. 280–281. On Saint-Bonnet see also R. Bergeron, "Saint-Bonnet-le-Château, vieille ville industrielle du Forez," in *Etudes Foréziennes*, II bis (1972), pp. 133–152.

25. Although evidence concerning the social composition of the supporters of the revolution in Saint-Etienne is scant, Colin Lucas had done a wonderful job in assembling a picture of the revolutionaries. While the most prominent supporters of the revolutionary Claude Javogues did not come from the people, some evidence indicates that arms-makers and metalworkers were the popular basis of support for Javogues in Saint-Etienne; see Lucas, *The Structure of the Terror*, pp. 50, 298–300. Lucas is more concerned with emphasizing the weight of wealthier sections of the population among the terrorists than with discriminating among the laboring population.

26. Abel Poitrineau, "Aspects de l'émigration temporaire et saisonnière en Auvergne à la fin du XVIIIe et au début du XIXe siècle," *Revue d'histoire moderne et contemporaine*, 9 (Jan.-Mar. 1962), pp. 40, 48–49.

27. Henri Baudrillart, *Les populations agricoles de la France*, 3e série, "Les populations du Midi" (Paris, 1893), p. 507.

28. "Mémoire sur les environs de Saint-Chamond, 1843," AG/MR 1266.

29. Before 1870, in all of the mountainous areas where small peasants were already an important force at the end of the eighteenth century, there was a tendency for small property to expand; see Merley, *La Haute-Loire*, pp. 358–359; and Garrier, *Paysans du Beaujolais et du Lyonnais*, pp. 292–293, 400–401. See also Baudrillart, *Les populations agricoles*, on the Haute-Loire, pp. 588–589, and the Haut-Vivarais, pp. 344–345. L. Gachon also describes the emergence of independent landholding in the Plateau du Livradois, in *Les populations rurales du Puy-de-Dôme*, vol. 33, Mémoire de l'academie des sciences, belles lettres et arts de Clermont Ferrand (Clermont-Ferrand, 1933), pp. 289–306.

30. For the views of one careful observer of Stéphanois agriculture, see "Reconnaissance d'une position militaire pour le but de couvrir la ville de Saint-Etienne, 1852," AG/MR 1266.

31. On the characteristics of rye, see M. Jasny, *Competition among Grains* (Stanford, Calif., 1940).

32. L. J. Gras, *Histoire de la rubannerie et des industries de la soie suivie d'un historique de la fabrique de lacets de Saint-Chamond* (Saint-Etienne, 1906), p. 708.

33. Armand Audiganne, *Les populations ouvrières de la France dans le mouvement social de XIXe siècle*, 2nd ed. (Paris, 1860), vol. 2, p. 91.

34. See Devon, "L'utilisation des rivières du Pilat," pp. 241–305; and Hedde, *Revue industrielle de l'arrondissement de Saint-Etienne*, pp. 24–25.

35. "Enquête de 1848—-Loire—Canton du Chambon-Feugerolles," AN-C956.

36. Gras, *Histoire de la rubanerie*, p. 726.

37. V. Jury, *Association française pour l'avancement des sciences*, sixteenth session, August 1897, vol. 2 (Saint-Etienne, 1897), pp. 125–126.

38. Eugene Tallon, *La vie morale et intellectuelle des ouvriers* (Paris, 1877), p. 38.

39. M. Beaunier, "Mémoire sur les mines de département de la Loire," *Annales des mines*, série 1, no. 1(1836), p. 59.

40. Poitrineau, "Aspects de l'émigration temporaire," pp. 18–29.

41. A. Beauquis, *Histoire économique de la soie* (Paris, 1900), p. 92.

42. "Enquête de 1848—Loire—Canton du Chambon-Feugerolles," AN-C956.

43. On the wages of scieurs-de-long, see Statistique de la France, Deuxième Série, Tome 12, *Prix et salaires à diverses époques* (Strasbourg, 1863). For the years 1853 and 1857, the ordinary wage is two francs thirty and two francs seventy-five at Saint-Etienne.

44. François Simiand, *Le salaire des ouvriers des mines de charbon* (Paris, 1907); average miners' salaries in the Loire for 1848, 1853, and 1857 are 2.88, 2.87, and 3.07 francs.

45. On migration in the Stéphanois region, see Jean Merley, "Éléments pour l'étude de la formation de la population stéphanoise à l'aube de la révolution industrielle," in *Démographie urbaine XVᵉ-XXᵉ siècle*, Centre d'histoire économique et sociale de la région lyonnaise, no. 8 (1977), pp. 261–275.

46. *Le Mercure Ségusien*, May 12, 1848.

47. Archives du Département de la Loire, Saint-Etienne, ADL 10M28.

48. "Enquête de 1848—mineurs de Rive-de-Gier," AN-C956.

49. James R. Lehning, *The Peasants of Marlhes: Economic Development and Family Organization in Nineteenth-Century France* (Chapel Hill, 1980).

50. Pierre Guillaume, "Les débuts de la grande industrie houillère dans la Loire, les mines de Roche-la-Molière et de Firminy sous la restauration," *Cahiers d'histoire*, 4:2 (1959), pp. 147–166.

51. Pierre Guillaume, *La compagnie des mines de la Loire: Essai sur l'apparition de la grande industrie en France* (Paris, 1966), pp. 144–145; and "Enquête de 1848—mineurs de Rive-de-Gier," AN/C956.

52. See the report cited in L. J. Gras, *Histoire de la Chambre de Commerce*, Saint-Etienne, 1910.

53. Guillaume, *La compagnie des mines*, p. 141.

54. W. J. Jackson, *James Jackson et ses fils* (Paris, 1893), pp. 63–65.

55. In 1813, the French government required mine owners to provide treatment and support for injured miners; this decree was reinforced in 1817. Most mine owners provided some minimum services by setting aside a small amount from the workers' salaries and supplying a company doctor. As companies grew larger, this attitude of grudging acquiescence changed. In 1842 the Fonderies et Forges de la Loire et de l'Ardèche established a company fund which provided a pension plan and allowed workers to participate in setting benefits, but it added, "Any worker who abandons work or leaves the mine for any cause whatsoever will lose by this sole act all rights to the fund." The fund established by the Compagnie des mines de la Loire was comparable, but more generous. Widows of miners killed on the job received 10 francs a month, those with families, 15; in the case of orphans the company promised to bring them up and teach them to be machinists, forgers, or carpenters—skilled jobs which could be performed in the mines. All the large companies seem to have provided services which went

well beyond those demanded by the government, which, in any case, were only regularly required for coal companies. Guillaume, *La compagnie des mines de la Loire*, pp. 146–149; AN/C956.

56. Guillaume, *La compagnie des mines*, pp. 144–145; and "Enquête de 1848— mineurs de Rive-de-Gier," AN/C956.

57. On the 1869 strike see Bernard Delabre, "La grève de 1869 dans le bassin minier stéphanois," *Etudes foreziennes*, 4 (1971), pp. 109–138; Fernard L'Huillier, *La lutte ouvrière à la fin du Second Empire* (Paris, 1947); and Michael Hanagan, "Proletarian Families and Social Protest in the Stéphanois," paper presented to the conference on "Work in France," Cornell University, April 1983.

58. "Enquête de 1871–75," AN/C3022.

59. Antoine Sylvere, *Toinu, le cri d'un enfant auvergnat* (Paris, 1980), p. 125. Ulysse Rochon also mentions that indebted peasants from the Haute-Loire frequently migrated to the Stéphanois region to earn money to get their farms out of debt. *La vie paysanne dans le Haute-Loire*, vol. 2 (Le Puy-en-Velay, 1936), p. 126.

60. For some examples of the effect of long-distance recruitment on labor militancy, see Gary S. Cross, *Immigrant Workers in Industrial France: The Making of a New Laboring Class* (Philadelphia, 1983); and Lawrence Schofer, *The Formation of a Modern Labor Force: Upper Silesia 1865–1914* (Berkeley, 1975).

5

Urban Structure, Migration, and Worker Militancy: A Comparative Study of French Urbanization

Leslie Page Moch

"The France of strikers is, first of all, the France of textiles[;] its capital is Roubaix."[1] This city's "monster mills" produced the factory proletariat exemplifying the working class that appeared in the nineteenth century—a conscious, militant working class that readily expressed its outrage in strikes. The city's workers struck in numbers to match the size of the mills that employed them; strikes in Roubaix were not modest affairs.

Little inclined to meet in closed rooms, to club together, to deliberate, the weaver loved movement, noise, mass demonstrations. The street was his domain, where—from one factory to another, one village to another—composite processions unfurled, carrying flags, beating drums, shouting and singing, in close order—15,000; 20,000 in Roubaix in 1880 or 1890.[2]

One protest in 1880 was an epidemic; it spread to 40,000 strikers, 14 communes, and 325 employers.[3]

Workers' protests, demonstrations, and strikes in the city of Nîmes in the Midi were quite different. There strikers were not weavers and mill workers, but shoemakers and dressmakers working at home or in small *ateliers* for piece rates. The bitterest conflicts, marked by the longest struggles and cruelest epithets, pitted cafetier against waiter and store owner against clerk. Like Roubasiens, Nîmois expressed their sense of injustice through strikes and demonstrations, but Nîmois labored in a city of workshops, offices, and stores, not factories. As a consequence, this heterogeneous labor force carried out less widespread and less successful strikes. For example, some 100 garment workers walked off the job at Leopold Landauer's workshop in April 1876 to protest the annual lengthening of the workday; every spring starting time shifted from seven o'clock to six o'clock in the morning. Landauer refused to keep winter hours, citing a tradition of 50 years. He threatened to replace shop workers with some of his 300 home workers. The strike lasted one day and was repeated 30 years later for identical motives. In the spring of 1906, Landauer's workers obtained only a 15 minute work break in their day, which continued to begin at six o'clock in the summer. "This one-day strike," the authorities were assured, "passed entirely unnoticed, and has as a consequence no influence whatsoever."[4]

In 1900, the labor forces and patterns of militancy in Roubaix and Nîmes were utterly different. This contrast was a product of the nineteenth century. Indeed, until the fall of Napoleon, Nîmes and Roubaix— and the regions of which they were a part—bore a striking resemblance to each other. Roubaix is located on the edge of Flanders, in a densely settled plain arbitrarily divided when the southern portion became part of France in the seventeenth century (see Map 5.1). Nîmes is on the Mediterranean plain just west of the Rhone River; it is an ancient town in the eastern portion of the culturally distinct province of Languedoc. Under the Old Regime, Roubaix and Nîmes each headed prosperous manufacturing regions. Most production was the work of rural folk, both in protoindustrial Languedoc and Flanders. In the Flemish countryside, textiles were produced in virtually every village, where spinning was year-round work and weaving was a winter vocation. In Languedoc, peasant families participated in raw silk production by raising mulberry trees to feed the silkworms, tending the worms or winding silk from the mature cocoons.[5] In addition, rural families produced hosiery, wool, and cotton.

This essay will trace the histories of Roubaix and Nîmes—and of their Flemish and Languedocian hinterlands—between the end of the Old Regime, when they so closely resembled each other, to the opening years of the twentieth century, when they stood in stark contrast. The protoindustrial rural production of the areas will be compared, along with the industrial and agricultural crises that abetted the proletarianization of rural labor. After an account of the decline of rural industry that followed technological innovation and rural crises, attention will shift to the city. The second section compares the distinct patterns of urban growth for Roubaix and Nîmes. Deployment of capital helps explain the different economic configurations of the two cities and, by extension, workers' contrasting labor experiences. In the final section, I compare the patterns of migration that produced the labor force of Roubaix and Nîmes and the relationship between migration and worker militancy. This general comparison explores why the two paths diverged: why Flanders moved from protoindustry to large-scale factory production and a radicalized proletariat, and why eastern Languedoc moved from

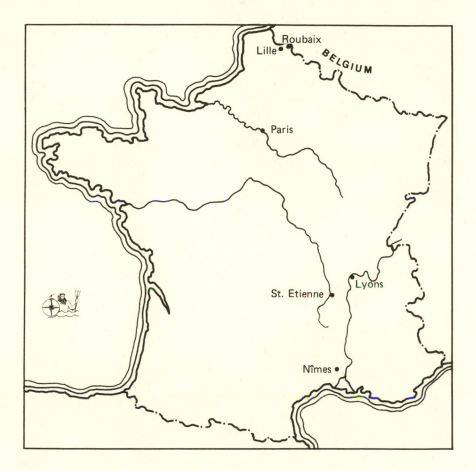

Map 5.1 France

protoindustry to artisanal production, commerce, and a less militant labor force.

In the eighteenth century, the cities were similar and their capitalist leaders were merchant-manufacturers (*marchands fabricants*). In the context of shifting markets and technological developments, nineteenth-century bourgeoisies made decisions about capital deployment that created separate paths of economic development. These developments stimulated distinct patterns of labor force recruitment and dissimilar patterns of labor force solidarity. Because twentieth-century Roubaix and Nîmes came to occupy opposite ends of the spectrum of industrial development, much of France is implicated in a comparison of their divergent paths. More important, they supply characteristic and enduring examples of militant and divided workers. The contrast between the two was produced neither by short-term economic fluctuations nor by factors reflecting their different geographic locations. The roots of militancy can be traced instead through a broadly based history of regional development. A long-term comparison of the two cities consequently can supply us with a meaningful spectrum of factors to consider in labor force development: capital transfers, urban structure, and migration. The development of these distinctive labor forces from common beginnings should help to sort out the roles of migration, urbanization, capital concentration, work, and family experience in the creation of worker militancy.

RISE AND DECLINE OF RURAL PRODUCTION

Roubaix's textile vocation was born from its territory, which had water and grass and, from Roman times, sheep.[6] Wool production and the production of linen from locally grown flax flourished by the eighteenth century. In 1781, when fewer than 8,000 people lived in Roubaix, it employed about 40,000 rural textile workers; 8,300 were weavers and the others combers, spinners, and preparers.[7] The hierarchy of workers descended from the weaver who owned his loom, house, some parcels of land, and livestock, to the proletarian comber or spinner, who earned little and owned virtually nothing. Women's role in textile production was crucial for all families. In his classic study of the peasants of the region, Georges Lefebvre observed that although weaving was a winter vocation for males, at all times of the year "as soon as she had any leisure, the female peasant, from the wife of a poor day laborer to the farmer's wife, turned her spinning wheel."[8] Textile production enabled peasants to survive on the densely settled Flemish plain, so an increasing number added spinning and weaving to farming or replaced it altogether. In many villages, the majority of families farmed no land or so little that they were effectively proletarians, dependent on wages from textile work or farm labor.[9] Their dependence made them the natural allies of the merchant, who was eager to weaken the web of state regulations inhibiting uncontrolled exploitation of rural labor. Under the Old Regime, the state restricted and protected the guilds of cities like Lille, Roubaix's powerful, distinguished neighbor. When restrictions on manufacturing in and around Roubaix were lifted in 1777, merchants rushed to employ cheap rural labor; textile production now became the chief occupation. Flemish linens and woolens found markets inside and outside France. Piece rates did not rise with the merchant's prosperity; rather, the laborer, who had no contact with the market, was paid notoriously low rates and often paid the middleman out of his own pocket.[10]

The wage-dependent rural people of eighteenth-century Flanders were in many ways like the people of Languedoc, for whom raw silk became a crucial cash crop.

Considered at the beginning as a complementary resource and used to fix property boundaries or to support the walls of terraced mountain fields, the mulberry tree then became *la pièce maîtresse* of the economic equilibrium of the Cévennes and the Gard. Associated with other crops, such as wheat, or even planted in vineyards, it literally invaded communities. It even penetrated villages and towns, and invaded the hearts of large cities. Everywhere it permitted the working of silk—becoming on the eve of the Revolution one of the fundamental products of Eastern lower Languedoc, truly pulling from misery this area so poorly provided by nature.[11]

In the late spring silk larvae hatched, then devoured mulberry leaves voraciously for a period of about six weeks before forming cocoons in specially heated chambers of peasant houses. In July women worked intensely, dissolving the cocoons in boiling water and drawing the slender thread of silk, which was then spun and woven year-round. The production of silk hose was equally a rural vocation; by 1778 hose was produced on 7,000 knitting frames in the department of the Gard. Languedoc's most important textile, however, was wool, spun year-round as in Flanders and woven from November to May in the mountains. The people of the Protestant Cévennes mountains north of Nîmes, in fact, produced 70,000 pieces of wool cloth at their peak in 1761.[12] Languedociens, from the secure land holder and silk breeder to the impoverished wool spinner, depended upon silk, textile, and hosiery production for cash. Women provided essential labor as seasonal silkworm tenders, silk thread harvesters, and year-round spinners. By their labor-intensive home work, rural workers made Languedoc one of the flourishing industrial areas of eighteenth-century France. The peasants of Languedoc, like those of Flanders, were allies of the merchants, whose interests lay in low labor costs and relative ease of avoiding state supervision in the countryside. "How difficult it is," exclaimed the king's intendant Ballainvilliers during a silk harvest, "to execute the law to the great quantitiy of people dispersed in hamlets and the countryside!"[13] Merchants of mountain-produced hosiery, wool cloth, and raw silk were concentrated in Nîmes. Their power over peasant producers was enhanced by the export market, located in the prosperous ancient city of Beaucaire on the Rhône River near the Mediterranean Sea. Rural workers who spun, wove, and knit during the cold upland winters had no contact with the rich atmosphere and comfortable climate of Beaucaire.

As capitals of protoindustrial hinterlands, Roubaix and Nîmes alike

might be called "cities without frontiers" because, like Lyon as described
by Yves Lequin, they "projected their dynamism on often very distant
villages."[14] Villagers in both regions fit into the general category of protoindustrial laborers, and with the exception of workers in some mills
set up for the annual harvest of raw silk, most worked in small familial
units.[15] Rural producers in Flanders and Languedoc did enrich the Roubaix and Nîmes merchants, but the quantity of accumulated capital does
not match that later accrued by factory production. Both protoindustrial
labor forces primarily produced for export and lived from piece rates
for textiles, hose, and raw silk. Merchant-industrialists consequently
dominated the bourgeoisie of both towns. In Nîmes, for example, 83 of
the top 103 taxpayers in 1774 called themselves *marchands fabricants*.[16]
An intimate relationship with the hinterland grew as rurals became increasingly dependent on the city's cash and merchants became dependent on villagers' labor, yet the cities and their regions differed in important
ways. While Nîmes was the undisputed capital of silk weaving and the
hosiery market-place, Roubaix was much smaller than Nîmes and chafed
at the prosperity of its privileged provincial capital of Lille. It was in-
distinguishable from other towns around Lille at the opening of the
nineteenth century with its population of barely 8,000. Nîmes at the
same time housed about 35,000 citizens. Another factor enhanced Nîmes's
regional importance: on the sparsely populated Mediterranean plain,
where people had concentrated in towns for centuries, Nîmes stood out
more from the surrounding countryside than Roubaix, a smaller and
less distinct unwalled town on the densely populated Northern plain.
Because Languedoc had neither the rich soil nor the water of Flanders,
it was less densely populated, and its people were less proletarian in the
age of flourishing rural industry.

Crises in the countryside and the development of mechanized production together strangled rural production in Flanders and Languedoc
during the nineteenth century. French Flanders's wool production was
nearly eliminated even before the Revolution by competition from finer
English wools; cotton production grew in its stead between 1789 and
1815. At the end of the Napoleonic wars, Belgian Flanders immediately
felt the competition of mechanized linen cloth and thread production,
only beginning in the cities of French Flanders, but in full swing in
England. English linen was less firm and strong than handwoven Belgian
linen, but it cost the consumer one-third to one-half as much. The countryside was quickly impoverished as orders for linen fell and rural looms
slowed or came to a standstill. Workers began leaving the villages for
Lille, Tourcoing, and Roubaix because Flanders could support few idle
hands.[17] In Languedoc, silk production thrived as the region's speciality.
In 1853 the *département* of the Gard alone produced a quarter of the
nation's mulberry trees and one-sixth of its silk (4,400 tons), worth far

more than the region's modest wine production. Disaster suddenly struck, brusquely ruining the region's peasantry; the deadly disease *pébrine* struck the silk larvae in 1855. This ruined the silk crop and necessitated the purchase of Japanese cocoons. By the time *pébrine* was successfully combated (thanks to the work of Louis Pasteur), the completion of the Suez Canal delivered the final blow to local silk production. Rural mill work and hosiery production shared the fate of the raw silk industry. Wool production in Languedoc suffered competition from mechanically produced woolens. As the textile arts flourished in Flanders and Alsace, then, the industry of cotton thread, wool, and silk diminished in lower Languedoc.[18]

Rural industry was not quickly extinguished, however; the people of both Flanders and Languedoc—like the Lyonnais and Lombards described in chapters 4 and 6—hesitated to join the urban proletariat. Handloom weaving persisted into the twentieth century in Flanders, even when starvation pay rates forced families to work the sugarbeet harvest during summers in order to subsist.[19] Urban workers would return to the countryside during the dead season to harvest sugarbeets. Peasant silk producers in Languedoc's Cévennes mountains persisted in silk production, even when only protective tariffs and subsidies gave them any profit. Peasants from the Lozère worked in the mines of the Gard in the winter and returned to subsistence agriculture during the growing season. Cévenols and Lozèrians alike worked the grape harvest in the fall on the Mediterranean plain.[20]

URBANIZATION AND CITY WORKERS

The slow deindustrialization of rural Flanders and Languedoc accompanied radically different rhythms of urbanization. In the case of Roubaix, factory industry created the city. Expansion began with mechanized cotton mills in the 1820s. In the next decade, Roubaix turned to wool, then expanded wool production to massive proportions with the use of mechanical wool combing. In 1851, the town had grown to nearly 35,000. By the end of the century, Roubaix had become a city of 125,000 where machine workers tended the combing, spinning, and weaving of wool in mills employing up to 1,500 workers.[21] Urbanization and industrialization went hand in hand. Roubaix fits the stereotype of change in the nineteenth century; its factories were those that feed our images of the industrial revolution, and its rapidly expanded population fit the imagined masses drawn into industrial work.

Roubaix's industrial expansion was fired by the city's enterprising bourgeoisie who, like Jean-Baptiste Motte-Bredart, built mills in one generation and through reinvestment and diversification created both a family dynasty and a successful textile industry. At the turn of the

century, families invested about 300,000 francs to create a wool weaving
mill, 1 million for a wool spinning mill, 4 million for the largest wool
combing mills. Bourgeois capital was carefully spent; little was squan-
dered on leisure, travel, or sons who lived from their investments. Sons
worked in family mills, entered the textile business, and reinvested family
capital.[22]

In Roubaix, where the largest group of workers was employed by the
textile industry, the factory proletariat outnumbered the handloom
weavers by the end of the century, and the factory whistle called most
people to their jobs. Mechanization required time discipline, and workers
tended machines by the hour; overseers enforced discipline by curtailing
breaks. In addition, the factory increasingly intruded into workers' religious lives between 1850 and 1914 as the devout bourgeoisie of the
city encouraged prayers in the workplace and cults with names like Our
Lady of the Factory. Statues of the Virgin appeared in shops and offices.
Employers arranged catechism classes for children and gave them gifts
on the occasion of their first communion. Nuns supervised many wom-
en's workrooms.[23]

The proletarian family survived by deploying family members' labor
and pooling wages. Because textile factory tasks were segregated by age
and sex, family members rarely worked together; nevertheless, parents
and children, men and women, labored in Roubaix's mills. Husband and
wife would both be employed until there were two or more children;
then the wife dropped out of the labor force. As children grew, they
took their mother's place in the factory, and parents would attempt to
keep them—and their wages—at home as long as possible. At the end
of the nineteenth century, compulsory education and child labor laws
restricted children's work, so more married women found employment.
The incidence of married women's work nearly doubled between 1872
and 1906, by which time 39 percent of married women were employed
for wages.[24]

The structure of the work experience and patterns of family dependence encouraged worker solidarity in Roubaix. Often all family wage
earners depended on textile employers. The fact that textile workers
dominated the labor force encouraged solidarity among them. Also,
worker exploitation and irritating factory discipline were manifest in
such settings. Roubaix must have reminded the English traveler of
Manchester, because in both towns industrial capitalism had produced
a sharp contrast between the conditions of the bourgeoisie and the mass
of workers. Bourgeois mansions on the outskirts of both cities contrasted
sharply with laborers' mean slum housing.[25]

Nîmes's history of growth and industry provides a marked contrast to
that of Roubaix. In the early nineteenth century, the city (of about
35,000) was a capital for the production of silk cloth and other textiles

as well as hosiery. Despite market crises, Nîmes grew from about 35,000 to nearly 54,000 people by 1851. In the 1850s, a three-pronged disaster destroyed the city's industry. First was *pébrine*, which undermined silk weaving. Then the fair at Beaucaire, which for centuries had provided Nîmes's most important outlet for sales to Paris and abroad, closed. Its failure reflected the victory of the railroad over river transport, of the maritime port over the river port, of the permanent economic center over the annual fair market.[26] Finally, the inexpensive silks, taffetas, shawls, rugs, and upholstery fabrics produced in northern France, in England, and in the United States created competition that the artisans of Nîmes could not match.

Unlike Roubasiens, Nîmois of the bourgeoisie were unwilling to invest in mechanized mills largely due to the attractive alternative of investing in the wine industry. Industrial profits easily could be invested in vineyards, but once used, profits could not be used to purchase steam engines or automatic looms. Once archaic technology reduced industrial profits, the temptation to move definitively from manufacturing to vineyard management became irresistible. "It is thus," concludes Raymond Dugrand, "that in a generation, industrialists became absentee wine growers.... The vineyard killed true industry."[27] During the 1860s, Nîmes's textile industries collapsed and the population of Roubaix surpassed that of Nîmes. Nîmes grew by a third (from 60,000 to 80,000) between 1880 and 1900. It was, by the turn of the century, no longer an industrial city.

The example of Nîmes demonstrated how the paths of urbanization and industrialization could and did diverge. The city grew at the expense of the countryside, developing as a trade and commercial center rather than as a producer of manufactured goods. Its typical laborers were not factory proletarians, but railroad and tramway workers, commercial and government clerks, barbers, waiters, day laborers, and domestic servants—all workers in the tertiary sector, which expanded even more than France's industrial labor force between 1850 and 1900.[28]

In Nîmes, family industrial employment ceased to be a common experience. Where artisan weaver families had worked together in 1850, only a few shoemakers worked *en famille*. Manufacturing, such as it was, usually consisted of work in homes for shoemakers or seamstresses, or in small workshops for the leather cutter or sewing machine operator. This was not the work of the majority; a maximum of 10 percent of Nîmois worked in garment and shoe industries by 1906. Many skilled laborers were able to avoid employer-imposed time discipline. The city's shoemakers, for example, were among the most devout celebrants of the weekly holiday called "Saint Monday" and patrons of Monday night theater. Those whose lives were subject to time discipline were the railroad workers, the clerks, and the seamstresses whose employers—state

or private—demanded obedience to the clock.[29] Religion did not enter
the workplace in the same way as in Roubaix because in Nîmes many
members of the bourgeoisie were Protestant and most workers were
Catholic. Consequently, employers did not encourage worker devotion.

As Nîmes deindustrialized, its families' strategies for survival necessarily changed. Family artisanal production gave way to wage pooling.
In two ways this differed from the family-work nexus in Roubaix. Nimois
families did not share an employer or even an industry; more commonly
the daughter was a seamstress and the son and father were day laborers,
railroad workers, or clerks. Moreover, wives and children were less likely
to be employed in Nîmes than in Roubaix, both because there were
fewer employment opportunities and because Nîmes was an increasingly
white-collar town. By 1906, clerical workers accounted for 17 percent
of its labor force, shopkeepers for 6 percent, and the bourgeoisie for 11
percent—over a third in total.[30] As a consequence, a greater proportion
of Nîmois were foregoing their children's wages and instead investing
in their education or training for clerical work. Nîmois families pooled
wages when necessary, but a significant proportion had to make do on
the wages of husbands and adult children. The lack of employment for
wives and children may have undercut male workers' ability to protest,
because they were unlikely to have wages to draw on besides their own
during a strike.

Moreover, the evolution of Nîmes's economy fragmented structural
opportunities for worker solidarity because subgroups were created with
different potentials for radicalism. What remained of the industrial labor
force, while very united by occupation, had little chance of success in
strikes. Industrial enterprise in Nîmes was precarious, so demands for
wage increases, for example, were futile. At the end of a successful
shoemakers' strike in 1904, a report predicted, "If the strikers solicit
another rate increase next season . . . many small *patrons* will be obliged
to close their establishments."[31] Service workers lacked the traditions of
solidarity that strengthened Nîmes's industrial sector. And the white-
collar workers, so important in Nîmes, did not identify with laborers and
were not sympathetic allies. In the midst of a printers' strike in 1906, a
local newspaper took the view that these skilled laborers could not pose
as victims: "It suffices to compare their salaries to those of commercial
or administrative clerks who work twelve to fourteen hours a day for a
much inferior salary."[32] The importance of the tertiary sector and of
white-collar work in Nîmes undercut chances for broad united support
of worker militancy.

MIGRATION AND MILITANCY

Migration played a crucial role in labor force formation for the growing nineteenth-century cities. Men and women born in small towns and

villages found work in urban areas and increasingly became lifelong city residents. These newcomers, their origins, and their urban occupations consequently provide a major clue to the creation of worker solidarities and to our comprehension of the urban workers' experience.[33] In Roubaix and Nîmes, rhythms of urbanization, patterns of worker origins, and migrant occupations together created distinct places for migrants. Roubaix grew so rapidly—quadrupling between 1820 and 1850, then more than tripling before 1900 to 125,000—that migrants were responsible for most city growth. French came from south of the city and from French Flanders to the west. Belgians, particularly the Flemish, streamed into Roubaix, attracted by the possibility of relatively high wages. Indeed, Belgians outnumbered French in Roubaix in the 1870s and 1880s. With time, urban sprawl and improved transportation made it less necessary for Belgians actually to live in France. As a consequence, up to 40,000 workers commuted to Roubaix daily or weekly in 1905—passing the small, bleak customs posts by train, tram, bicycle, or on foot.[34] They were called *pots de beurre* by the French for the packets of food they carried. In the city Belgians formed a separate community defined by religious culture, language, and economic specialization. They were among the most devout in this religious region. Belgians rarely divorced and probably bore fewer illegitimate children than the French in Roubaix. Because many spoke neither French nor its Flemish dialect, the Bishop of Ghent assigned Flemish-speaking priests to the city. The inability of many to speak French made the Belgians most visible; it separated them from the French at church and at public gatherings such as political meetings, and prevented less formal social interaction.[35] Belgians worked in certain jobs—the Walloons in the building trades and the Flemish in textiles. In 1872 Belgians, for example, were 90 percent of the city's *terrassiers* (laborers in earth-works). While natives were most of the remaining handloom weavers, lowerpaid mechanized weaving and the factory jobs of comber and washer were Belgians' occupations. Even in the factory, where tasks were rigidly assigned by age and sex, Belgians clustered in certain areas. They also grouped together in some of the city's worst housing, the cramped and unhealthy row houses called *courées*.[36]

Just as the pre-revolutionary merchant was eager to exploit rurals' acceptance of low piece rates, the nineteenth-century industrialist was eager to employ Belgians in his factory. Belgians would accept low wages in France because wages were 30 to 40 percent lower at home. They could be, and were, strikebreakers. Moreover, they were used by Roubasien employers to threaten labor militancy. Consequently, a barrier of hostility separated French migrants and native-born Roubasiens from this important migrant group.[37]

Because Nîmes's growth was relatively slow, it did not require as many migrants as Roubaix. In its crisis-ridden days as a silk producer, Nîmes

was fed by the indigenous labor force, streams of artisans from the silk
towns of Lyon and Avignon, and its regional hinterland of the Cévennes
mountains, the *département* of the Gard and the southern rim of the
Massif Central in the Lozère.[38] With deindustrialization of the city and
countryside, migrant streams from other silk centers ceased, and Nîmes
grew through the influx of rural and small-town people from its regional
hinterland. By the twentieth century, nearly 70 percent of the migrants
in Nîmes originated in eastern Languedoc (the departments of the Gard,
the Lozère, the Hérault, and the Ardèche), and another 10 percent came
from more peripheral neighboring departments.[39] Migrants to Nîmes
had particular characteristics, but they were not perceived as distinctly
as Roubaix's Belgians. Most were Catholic; this is not surprising in Catholic France, but it is noteworthy in Nîmes, where Protestants had long
been an important minority, the leaders of radical politics, and the dominant members of the bourgeoisie. The city became increasingly Catholic
because migrants following traditional paths from the Protestant Cévennes were outnumbered by those from the more remote Catholic Lozère and Massif Central.[40] Language did little to set migrants apart because
the mountain patois, a *langue d'oc*, was comprehensible to Nîmois. Nonetheless, migrants in Nîmes did cluster in particular economic categories;
males took the city's unskilled and semi-skilled occupations—they were
the *terrassiers* and railroad workers. Female migrants were Nîmes's domestic servants and *concièrges*. By contrast, native Nîmois had a firm
grasp on clerical jobs, skilled labor, and the city's industries; they were
the shoemakers and garment specialists.[41] A comparison of migrants
from a Protestant Cévenol town with those from two communes in the
Catholic Lozère shows how traditions of migration, migrants' social origins,
aspirations, and urban opportunities steered the Cévenols into clerical
jobs, the city's industries, and the bourgeoisie—and Lozèrians into semi-
skilled and unskilled service, transport, and construction jobs. Migrants
to Nîmes did cluster together, but the groupings were based on a combination of religious affiliation, economic background, and geographical
origins, rather than just birthplace. There was an undercurrent of tension in Nîmes, but the tension set liberal Protestant against conservative
Catholic, not native against newcomer. One Protestant artisan recalls:

As for Catholicism, it was so far from us, from our ideas, although socially very
close, that we spoke of it very little, and then only to condemn it severely. It was
then to recall the wars of religion, and especially the more recent extortions,
the crimes of the White Terror in 1815. This was no longer really a religious
judgment, it was a political judgment.[42]

In both cities migrants fed into particular political, cultural, and economic constituencies. They did so not because their origins were more

or less distant, or even foreign; rather, by their training and associations, migrants entered particular jobs. In Roubaix and Nîmes alike, these were the occupations expanding at the time of their arrival—in Roubaix, the mechanized textile industry; in Nîmes, the transport and service hierarchies. These similarities remind us that migration is a selective process; in the urbanization of France this meant that particular groups left village and small town for destinations and opportunities about which they had information.[43]

How did the different patterns of migration to the two cities affect worker militancy? Roubaix was the site of frequent and large strikes beginning in 1880. Its textile proletariat, weavers in particular, struck to protest falling rates and pressure to increase productivity by minding two looms. The discipline of the factory was a second target, "the rigor of schedules, the cloistering, the bell, the irritating regulations, brandished by hated 'prison guards.' "[44] According to Michelle Perrot, the detested conditions of labor encouraged frequent and spontaneous strikes: "The prompt solidarity of the textile mills shows what discontent lurked there, constant, latent."[45] This burst out in bitter strike songs and epithets like one written on the wall of a Motte weaving factory in 1882: "Our idle bosses, these ambitious thieves."[46] A large strike occurred in April 1880 when power loom weavers walked off their jobs in one Roubaix factory; this quickly became a general strike of over 40,000 workers. Ten years later, a May Day general strike of 15,000 workers planned for one day spread to 35,000 workers, some of whom remained on strike for two weeks; this was Roubaix's largest strike. Nearly the entire labor force participated. Then in 1903 and 1904, Roubaisiens participated in a series of textile strikes in response to woolens crises. The 1904 Roubaix strike began on a spring day when some 18,000 to 25,000 workers walked off the job. In all cases, the strikers pleaded their cause with public meetings, demonstrations, and parades.[47]

Nîmes's strikes and demonstrations were smaller, more varied, and less successful. Industrial workers in small ateliers—rug weavers, sewing machine operators, corset makers, and shoemakers—protested the injustice of the rate reductions, machine usage fees, lay-offs, and 11 hour workdays. Their complaint was owners' nonstop exploitation, exacerbated by the difficult times plaguing Nîmes's industry. Many strikes failed. When 20 rug weavers walked off the job in 1892 to protest a 50–centime rate cut, the shop owner refused to relent because the market for rugs was very poor; no other weavers joined the strike. Ill-paid seamstresses who sewed corsets, hunting vests, and suits struck in groups of 15 to 25 at the turn of the century to protest rate reductions; they, too, were unable to maintain their salaries. Workers whose production was more central to the Nîmes economy fared better. When 45 coopers and barrel binders chose to strike just before the 1904 grape harvest, their demands for a wage increase were met within the week. Likewise, the 76 carters employed by the company that contracted with the Paris-Lyon-Marseilles rail line to unload and distribute freight demanded a wage increase and marched up to the Bourse du Travail to form a union in 1900. Their demand was granted with dispatch.[48]

Striking manufacturing workers could draw on a supportive indigenous community that had suffered together through the decline of textile production in Nîmes. Consequently, workers in this sector were most likely to strike and could garner resources from the laboring community. For example, when shoemakers who worked at home for one company struck for a rate increase in November 1904, entrepreneurs retaliated by closing down all production. In response shoemakers all over the city—3,000 in all—quickly expressed their solidarity by striking en masse. The shoemakers' union grew and a union of female boot stitchers was formed. The strike hit families especially hard, because most shoes in Nîmes were produced at home, where wives and children often helped make baby shoes and boots. Strikers turned to the community for funds, taking collections house-to-house and in cafes, receiving private donations, 100 francs from the Bourse du Travail, and 1,000 francs from the municipal council. After ten days, the shoemakers returned to work for an arbitrated compromise raise and thus bought some time from the city's declining industry.[49]

It was not until after 1904 that service workers such as barbers and waiters began to strike in Nîmes. These workers had neither industry's traditions of labor militancy nor legal protection from exploitation. They were fighting in unexplored territory, and the virulence of their battles reveals the bitterness of the city's servants, who had neither a time-honored day of rest nor the dignity of a productive skill. For example, in 1907 waiters fought for the right to a weekly holiday, tips, a reduction of fines for breakage, and reduced hours of work (which were as long as 14 hours a day). Demonstrations, vandalism, and catcalls at nonstrikers were part of the struggle. Citywide, barbers and hairdressers demonstrated for Sunday holidays and work stoppage at 8 P.M., and carbolic acid destroyed the storefront of a hairdresser who refused to close.[50]

One of the most solidly united groups of workers in this white-collar town was the clerks, who early on had a large mutual aid society and union. Many of its members were Protestants who worked in large stores and offices, and the majority of white-collar workers were native to Nîmes. Commercial clerks launched an earnest campaign to close stores on Sunday afternoons in the 1890s. It peaked in 1901, when a parade led by children, with some 80 women and 150 men, demonstrated in favor of store closings. On August 11, the demonstrators left stink bombs in the city's department stores. When an ex-deputy of the conservative party ostentatiously made a purchase, he accepted a pamphlet explaining the demonstration, remarking that the "paper would also be good to w . . . his behind."[51] The police subsequently intervened to protect him. As furious as the demonstration was, it was not a strike. More important, clerks sought the solidarity of the buying public—not laborers—with posters from the Bourse du Travail. Moreover, they urged the public to share their outrage at the police, who, according to one poster, treated female clerks "like prostitutes."[52] Clerical workers' militancy reflects their united community, aspirations to upward mobility, and rejection of a blue-collar identity. In Nîmes, then, three distinct kinds of wage earners used strikes and demonstrations to express their grievances: workers in the city's struggling industries; workers in the expanding service sector who fought to define exploitation in the face of employers' unregulated demands; and retail clerks.[53]

The role of newcomers to the city in strikes and demonstrations is complex. Some Belgians were unwilling to strike and worked as strike-breakers, while others were willing participants and even leaders of strikes in Roubaix. "Belgian workers can be divided into two categories," writes Nicole Quillien: "One is composed of Belgians who settled in France, who often became French citizens in the end and who had participated in socialist activities in their home country—these were integrated into the milieu of the French worker."[54] This group gave direction and support to the massive strike of 1880. Active Belgian socialists and naturalized French citizens, many had been born in Roubaix. Indeed, nearly half of Roubaix's foreigners had been born in the city by the mid-1880s.[55] "But there were also large contingents of Flemish workers," Quillien continues, "who lived in certain neighborhoods of Roubaix; they remained grouped together and even continued to ignore French, or could neither read nor write; there were also those who returned home each week and who did not participate in the life of the region."[56] These were the strikebreakers—encouraged by the *patronat*, feared and hated by militant workers—who broke the back of the 1903 and 1904 textile strikes. Many were border-dwellers (*frontaliers*) who did not consider Roubaix their home.

Most strikers in Nîmes worked in areas dominated by native Nîmois. The many textiles crises suffered by indigenous industrial workers had produced citywide solidarity. For them, the legalization of strikes in 1864 had a stimulating and liberating effect; a strike movement quickly spread that summer for which all members of the trades donated 50 centimes weekly to a strike fund. The *procureur général* reported: "Workers name delegates who meet and draw lots for the manufacturer for whom work will cease until the wage increase is granted. Meanwhile, the workers in shops where work continues club together to assure those who are not working two francs per day."[57] The legalization of unions in 1884 fostered one of France's first Bourses du Travail in Nîmes, which offered the city's workers a meeting place, material support, and publicity. Nîmes's seamstresses formed France's first all-female union in 1889.[58] Shoe-makers and clerks formed active unions as well. The workers of Nîmes had a history of contention and solidarity, probably born both of the city's divided society and of the long sufferings of its working population. Like Roubaix, Nîmes had a high strike rate.[59] But Nîmes offered insuf-ficient employment to its working-class men and women.

The laborers of Nîmes were divided by geographical origin, but be-cause of the city's social and economic history, this division was mani-fested in the preservation of industrial jobs for natives and members of long-standing migration streams.[60] Regional identification permeated this city. Its people were bound to the hinterland by family ties that stemmed from a long history of trade and human exchange with the countryside.[61] Perhaps this explains the virulence of clerks' demonstra-tions against the department store La Maison Universelle, which insisted on operating seven days a week; the store was owned and run by a Parisian. On a Sunday afternoon in August 1901, 4,600 demonstrators and onlookers gathered in front of La Maison Universelle. They whistled and chanted in patois to its owner, Maubé, to pack his bag: "Moun pauré Maubé, faï ta malo!"[62]

What is the link, then, between migration and the creation of urban solidarities? No automatic association connects migration to militancy. Neither the act of migration itself, the distance traveled, nor foreign origins seem to have either divided the migrant from, or bound him to, the urban working class. Migration and labor solidarity joined instead at two points. The first was the areas of the labor force into which migrants fed; specializations varied by the conditions of departure and the timing of arrival. For example, rural conditions and urban economics together sent Flemish Belgians into mechanized wool production and Lozèrians into railroad work, construction, and domestic service. Some work, such as in large textile mills, allowed opportunities and conditions for the formation of worker solidarities, while others—domestic service being the most obvious example—did not. The second way in which migration and solidarities were linked was the degree to which newcom-ers were open to joining class-based groups. Some migrants, like the Belgian socialists in Roubaix, were leaders among radicalized workers. The mountain-born filemakers of Saint-Etienne and the glassworkers of Carmaux, who moved in national networks, were radicalized when the preeminence of their skilled labor was threatened.[63] Other migrants were less willing to strike because they were not part of the worker community, like the border-dwellers who lived in Belgium and worked in Roubaix, or because their ideology discouraged rebellions against authority. This was true both of sections of Nîmes's working class—some still royalists under the Third Republic—and of Roubaix's most devout Catholic workers. Migration is indeed a major clue to the formation of urban solidarities, but it must be read in the context of the urban society and the economy that greet the migrant.

Roubaix and Nîmes represent opposite ends of the spectrum of urban environments in France—one a red brick city of factories with smoking chimneys, the other an ancient agglomeration of homes, shops, and public buildings roofed in red tile. The differences between them are deceptive, however, because the two towns and their hinterlands underwent the same processes between 1750 and 1914. Protoindustrialization peaked at the close of the Old Regime, part of the merchants' long struggle to free production from the medieval monopoly of urban guilds. In both Flanders and Languedoc, the development of mechanized textile production threatened rural production and impoverished rural workers. In Languedoc, competition was exacerbated by the natural disaster of *pébrine* and competition from the world silk market with the completion of the Suez Canal. The concentration of capital in Roubaix's mills pulled workers into an area of explosive expansion, whereas capital invested in Languedocian vineyards produced smaller cities on the Mediterranean plain. There, the rural wine industry produced a prosperous trade and tertiary sector that attracted migrants. In both cities, workers came from the surrounding region, especially from Belgium, and the uplands of Languedoc; but while a national boundary had divided Belgians from Roubaix during its days as a center of cottage industry, centuries-old connections joined the people in Nîmes to its hinterland. Consequently, the combined effects of human migration and capital deployment produced the paradoxical contrast between the labor forces of Roubaix and Nîmes—one a highly conscious yet deeply divided industrial proletariat, the other a labor force of laborers and white-collar wage earners divided by religious affiliation and varying ambitions, yet joined by occupational solidarities and regional culture.

NOTES

Many thanks to Michael Hanagan, John Merriman, Judy Reardon, and Charles Tilly for their comments on an earlier version of this essay.

1. Michelle Perrot, *Les ouvriers en grève, France 1871–1890* (Paris, 1974), p. 352.

2. Ibid., p. 356.

3. Ibid., p. 13.

4. *Archives départementales du Gard* (hereafter cited as ADG), series 14 M, 445, Strike Reports; Jean-Michel Gaillard, "Le mouvement ouvrier dans le Gard (1875–1914)," Mémoire de Maitrise d'Historie, Université de Nanterre, 1969, pp. 155–157.

5. Raymond Dugrand, *Villes et campagnes en Bas-Languedoc* (Paris, 1963), pp. 377–378; Georges Lefebvre, *Les paysans du Nord pendant la Revolution française* (Bari, 1959), p. 290.

6. Jean Piat, *Roubaix, capitale du textile* (Roubaix, 1968), p. 23.

7. Louis Trenard, *Historie d'une metropole. Lille, Roubaix, Tourcoing* (Toulouse, 1977), p. 253.

8. Lefebvre, *Les paysans du Nord*, p. 297.

9. Ibid., p. 289; Trenard, *Histoire d'une metropole*, p. 244.

10. Lefebvre, *Les paysans du Nord*, pp. 301–305.

11. Dugrand, *Villes et campagnes*, p. 378.

12. Production was about half that figure on the eve of the Revolution; ibid., p. 377.

13. Quoted by Léon Dutil, *L'état économique du Languedoc à la fin de l'ancien régime (1750–1789)* (Paris, 1911), p. 452.

14. Yves Lequin used this phrase to describe the silk-working towns of the Lyonnais. *Les ouvriers de la région lyonnaise (1848–1914)*, vol. 1 (Lyon, 1977), p. 43.

15. Charles Tilly, "Flows of Capital and Forms of Industry in Europe, 1500–1900" CRSO Working Paper, N. 263, (Ann Arbor, 1982), p. 8.

16. Dugrand, *Villes et campagnes*, p. 386.

17. Fermin Lentacker, *La frontière franco-belge: étude géographique des effets d'une frontière internationale sur la vie des relations* (Lille, 1974), pp. 121–122; Michel Raman, "Mesure de la croissance d'un centre textile: Roubaix de 1789 à 1913," *Revue d'histoire économique et sociale* 51 (1973), pp. 474–475.

18. Dugrand, *Villes et campagnes*, p. 391.

19. Louise A. Tilly, "Linen Was Their Life: Family Survival Strategies and Parent Child Relations in France" CRSO Working Paper, N. 223, (Ann Arbor, 1981); Louise A. Tilly and Kathryn Tilly, *Mémé Santerre: A French Woman of the People* (New York, 1985).

20. René Lamorisse, *La population de la Cévenne languedociene* (Montpellier, 1975), pp. 216–228; Leslie Page Moch, *Paths to the City: Regional Migration in Nineteenth-Century France* (Beverly Hills, Calif., 1983), chap. 2.

21. Georges Franchomme, "L'évolution démographique et économique de Roubaix de 1870 à 1900," *Revue du Nord* 51 (Apr.-June 1969), pp. 223–224; Raman, "Mesure de la croissance d'un centre textile," p. 492; Trenard, *Histoire d'une metropole*, p. 322.

22. Studies of the bourgeois families of the region draw from rich documentation. See David Landes, "Religion and Enterprise: The Case of the French Textile Industry," in *Enterprise and Entrepreneurs in Nineteenth- and Twentieth-Century France*, ed. Edward C. Carter, III, Robert Forster, and Joseph N. Moody (Baltimore, 1976), pp. 43–78; Gaston Motte, *Les Motte. Etude de la descendance Motte-Clarisse, 1750–1950* (N.p., n.d.), p. 138; Bonnie G. Smith, *Ladies of the Leisure Class: The Bourgeoises of Northern France in the Nineteenth Century* (Princeton, 1981); Louise A. Tilly, "Rich and Poor in a French Textile City," in *Essays on the Family and Historical Change*, ed. Leslie Page Moch and Gary Stark (College Station, Tex., 1984).

23. Yves-Marie Hilaire, "Les ouvriers de la région du Nord devant l'Eglise catholique (XIXᵉ et XXᵉ siècles)," *Mouvement sociale* 57 (Oct.-Dec. 1966), p. 192; Landes, "Religion and Enterprise," p. 77; Tilly, "Rich and Poor."

24. Louise A. Tilly, "Occupational Structure, Women's Work, and Demographic Change in Two French Industrial Cities, Anzin and Roubaix, 1872–

1906," in *Time, Space and Man: Essays on Microdemography*, ed. Jan Sundin and Erik Soderlund (Atlantic Highlands, N.J., 1979), p. 125.

25. Jacques Prouvost, "Les courées à Roubaix," *Revue du Nord* 51 (Apr.-June 1969); Tilly, "Rich and Poor."

26. Pierre Léon, "Vie et mort d'un grand marché international, la foire de Beaucaire," *Revue géographique de Lyon* 4 (1953), p. 327.

27. Dugrand, *Villes et campagnes*, pp. 401–402.

28. André Armengaud, "Industrialisation et démographie dans la France du XIXᵉ siècle," in *L'industrialisation en Europe*, ed. Pierre Léon, François Crouzet, and Raymond Gascon (Paris, 1972), p. 188; see also R. M. Hartwell, "The Tertiary Sector in the English Economy during the Industrial Revolution," in *L'industrialisation en Europe*, ed. Léon, Crouzet, and Gascon, pp. 213–227.

29. Moch, *Paths to the City*, chap. 5.

30. Ibid., chap. 2. For an elaboration of the difference between work and family patterns in Roubaix and Nîmes, see Leslie Page Moch and Louise Tilly, "Family, Migration, and Labor in Three French Cities" (meetings of the Social Science History Association, Bloomington, Ind., 1982).

31. ADG, series 14 M, 534, Strike Reports, 1904–1907.

32. Ibid., undated newspaper clipping found in Strike Reports.

33. See also John Merriman, ed., *Consciousness and Class Experience in Nineteenth-Century Europe* (New York, 1979), p. 7; Judy A. Reardon, "Belgian and French Workers in Nineteenth-Century Roubaix," in *Class Conflict and Collective Action*, ed. Charles Tilly and Louise A. Tilly (Beverly Hills, Calif., 1981), pp. 181–182; Charles Tilly, "Migration in Modern European History," in *Human Migration: Patterns and Policies*, ed. William McNeill and Ruth Adams (Bloomington, Ind., 1978).

34. Great Britain, Board of Trade, *Cost of Living in French Towns. Report of an Inquiry by the Board of Trade into Working Class Rents, Housing and Retail Prices, together with the Rates of Wages in Certain Occupations in the Principal Industrial Towns of France*. Presented to both Houses of Parliament by Command of His Majesty, CD 4512, 1909, p. 276; Lentacker, *La frontière franco-belge*, p. 267.

35. Claude-Hélène Dewaepenaere, "L'enfance illegitime dans le département du Nord au XIXᵉ siècle," in *L'homme, la vie et la mort dans le Nord au 19ᵉ siècle*, ed. Marcel Gillet (Lille, 1972), pp. 151–153; Noëlle Dombrowski-Kéerle, "Le divorce dans le Nord de 1884 à 1914 (Aspects démographiques et sociaux, étude statistique)," in *L'homme, la vie et la mort*, ed. Gillet, pp. 185–186; Franchomme, "L'évolution démographique et économique de Roubaix," pp. 211–212.

36. Franchomme, "L'évolution démographique et économique de Roubaix," p. 210; Reardon, "Belgian and French Workers," pp. 174–178; idem, "Belgian Workers in Roubaix, France, in the Nineteenth Century," Ph.D. dissertation, University of Maryland, 1977, pp. 234–236.

37. Reardon, "Belgian and French Workers," pp. 180–181.

38. Armand Cosson, "Industrie de la soie et population ouvrière à Nîmes de 1815 à 1848," in *Economie et société en Languedoc-Roussillon de 1789 à nos jours*, ed. Gérard Cholvy (Montpellier, 1978), pp. 208–209.

39. Moch, *Paths to the City*, chap. 3.

40. Jean-Daniel Roque, "Nouveaux aperçus sur l'Eglise protestante de Nîmes dans la seconde moitié du XIXᵉ siècle," *Bulletin de la Société de l'Histoire du Prot-*

estantisme 120 (1974), pp. 54–57; Alain Rouquette, "Une 'colonie' gévaudanaise dans les basses-Cévennes: les lozeriens à Anduze," *Cévennes et Gévaudan, Actes du 46ᵉ Congrès de la Fédération Historique du Languedoc Méditerranéen et du Roussillon* (Mende, 1974).

41. Moch, *Paths to the City*, chap. 5.

42. Paul Marcel, *Souvenirs d'un passé artisanal* (Nîmes, 1967), p. 37.

43. Moch, *Paths to the City*, chap. 2.

44. Perrot, *Les ouvriers en grève*, p. 354; Tilly, "Rich and Poor."

45. Perrot, *Les ouvriers en grève*, p. 355.

46. Ibid., p. 613.

47. Ibid., pp. 352–356.

48. ADG, series 14 M, 534 and 445, Strike Reports, 1899–1900 and 1904–1907.

49. ADG, series 14 M, 534, Report of Shoemakers' Strike, November 1904.

50. ADG, series 14 M, 534.

51. *Petit Républicain du Midi*, August 13, 1901.

52. ADG, series 6 M, 1622, Poster; Gaillard, "Le mouvement ouvrier," pp. 102–103.

53. See Theresa McBride, "A Woman's World: Department Stores and the Evolution of Women's Employment, 1870–1920," *French Historical Studies* 10 (Fall 1978), pp. 664–688; Michael B. Miller, *The Bon Marché: Bourgeois Culture and the Department Store, 1869–1920* (Princeton, 1981).

54. Nicole Quillien, "La S.F.I.O. à Roubaix de 1950 à 1914," *Revue du Nord* 51 (1969), p. 277.

55. Franchomme, "L'évolution démographique et économique," p. 210; Perrot, *Les ouvriers en grève*, pp. 464–465; Reardon, "Belgian Workers in Roubaix, France, in the Nineteenth Century," pp. 169–172.

56. Quillien, "La S.F.I.O. à Roubaix," p. 277.

57. Archives Nationales, Paris, series BB, 18, 1698, quoted by Perrot, *Les ouvriers en grève*, p. 75.

58. Victorien Bruguier, *La Bourse du Travail à Nîmes* (Nîmes, 1925); Gaillard, "Le mouvement ouvrier," pp. 16, 102.

59. Both Nîmes and Roubaix experienced an annual average of over 30 strikes per 100,000 industrial workers during the period 1910–1914; Edward Shorter and Charles Tilly, *Strikes in France, 1830–1968* (New York, 1974), pp. 271–278.

60. Moch, *Paths to the City*, chap. 5; see also Lequin, *Les ouvriers de la région lyonnaise*; William Sewell, Jr., "Social Mobility in a Nineteenth-Century European City," *Journal of Interdisciplinary History*, 7 (1976), pp. 217–233.

61. Moch, *Paths to the City*, chap. 3. (My poor Maubé, pack your bags!)

62. *Petit Républicain du Midi*, August 13, 1901.

63. See Michael P. Hanagan, *The Logic of Solidarity: Artisans and Workers in Three French Towns, 1871–1914* (Urbana, Ill., 1980); Joan W. Scott, *The Glassworkers of Carmaux* (Cambridge, Mass., 1974).

6

Lyonnais, Lombardy, and Labor in Industrialization

Louise A. Tilly

Industrialization does not happen to whole countries. Nor does it happen to individual communities, even if those communities are great cities. Industrialization, properly understood, almost always occurs region by region. In the typical European experience, the growth of manufacturing in large units of production—for that is what most of us mean by industrialization—occurred through an interaction of one or more cities and a contiguous region. In the course of that interaction, not only labor but also capital, entrepreneurs, technology, markets, and the very sites of particular kinds of production moved back and forth between a dominant city and its hinterland. Most often, the dominant cities served as centers of markets, capital accumulation, entrepreneurship, communication, and consumption long before they became important loci of manufacturing.

There the variation begins. When Yves Lequin, historian of industrialization in Lyon and the Lyonnais, speaks of the "multiple paths of industrialization," he speaks from an awareness of the distinctive itineraries of different regions of Europe in the nineteenth- and twentieth-century period of concentration.[1] Lequin's exemplary analysis of the Lyonnais points the way to understanding the transformation of a number of other European regions.

One of the more surprising results of a close look at the hinterlands of the great capital-accumulating cities in Lequin's work and elsewhere has been the revelation that much of Europe's industrial expansion during the seventeenth to nineteenth centuries took place in rural areas. For that rural expansion of manufacturing, Franklin Mendels's term "protoindustrialization" has come into fairly wide, if disputed use. Whatever judgment one might make of the term's ultimate utility, its development over the last decade has contributed to a systematic reexamination of the Industrial Revolution, industrialization, and processes linked to them. Proponents of the concept have demonstrated the expansion of rural, village, and small-town manufacturing in seventeenth- and eighteenth-century Europe. Mendels, Pierre Deyon, and others have argued that the first European industrialization was located outside the old urban centers and that it employed rural labor.[2] For many ordinary Europeans, proletarianization, the imposition of the necessity to sell one's labor power, was a process experienced not in an urban factory, but in rural settings and dispersed units of production. The work of the proponents of protoindustrialization challenges theories of the Industrial Revolution and the process of industrialization, which posit sharp breaks with past experience, unidirectional progress, and an entrepreneurial/ technological nexus marked by the emergence of large-scale factories with inanimate sources of power. Peter Kriedte, Hans Medick, and Jurgen Schlumbohm, in their brief for the conceptual usefulness of protoindustrialization, have argued further that the process is the key to primitive capital accumulation and the emergence of a wage-earning, immiserated proletariat that provided the labor force for later large-scale industrialization.[3] Charles Tilly warns against a return to a "stage" orthodoxy that simply adds a newly defined, compulsory stage to older evolutionary accounts. For him, industrialization is not a linear process but a dialectical one in which "transfers of capital simultaneously caused rises in the industrial activity of some regions and declines in the industrial activity of others."[4]

These analyses have shown that the spatial distribution of economic activity and demand for labor is related in systematic ways to the organization of production. Especially in textile production, the movement of capital to the countryside was a result of urban entrepreneurs' search for cheap labor that they could control. The return of textile production (now in factories) to the cities, and the installation of new metal and engineering industries in urban settings were consequences of capital concentration and the large-scale units it established. An *urban* proletariat, then, developed in the late nineteenth century, cut off from agricultural work and rural location. Labor, like capital, is movable, and its geographic location, as well as its relationship to the means of production, is problematic. As protoindustry faded, the countryside deindustrialized and its remaining population returned to agriculture.

Urban concentration and the urban factory were not, however, the end of the process. Observing the nineteenth-century industrial city, and following its vicissitudes, reveals continuing change of the organization of production, forms of economic activity, and characteristics and location of the labor force. Pushing this argument to the present brings us uncomfortably close to home, with the deindustrialization of the heavy

manufacturing cities of old industrial regions in Western Europe and
the United States. Contemporary analysis lies outside the scope of this
paper, which examines only two industrial cities—Lyon, France, and
Milan, Italy—and their regions in the nineteenth century. It focuses on
the process by which their economies changed: first, the dispersion of
industry to the countryside, next, reconcentration of new forms of industry in the city; and finally, its reexport to suburbs and smaller regional
cities and the specialization of the metropolis in service and commerce.
This process is examined by tracing the changing sectoral distribution
and organization of production in the urban capital, and the spatial
distribution of labor in response.

The time perspective is a long one; highly aggregated movements of
labor are described. Yet the unit of analysis, the region, keeps the historical account anchored in concrete historical experience. This is not a
fine-grained study of the formation of a working class, but a broadly
sketched comparison of labor migration and labor-force formation over
a long period for two cities and their regions. That this was the consequence of the flows of capital and the productive activity it promoted is
simply assumed. The central problem is understanding the regional
arena of the movements of capital and labor to meet and overcome
problems of labor supply and discipline engendered by increasing demand. From this perspective, capital looks less innovative and inten-
tional, more reactive to its problems—which are often imposed by labor
in its efforts to protect or forward its interests. On the other hand, it
also suggests that urban industrial labor's development of organization
and mobilization in the late nineteenth century was at least partially
dissipated by the changing location of production and by changing characteristics of the work force, in addition to changing work processes and
efforts to control workers. Such outcomes were a consequence of this
dialectical relationship.

The chapter looks first at the economic development of Lyon and the
Lyonnais and concomitant movements of labor. It then turns to Milan
and Lombardy for a comparative analysis. It concludes with brief re-
marks about the implications for labor organization and collective action
in the period before World War I.

LYON AND THE LYONNAIS

The ruralization of Lyon's industry lagged chronologically behind that
of other French cities. Pierre Cayez speaks of Lyon as one of the "rare
large . . . cities, probably the only one" whose economy was still largely
based on manufacturing at the end of the Old Regime.[5] Lyon nevertheless eventually experienced a "hemorrhage . . . the departure to its
hinterland of workshops and looms."[6] Certain rural industries such as

hatmaking and cotton, linen, and wool spinning and weaving had earlier developed a protoindustrial connection with merchant putters-out in Lyon. Only in the nineteenth century, however, did the predominant silk industry begin to put out work to looms outside the center city. About 64 percent of the region's silk looms in 1833 were in the city proper and in the close-in suburbs—Croix-Rousse and La Guillotière— now part of the city; at mid-century the proportion was 51 percent. The suburban proportion had not changed; it was the city's share that fell by more than a quarter. Almost half the region's silkweaving looms were outside the metropolis.[7] An urban-rural division of labor had developed with skilled, specialized, high-fashion weaving done in the city and its close suburbs. Cruder plain weaving was done in the more distant countryside. In the nineteenth-century system, merchant - manufacturers could simply cut off orders to their relatively distant rural weavers, who owned their own looms, when there was not enough work to go around. The protoindustrial organization and ruralization of silk weaving, by keeping workers in rural areas, prepared the way for the decentralization of factory silk spinning and weaving in the latter part of the nineteenth century and the changeover of Lyon's urban center to activities supplementing weaving and new products such as chemicals and machines.[8]

Yves Lequin describes industrialization and urbanization in the Lyonnais region (taken broadly and loosely) as fluid and interrelated processes. Around 1850, he writes, Lyon was a city "without frontiers— [which] attracted, to be sure, but more important, projected its dynamism frequently on very distant villages; more often than men moving toward industry, jobs sought out men."[9] The region had a "working class already strongly marked by diversity; there were few clearcut choices made between agricultural and industrial work but rather all the intermediate situations; the workers, here and there, owned the means of production; changing activity did not mean geographic mobility, and industry moved toward its labor force at least as often as the peasant to the factory; urban centers themselves put down the roots of their industrial development in the countryside."[10] At least until the middle of the nineteenth century, "the regional form of industrialization was only sometimes characterized by the formation of large units of production and the geographic concentration of the labor force."[11]

The old organization and prosperity of the Fabrique of the Lyon silk industry, based in the city on handweaving of fibers reeled, thrown, and spun elsewhere, and the mining and metal/machine industry of the nearby Stéphanois, continued to grow until the late 1870s. The organization of the Fabrique—"urban [bee]hive and rural swarming (*essaimage*), concentration of the administration of the business and scattering of the manufacturing"—was reproduced in other sectors.[12] During the period 1876–

86 a severe depression hit the silk industry in Lyon especially, also provoking a crisis in the Saint-Etienne region.

A "restructuring of the Fabrique followed, involving a break with [its] former organization and long-standing modes of behavior."[13] Power looms replaced the hand looms, and weaving moved from the city of Lyon to smaller cities in the region. New industries located in the city— chemicals, for example. Previously scattered machine works were attracted to Lyon and to Saint-Etienne, with mechanization and growth in scale. For Lyon, this involved building railroad cars, trams, bicycles, and eventually automobiles and electrical equipment. Interestingly, Lequin concludes that there was a kind of stability in industrial areas, if not of sectoral activity: "[A] global industrial map in 1914 would not differ greatly from one of 1850, with some minor exceptions."[14] The industrial labor force moved with its jobs from declining rural areas of metallurgy, nail and tool making. "In part, it is industry that feeds industry." Women and children migrated from areas in which protoindustrial textile production had prevailed to new spinning and weaving mills in small regional cities. The new mills tapped young females from peasant families at a premarital wage-work phase of the life cycle.[15]

The depopulation of the agricultural countryside came in the mid to late 1890s[16]—again a paradox: "People did not leave agriculture (and the countryside) but often, rural industry in the countryside, for the city [Lyon].... there, these rural to urban migrants found work in the urban service sector."[17] Lequin concludes: "The working class of the 1900s is a conjuncture of three streams: the remnants of the old traditional sectors, the flower of the 'industrial revolution,' and tertiary workers called forth by the precocious sophistication of the regional economy.... The successive phases of economic development telescoped on themselves to shape the characteristic working class: the industrial proletariat was hardly visible before it began to dissolve in salaried service workers."[18] The consequences of the geographic redistribution of economic activity and classes by the eve of 1914 were a less numerous industrial working class, a new concentration of service and administrative workers in the city proper, and suburbs—the site of chemical and engineering plants— populated by a new industrial working class.[19] In Lyon, a diversification of the working class went along with the decline of the Fabrique, a "tendency to crumbling sectors" rather than the classic mode of "the construction of a class with industrialization."[20] The silk industry and certain aspects of the metallurgical and machine industries decentralized to smaller regional cities.

The general outlines of industrial production and the movement of capital and labor in the Lyonnais by about 1914 were:

1. Protoindustrialization and decentralization of production as a strategy of urban capitalists to escape the limits on productive growth imposed by urban

artisans' corporate efforts to control recruitment of labor and organization of production;

2. Concentration of capital in the regional capital and growth of mechanized production in the metropolis and smaller regional cities;

3. Departure of industrial proletarians from the countryside; deindustrialization of formerly industrial rural areas;

4. Replacement of urban artisans and skilled workers by former rural industrial proletarians in new sectors of economic activity;

5. Growth of the urban tertiary sector, also fed by migration, and its characteristic labor force;

6. Suburbanization of urban industrial production and workers' residences; and

7. A regionally hierarchical economy with (a) a service and commercial metropolis, (b) smaller regional manufacturing cities feeding the capital's trade, and (c) an agricultural countryside.

LOMBARDY AND MILAN

We now turn to the case of Milan and its region, Lombardy, to compare the patterns of industrial change and distribution of labor (See Map 6.1). Immediate differences come to mind. The great wealth based on silk cloth production in Milan and other Lombard cities had declined in the seventeenth century. The center of European silk production moved to Lyon. A tax farmer from Milan, complaining about the economic problems of the city, gave a rough but correct explanation: "Formerly only here were artificers to be found, but now they have spread all over the world."[21] Only the most costly and luxurious silk products, requiring the greatest skill, remained the province of Milanese weavers.

Despite the much earlier decline of the Lombard cities, there was a development in common with the Lyonnais—the dispersal of industry in the countryside. The crisis was an *urban* one. Domenico Sella notes, for example, that "far from being the vanguard of the modern economy, they [the cities] must be viewed as anachronistic relics of a rapidly fading past."[22] In the countryside, raw silk and thread production grew rapidly. Linen and wool were spun and woven in cottages. Cotton weaving developed in the Gallarate–Busto Arsizio district. Rural mills for grinding grain, crushing ores, producing paper, fulling and dyeing cloth appeared. Small metal products like nails and arms were also produced on farms or in tiny rural workshops.

In the eighteenth century, Milan produced silk braid and ribbon, but the ruralization of other production continued.[23] The city enjoyed a certain prosperity as an administrative capital and as the locus of urban residences of wealthy landowners who were engaged in the trade of agricultural and rural industrial products (especially raw silk). In the

Map 6.1   Lombardy

second half of the century, larger-scale cotton spinning and pottery factories, sometimes investments by non-Milanese entrepreneurs, began to go up on the outskirts of Milan, in Como and in Monza, as well as in smaller cities.[24] However, the period of the French Revolution and Napoleon, with French occupation and, later, a satellite republic in Lombardy, were years of stagnation or worse.

Once Austrian hegemony was restored, however, silkworm cultivation and the production of raw silk reemerged in response to pent-up demand in England and on the continent. New Austrian regulations also promoted cotton manufacture, still primarily organized on a domestic basis.[25]

The form and organization of the economic activity of rural Austrian Lombardy, whether agriculture or manufacturing, can be neatly classified in terms of intraregional specialization. In the Alps there were small peasant family holdings—purely agricultural—raising cattle, chestnuts, and cereals for household subsistence. In the hill zone lived tenant share farmers (*mezzadri*) with small, family-run leased holdings on which mulberry trees, grapes, and cereals were raised. The mulberry leaves produced the cash crop, the cocoons from which silk was reeled. The landlord's share was the cocoons and grapes, and small workshops or reeling mills were established on estates for the first steps of silk production. A very differently organized agriculture was found in lower Lombardy in the wide plain of the Po River. There, large irrigated farms with wage-earning work forces grew cereals and rice, and produced cheese for urban markets.[26]

Manufacturing was located primarily in the hill area and on the northern edge of the plain, whether in towns or in the countryside. Urban production, on the other hand, changed relatively little over the prerevolutionary period, except that certain new products, such as carriages were introduced. There was a rapid increase as well in silk spinning and weaving.[27] Mining and metallurgy, located near the mines in Brescia, Bergamo, and Como, were, however, in decline. The arms manufacture of Lecco was the only branch of the industry still relatively active.[28] Greenfield calls this a "manufacturing region," and notes that the concept, as he uses it,

will not suggest the visible signs of the presence or absence of industry familiar to us—neither smoke stacks nor even great mills, not to mention milltowns and "black districts." Except for the silk reeling mills that were springing up on farms or collecting in the country towns, it would generally be necessary to go into the peasant's cottage or to watch the string of horses or wagons on the road to town to detect the presence of industrial activity, for the manufacturing industry of the region was widely and increasingly diffused through the countryside as the part-time occupation of the peasants and their families.... Nevertheless the region embraced a very considerable industrial activity.[29]

By the 1840s, silk production had increased greatly, and exports were more likely to be in some refined form. Silk weaving, although always much less important than in Lyon, had also increased, mostly in Como and Milan.[30] New mechanized cotton spinning mills were installed during the early Restoration years in Busto Arsizio, Gallarate, Monza, and Solbiate—all in the Alto Milanese.[31] Linen and wool weaving and much cotton weaving remained primarily domestic industry. Bruno Caizzi calls this combination "halfway between agriculture and industry," and its labor force "hybrid."[32] Larger-scale metallurgy also appeared: the Falck iron and steel mills, installations of quite a different order than the old metallurgy, were established in 1840 at Dongo by an Italian-Alsatian partnership. The machine industry more often was located in Milan, especially in the late 1840s, with plants that manufactured textile machines, track, and rolling stock for the new railroads.[33]

All the textile branches employed women, but the large new spinning mills crowded young women and children into disciplined shops where they worked long hours. Cesare Correnti remarked in alarm that "the degradation of the race is evidence in several Lombardese industrial districts in which it is difficult to find healthy active young men for military service."[34] It seems likely that factory-industrialized labor of some family members in the regionally dispersed mills took the place of earlier home protoindustry and made it possible for *mezzadri* to remain in agriculture in a period of low prices. Both protoindustry and the early mills paid wages below the cost of maintaining an individual worker; hence they were dependent on a labor force that was fed, partially at least, by another economic activity—the family farm. Kent Greenfield argues that "the manufacture of Lombardy grew directly o   of its agriculture; the atmosphere that its industrial life breathed, high and low, was that of a community of agriculturalists."[35] The site of mills was near the source of supply, farms with mulberry trees, rather than in cities. Industrialized cotton spinning was concentrated, not in the major cities, but in the close-in Alto Milanese where water power was available. Both silk and cotton mills were located, then, near available cheap labor— underemployed members of farm households, an aspect that Greenfield did not emphasize.[36] The early textile industrialization of Lombardy thus built on the base of rural industry that had developed following the seventeenth-century urban crisis in manufacturing.[37]

The Revolution of 1848, during which the Five Day Uprising of Milan expelled the Austrians from the city, interrupted economic growth in Lombardy. Austrian policy became more restrictive in the second Hapsburg restoration. Even more damaging, however, was the cataclysmic mulberry tree disease that began in 1854 to destroy the silkworms' food. A 20–year crisis in the major agricultural cash crop of Lombardy began.[38] The last years of Austrian domination and the first years of Unification were difficult ones in Lombardy and Milan. Raw silk export was drastically reduced, and little new economic activity replaced it.

INDUSTRY IN MILAN AND LOMBARDY AFTER UNIFICATION

In the immediate postunification period (the 1860s), there were few changes and little progress in the metal and machine industries. Around

1870 and after, the iron industry of Lombardy entered a crisis aggravated by the smallness and dispersion of units, transport difficulties, and financial and technical backwardness. From then until 1886, a restructuring of metal manufacturing and engineering proceeded "from a patriarchal regime of small plants to—overall, and not without a hard selection process—a truly industrial regime."[39] The engineering sector showed great dynamism, especially in Milan, but also in smaller cities such as Legnano where demand for agricultural and textile machines led to new industries.[40]

Although Milan's population grew in the 1870s and the construction industry prospered with city "urban renewal" projects, other industrial growth was minimal. Gino Luzzatto, in an early work on Lombard economic development, wrote:

Outside of the machine building shops ... founded in earlier decades, except for a paper mill and very few other factories, Milan did not have large plants, which in this period were preferably built where they could make use of water power and an inexpensive workforce.[41]

By 1875, recovery from the worst of the silk crisis was under way in Lombardy, opening a decade of "development, slow and oscillating at first, more rapid sure and almost continuous during the last five years."[42] Most Milan businesses were small, as a report on the occasion of the National Exposition of 1881 pointed out, making up

an industry of small owners ... who built their business by ceaseless work with their own hands, acting at the same time as directors, engineers and bookkeepers of their shops. In Milan, perhaps more than anywhere else, there [is] a crowd of small and medium sized businesses modestly hidden but feverishly active.[43]

The city produced many consumer products, which the engineer and entrepreneur Guiseppe Colombo saw as its industrial destiny—to satisfy the many demands of civil life ... the refinement produced by the diffusion of culture into all social classes."[44] Colombo did not foresee preeminence for Milan in large-scale industry because of its lack of adequate power sources.

Even as he wrote these words, he nevertheless also praised the large machine shops already in place. Furthermore, railroad building was enlarging shipping and transport possibilities for all branches of manufacture. Edoardo Borruso argues that the installation of this communication system increased "demand for engineering products to such a degree as to consolidate and firmly entrench the primitive nucleus of the metal and engineering industry formed in the pre-unification period."[45] That railroad net (connected to the other side of the Alps through the Saint Gothard Pass in 1882) attracted new companies and heralded continuing prosperity for the Milanese firms that produced railroad cars and locomotives. Twenty-one businesses incorporated and set up headquarters in Milan between 1882 and 1887. Some of their names are still familiar: Pirelli (earlier a joint stock company, incorporated in 1883) and the Edison system, for example. The city continued to attract new business throughout the century. The Falck Metal Works moved to Milan in 1898, in response to the newly improved transport system for importing iron and exporting finished products.[46] Ironically, although Colombo believed in 1881 that the future of heavy industry in Milan was limited, he was personally instrumental in promoting the Società Edison's first electric generating station in Italy, which provided a reliable new source of power for the city. Meanwhile, the tariff of 1878 encouraged cotton spinning; the number of spindles in Lombardy doubled.

In 1886, the agricultural crisis that already had struck most of Europe reached Italy. A tariff war between Italy and France was especially damaging in Lombardy, from which raw silk was exported to the Lyonnais. New plant construction ended, and a financial crash followed in 1893. The cotton and silk textile industries of the hilly areas of Lombardy avoided the worst problems, for a tariff in 1887 protected their products. As the site of organizational headquarters of much of this textile industry, Milan shared some of its brighter economic aspects in contrast to the generally depressed Italian economy. The metal industry also was protected by the tariff, and importation of scrap iron facilitated the location of iron and steel plants in areas removed from the mines (which in any case were not very productive by this time). Important new plants were built in urban areas, although small or middle-sized units continued to dot the pre-Alpine hills. The reconstruction of the metal industry reduced the number of units by half in short order. Large new works were established in the late 1880s in Milan, Monza, and Saronna, while the older plants in Legnano expanded during the same period.[47] On the other hand, there was little work for Milan's engineering firms during the period around 1890, when government orders for railroad stock dried up.

The nationwide depression lasted until about 1896. Commercial relations with France were restored in 1898, and rapid economic growth resumed, lasting until about 1908. The metal and engineering industries in both Milan and Lombardy boomed as a consequence of free metal imports and demand for replacement of industrial plant equipment purchased in the earlier rapid growth period of the 1880s.[48] Electric power contributed to growth in these industries, while a new railroad line through the Simplon Pass and the return of the railways to state management brought new orders for rolling stock and tracks. Of the 16,000 engineering workers in Lombardy in 1901, 72 percent were in the zone of Milan, as was three-quarters of the motor power in the engineering industry.[49] Milanese companies supplied equipment for the expansion of the tram network in urban Lombardy, and several new companies appeared in time to be in on the first automobile boom.

Meanwhile, however, Europe as a whole had entered an overproduction crisis in cotton textiles. This time Lombardy's expansionary energy was not able to resist the downturn. From 1908 until the eve of the world war, Lombardy suffered from the collapse of cotton firms, reduced production in cotton textiles, and a silk industry that was compromised by foreign competition.[50] At about the same time (the second half of 1907), declining metal prices throughout Europe hurt that industry. The automobile industry had its first crisis in 1907,[51] and during 1908 and 1909 there was a sharp drop in railroad stock construction. Although there were some areas of recovery by 1914, the immediate prewar period was neither prosperous nor expansionary for Milan and Lombardy. Companies in the metal and engineering sectors used this period to further combine and concentrate; large new plants were built in the suburbs of Milan and in nearby cities (Pirelli in 1906; Breda and Falck in 1908). Their labor forces were no longer part of an older artisan and skilled worker tradition. By the eve of the war, the region's industry was "decidedly big business."[52]

In Milan and Lombardy, as in Lyon and the Lyonnais, then, there was

1. An initial movement of manufacture to the countryside (in Milan, this had occurred more than a century and a half before that in Lyon);
2. Development of protoindustry in rural areas where a labor force was available and partly employed (or in households partly employed) by agriculture;
3. Growth of industrialized textile production in regional towns and cities;
4. Development of new industries (engineering in both cases) in the capital city;
5. Growth of the urban tertiary sector, fed by rural to urban migration.

THE EVOLUTION OF THE MILANESE LABOR FORCE

The structure of the labor force in Milan from 1881 to 1911 followed the broad lines of the Lyonnais pattern.[53] There was a proportionate and absolute decrease in the number of persons employed in personal and domestic services and increased employment in distributive and administrative services. There was also a proportionate decrease of persons employed in small-scale, often artisanal industry. On the other hand, employment increased in both the home-based garment industry and in heavy industry, construction, and utilities.

In 1881, domestic and personal service was the largest single labor force category in the city; it employed more than 20 percent of the labor force. The manufacturing industries that employed most workers, then, were small scale. The largest category of manufacturing workers was in garment making, to a large degree carried out in small shops or homes. An 1893 survey of industrial plants in Milan with over ten employees accounted for only 10 percent—3,000 out of perhaps 30,000--of the garment workers in the city. Small shops for working wood, straw, leather, and fur, and food processing encompassed another 16 percent of the labor force. Although there were several very large machine shops, two paper mills, and a pottery factory, the work experience of the majority of Milanese in 1881 was outside the factory.

By 1901, a majority of the labor force was employed in manufacturing. The largest single occupational category remained domestic and personal service, but its proportion of the labor force had slipped by almost five percentage points since 1881. The garment industry was still the second largest employer, but its share had also declined, from 15.4 percent to 12.6 percent of the labor force. The industries that were growing rapidly, with more than twice as many persons employed in 1901 as in 1881, were metallurgy and engineering, chemicals, rubber, and glass; in the tertiary sector utilities, transportation and communications, and public accommodations were the leading employers. The largest numeric increase of workers occurred in metallurgy and engineering.

The 1911 occupational census reflects the economic transformation of the city in terms of scale of enterprise and producive capacity. The manufacturing sector employed 55 percent of the labor force in 1911. The largest numbers of workers were in the metal and engineering industries; the work force of this industry had increased by 83 percent since 1901. Garment making was still second in number of workers, but this industry had increased its workforce by only 22 percent during the decade. The other industry where employment had increased very rapidly was construction, with an 85 percent increase.

The tertiary sector, which in 1911 employed 43 percent of the labor force showed a shift toward employment in modern services—utilities, transportation, and communications. Domestic and personal service workers still formed the largest group of workers in the tertiary sector, but the absolute number had gone down by 11 percent since 1901. During the same years, employment in transportation, communications, and the production and distribution of energy had doubled.

Because it was an urban center populated by prosperous potential consumers, Milan continued to employ large numbers of workers in services and commerce, but modern services eventually predominated. Milan continued to be an enormous market for consumer goods, so it continued to be a center for producing them. For these reasons and because space for industrial expansion within the city limits ran out, the Milanese urban economy was never wholly dominated by heavy industry.

The changes in the labor force of the city mirrored the deep changes in Milan's economic activity; as in Lyon, the industrial working class emerged alongside a very large service sector that itself was growing and undergoing transformation. The Milanese working class of the 1900s, like that of Lyon, was constituted from three streams: "traditional" consumer manufacturing and craft workers; workers in newly industrialized sectors such as engineering; and tertiary (transportation, communication, and clerical) workers whose positions were based as much on Milan's role as center of a regional economy as on its industrial role.

NATIVITY OF THE LABOR FORCE AND MIGRATION

A static "snapshot" of the birthplace of the labor force is available only for 1881 and 1901. Between these two censuses, there was an across-the-board reduction of locally born workers in all categories of employment. The working population, as is the case in cities growing by migration, increasingly showed the effects of that migration. Non-locally born workers were highly concentrated in the (very small) primary and the (very large) tertiary sectors. Workers in manufacturing were much more likely to be locally born than workers in the other two sectors. Overall, in 1881 the manufacturing sector was 48 percent locally born; in the metal and machine industry it was 49 percent. The respective figures for 1901 were both 41 percent. Although more than half its workers were not born in Milan, manufacturing had much smaller proportions of migrants than did the services.

Since manufacturing workers were also younger than service workers, this suggests that by this period—the end of the century—at least some manufacturing workers may have been the second generation of an earlier migration in the 1860s or later. (There are no quantitative sources for this earlier migration, and I have found no descriptive evidence.) Within the manufacturing sector, there are some exceptions to this generalization. These were the construction industry, which most studies of urban migration have shown to be a major employer of male migrants, and the rubber industry, a new industry (Pirelli) that also employed many non-locally born workers. In both periods, professional, commerce, and service workers were much less likely to be locally born than were manufacturing workers. Persons working in public accommodations (restaurants, hotels) and domestic and personal service workers were, by a large majority (70 and 73 percent, respectively), immigrants.

Some understanding of these characteristics of occupational groups as well as other patterns of migration can be gained in the analysis of year-by-year registrations to the *Anagrafe*, the population register.[54] (Comparative data on the occupations reported by migrants are, however, available only from 1894 on.) Male manual workers were the largest category of immigrants over the entire period, but in 1911 the working-class share of the migration was 10 percent lower than it had been in 1894, while white-collar migration gained almost 10 percent in the period. The relative proportions of skilled and unskilled worker migrants were reversed, with the skilled contributing the higher percentage to the migration at the later period.[55] Women's occupations confirm the male patterns. The "housewife" category moved up 10 percent over the period, reflecting the higher proportion of skilled worker and white-collar migrants with wives who did not have to work. Milan was becoming less predominantly working class.[56] One reason for this was the increasingly common location of manufacturing plants in the suburban area around the city and rapidly growing working-class residential neighborhoods in the same districts.

The birthplace of migrants to Milan can only be imperfectly known with the aggregated data and rough classification of the *Dati Statistici*. The proportion of migrants that was born in the province of Milan itself was over 50 percent of the migration in 1888, 1896, and 1897; 40 percent or above in other years of the 1890s and up to 1905; and below 30 percent in 1906 and later. The 1901 and 1911 census reports give more detailed categories of place of birth: *provincie* for Lombardy and *compartimenti* for the rest of Italy. In 1901, 32 percent of the adult population of Milan was born in the city; in 1911 it was 31 percent. The percentage of *total* population born in other communes of the province of Milan was 22 percent in 1901 and 19 percent in 1911. Most of the inhabitants of Milan had been born in Lombardy (including Milan itself) in 1901 (83 percent) and 1911 (77 percent). Although after 1905 the Milanese migration came less often from the province of Milan, it was still composed, for the largest part, of persons born within 50 miles of the city.

In 1901 and 1911 most residents of Milan who were not born in the province of Milan came from southern Lombardy—the Po Valley agricultural area. In 1901, 26 percent of Lombardy natives came from the south (Pavia, Cremona, and Mantua); in 1911 the figure was 30 percent. This increase in the proportion of Milanese residents who were natives of southern Lombardy came at the expense of residents born in the northern provinces (Como, Bergamo, Brescia, and Sondrio) and those born in Milan province. This southern tendency is confirmed by calculating the ratio between Milan inhabitants born in a given province to the population of that province. The attraction ratio of Milan to its own province went down sharply between 1901 and 1911; that of Pavia sharply rose, by 16 percent. The Como ratio also increased, but more moderately (10 percent). This suggests that the migrants of the 1890s and the first decade of the twentieth century included an increased number of former wage-earning agricultural workers, who were the majority of workers in the Pavese or Cremonese. The apparent increase of migrants from southern Lombardy between 1901 and 1911 may have been, however, simply an artifact of the enormous growth of the city's working-class northern suburban belt and in the industrial cities of Sesto San Giovanni and Monza, in which new migrants from the north were likely to settle.[57]

The period of urban industrial growth at the end of the nineteenth century, then, saw a vast movement of workers from rural areas and small towns to larger towns and cities in Lombardy. Silk reeling, throwing, twisting, spinning, and weaving around Como, the cotton textile industry in the hill towns of the Alto Milanese, and the metal-mechanical industry of Milan attracted former rural workers. How many of these workers had worked in rural industry or in manufacturing in smaller cities? Although no quantitative answer can be offered, rural industry atrophied and disappeared; doubtless, some of its workers returned to agriculture. More of them migrated to the new urban industrial zones in Milan and smaller cities. As in the case of the Lyonnais, manufacturing workers followed jobs into urban industry. In Milan and Lombardy, as in Lyon and the Lyonnais, both industry and workers moved in systematic but disjunctive temporal patterns.

WORKER ORGANIZATION AND COLLECTIVE ACTION

Although the full meaning for worker organization and collective action of the processes just described cannot be discussed here, it is worth suggesting some possible connections.[58] Both cities had strong artisan–skilled worker corporate traditions that informed worker opposition to employer efforts to concentrate and control. The two revolts of the Canuts of Lyon in the 1830s and the Revolt of the Micca in Milan in 1886 occurred during times of great pressure on small-scale organization of production and worker control, with defensive mobilization by artisan elements. The push for labor organization of the late 1880s and 1890s was initiated and to some extent carried out by leaders from older corporate groups; new industrial workers picked up the message and organized in waves. In both cities, however, employer resistance and state repression effectively slowed down further worker organization and mobilization in the next decade.

A conversion to syndicalist direct action after 1900 followed a period of reformist coalition building. Syndicalism failed in turn also, as employers' cooperation in defense of their interests increased. A 1907 report about the Milan worker organizations shows that the metal/machine workers, for example, had undergone a cyclical process since the early 1890s of union growth, strikes, disintegration, and fragmentation, followed by renewed growth. The report concluded that this pattern was due to the high proportion of unskilled jobs constantly being filled by the "uninterrupted migration from the country" which introduced "rough elements, who brought unrestrained appetites and impulses to the union."[59] Whether or not their impulses were unrestrained, these new unskilled unionists had different interests from earlier artisans or skilled workers; it was difficult for them to agree on collective goals.

Lequin concludes the second volume of his study with regret that the Lyonnais workers of 1914 were very different from those he had described for 1848, the starting date of his study. The latter were militant artisans, republicans, and socialists; the late nineteenth-century workers had seemed to triumph, for "their numbers made them strong, they were able to impose corporative demands and uphold the principles of organized labor against still-divided capital. But then, very quickly, everything broke down." The strikes of 1906 were not a sign of worker strength, but of divisions over tactics in the face of the new resistance from employers. "The prewar working class was an uneasy, dissatisfied group, disarmed before a new industrial world." Worker mobility was at least part of the cause of this outcome, he believes: "The economic transformation of the region had destroyed the old groups and their strength."[60] In both Lyon and Milan, the divided, diverse, and shifting reality of the labor force was a ripe target for a capitalist class building coherence and organization.

CONCLUSION

The comparison of the Lyonnais and Lombardy suggests a general framework for the process of industrial change emphasizing spatial redistribution of labor and the concentration of capital. Industrialization was not simply an urban phenomenon but a reciprocal process of urban change along with agricultural and rural industrial change, and a shifting relationship of metropolis with smaller cities of its region. The impetus to change was not the intentionality of foresightful or innovative capitalists but the reaction of capitalists to problems of labor supply and control. In the process, the countryside deindustrialized and the central city extruded older industry into regional cities, itself becoming a center of capital formation and concentration—an administrative center with a larger consumer industry and the locus of a large-scale, technically advanced machine industry. Regional hierarchical economic systems were the result. The urban labor force developed from older urban artisanal elements—migrants from industrial work in the countryside who followed textile work into regional cities, or machine industry into the center city—and ex-agricultural migrants who entered service or a narrow range of unskilled industrial jobs in the metropolis.

By the early twentieth century, capitalist decisions about industrial location and concomitant movements of labor had produced a metropolitan urban center populated primarily by middle-class and service workers, while industrial workers clustered in the suburbs and satellite cities. Each city and region had its particular economic history, its own path of industrialization, its own labor movement and strike patterns. Regional patterns of industrialization in nineteenth-century Europe nevertheless involved common aspects of labor migration and capital concentration, with similar implications for workers' movements.

NOTES

An earlier version of this paper was presented at Round Table II, "Habiter la Ville," held at the Pierre Léon Center, University of Lyon, May 15–16, 1981. Thanks to colleagues at that conference, Professors Ira Glazier, Jacob Price, and Domenico Sella, for their comments on that earlier version. Most of the ideas were discussed with Charles Tilly, whose advice was most important.

1. Yves Lequin, *Les ouvriers de la région lyonnaise (1848–1914)*, Lyon: Presses universitaires de Lyon, 1977; quotation is the title of vol. 1, chap. 1.

2. Franklin Mendels, "Proto-Industrialization, The First Phase of Industrialization" *Journal of Economic History*, 32 (1972), 241–261; Pierre Deyon, "L'enjeu des discussions autour du concept de 'Proto-Industrialisation,' " *Revue du Nord*, 61 (1979), 9–18; Pierre Deyon and Franklin Mendels, "Programme de la Section A-2 du Huitième Congrès International d'Histoire économique: La Proto-industrialisation: Théorie et réalité (Budapest, 1982)," *Revue de Nord*, 68 (1981), 11–19.

3. Peter Kriedte, Hans Medick, and Jurgen Schlumbohm, *Industrialization before Industrialization: Rural Industry in the Genesis of Capitalism*, (translated by Beate Schempp), Cambridge, England: Cambridge University Press, 1981. Protoindustrialization has also served as a link between population change and economic developments. See David Levine, *Family Formation in an Age of Nascent Capitalism*, New York: Academic, 1977.

4. Charles Tilly, "Flows of Capital and Forms of Industry in Europe, 1500–1900," Section A-2, Eighth International Congress of Economic History, Budapest, August 1982, 21.

5. Pierre Cayez, "Une proto-industrialisation décalée: La ruralisation de la soierie lyonnaise dans la première moitié du dix-neuvième siècle," *Revue du Nord*, 63 (1979), 95.

6. Deyon, "L'enjeu des discussions," 11.

7. Ibid., 98.

8. Ibid., 102.

9. Lequin, *Les ouvriers*, 43.

10. Ibid., 45.

11. Ibid., 52.

12. Ibid.

13. Ibid., 84.

14. Ibid., 104.

15. Ibid., 135, 136.

16. Ibid., 143.

17. Ibid., 152.

18. Ibid., 158.

19. Ibid., 201–203.

20. Ibid., 186.

21. Quoted in Domenica Sella, *Crisis and Continuity: The Economy of Spanish Lombardy in the Seventeenth Century*, Cambridge, Mass.: Harvard University Press, 1979, 104.

22. Ibid., 136; see also Bruno Caizzi, "La crisi economica del Lombardo-Veneto nel decennio 1850–59," *Nuova Revista Storica* (1958), 205–222.

23. Bruno Caizzi, *Storia dell'industria italiana del XVIII secolo ai giorni nostri*, Turin: Unione tipografico-editrice torinese, 1965, 69–70; Mario Romani, "L'economia milanese nel Settecento," in *Storia di Milano*, vol. 12, Milan: Fondazione Treccani degli Alfieri, 494–495.

24. Caizzi, *Storia dell'industria*, 99, 109, 111, 135, 138, 140–141; Romani, "L'economia milanese," 537, 541.

25. Romani, "L'economia milanese," 677, 679; Ira Glazier, "Il commercio estero del Regno Lombardo-Veneto dal 1815 al 1865," *Archivio Economico dell'Unificazione italiana*, Series 1, 15, 1965, 1–47, discusses the Austrian tariff regime and trade regulations.

26. Kent Roberts Greenfield, *Economics and Liberalism in the Risorgimento: A Study of Nationalism in Lombardy, 1814–1848*, Baltimore: Johns Hopkins, 1965 (originally published 1934), 9–33; Romani, "L'economia milanese," 689–691; Raffaele Ciasca, "L'evoluzione economica della Lombardia dagli inizi del secolo XIX al 1860," in *La Cassa di Risparmio delle Provincie Lombarde nella evoluzione economica della regione, 1823–1923*, Milan: Alfieri and Laeroix, 1923, 362–365; Ferdinando Milone, *L'Italia nell'economica delle sue regioni*, Turin: Einaudi, 83–115.

27. Bruno Caizzi, *L'economia lombarda durante la Restaurazione (1814–1859)*, Milan: Banca Commerciale italiana, 1972, 15–40; Romani, "L'economia milanese," 693.

28. Greenfield, *Economics and Liberalism*, 90–92; Caizzi, *L'economia lombarda*, 151–182.

29. Greenfield, *Economics and Liberalism*, 82–83.

30. Ibid., 84–86; Romani, "L'economia milanese," 702; Caizzi, *Storia dell'industria italiana*, 230–239; Caizzi, *L'economia lombarda*, 15–40; Ciasca, "L'evoluzione economica," 372–373. See Glazier, "Il commercio estero," for evidence gleaned from Austrian government export records.

31. Romani, "L'economia milanese," 694: Caizzi, *Storia dell'industria italiana*, 210–216; Greenfield, *Economics and Liberalism*, 86–96; Ciasca, "L'evoluzione economica," 375.

32. Caizzi, *L'economia lombarda*, 111–133.

33. Caizzi, *Storia dell'industria italiana*, 247–254; Caizzi, *L'economia lombarda*, 159.

34. Quoted in Romani, "L'economia milanese," 717–718; other contemporary comment on the dangers or advantages of the new organization of production is discussed in Caizzi, *L'economia lombarda*, 41–46.

35. Greenfield, *Economics and Liberalism*, 92–93; Caizzi, *L'economia lombarda*, 46, notes also that in wool production, "spinning and weaving were interwoven in the form of domestic industry or small shops in the eastern parts [of Lom-

bardy]." Edoardo Borruso, "Evoluzione economica della Lombardia negli Anni dell'Unificazione italiana," *Quaderni storici*, 32 (1976), 520, although insisting that this process was "non-revolutionary," acknowledges that it had "a certain relevance for the introduction to the province of more technically complex methods [of production] and promoting the employment of a labor force eventually totally detached from purely agricultural work."

36. Caizi, *L'economia lombarda*, 98–100, notes that the problem of disciplining rural silk workers and improving the quality of their product preoccupied silk merchant capitalists.

37. Sella, *Crisis and Continuity*, 137.

38. Romani, "L'economia milanese," 733–734; A. M. Galli, "Il comasco nella 'grande crisi' bachiola (1854–1874)," *Economia e storia*, 14 (1967), 185–229; Caizzi, *L'economia lombarda*, 46–53; Borruso, "Evoluzione economica," 520–523; see also Glazier, "Il commercio estero," for collapse of the export trade.

39. G. Scagnetti, *La siderurgia in Italia*, Rome: Industria tipografia romana, 1923, 167, quoted in Luciano Davite, "I lavoratori meccanici e metallurgici in Lombardia dell'Unità alla Prima Guerra mondiale," *Classe*, 5 (1972), 337.

40. Davite, "I lavoratori," 338–339.

41. Gino Luzzatto, "L'evoluzione economica della Lombardia dal 1860 al 1922." in *La Cassa di Risparmio*, 468.

42. Ibid., 465.

43. C. Saldini, "L'industria," in *Milano 1881*, Milan: Ottino, 1881, 365.

44. Giuseppe Colombo, "Milano industriale," in *Mediolanum*, vol. 3, Milan: Vallardi, 1881, 40.

45. Borruso, "Evoluzione economica," 530–531.

46. A. Frumento, *Imprese lombarde nella storia della siderurgia: il contributo dei Falck*, Milan: Acciaierie e ferriere Lombarde Falck, 1952, 128.

47. Davite, "I lavoratori," 337, 341.

48. Stefano Fenoaltea, "Reflessioni sull'esperienza industraile italiana dal Risorgimento alla Prima Guerra Mondiale," in G. Toniolo, ed., *Lo sviluppo economico italiano, 1861–1940*, Bari: Laterza, 1973; see also Davite, "I lavoratori."

49. Davite, "I lavoratori," 351–352.

50. Luzzatto, "L'evolutione economica," 486.

51. Davite, "I lavoratori," 356–358.

52. Ibid., 366.

53. The statistical material on labor force is drawn from the published reports done by the city of Milan on the results of the population censuses of 1881, 1901, and 1911: Giunta Communale di Statistica, *La Popolazione di Milano secondo il Censimento 31 dicembre 1881*, Milan, 1883; Commune di Milano, *La Popolazione di Milano secondo il Censimento del 9 febbraio, 1901*, Milan: Reggiani, 1903; Commune di Milano, *La Popolazione di Milano secondo il Censimento eseguite il 10 Giugno 1911*, Milan: Stucchi, Ceretti, e C., 1919.

The three publications report numbers of workers by occupation, status, sex, age, residence, and nativity in industrial categories. Because categories of occupation and industry changed from census to census, occupations were used to regroup into comparable categories across the three censuses. Age, nativity, status, and residence information was not available in the same form for every census but was analyzed when it was given and compared when possible.

Further information on the censuses and other data gleaned from them can be found in Louise A. Tilly, "The Working Class of Milan, 1881–1911," Ph.D. dissertation, University of Toronto, 1974.

54. The annual report of the Anagrafe was presented in tabular form in the Milan statistical service publication, *Dati Statistici*, published yearly by the Commune of Milan.

55. Occupational titles by themselves are only rough indicators of skill level; hence the skill classifications used here are very approximate.

56. See also Aldo De Maddalena, "Rilievi sull'esperienza demografica ed economica milanese dal 1861 al 1915," in *L'Economia italiana dal 1861 al 1961*, Milan: Giuffrè, 1961, 79–103.

57. The material being discussed here tells us nothing about the *destination* of Lombard migrants, many of whom migrated elsewhere in the province or outside the province altogether. The subject here is simply the *origins* of those who came to Milan. Francesco Coletti, "Zone grigie nella populazione di Milano," in Carlo Carozzi and Alberto Mioni, eds., *L'Italia in Formazione. Ricerche e saggi sullo sviluppo urbanistico del terrotorio nazionale*, Bari: De Donato, 1970, 107–109; see also Giancarlo Consonni and Graziella Tonon, "Casa e lavoro nell'area milanese. Dalla fine dell' Ottocento al fascismo," *Classe*, 14 (1977), 193–208.

58. This section is based on Lequin, *Les ouvriers*, vol. 2, and Louise A. Tilly, "The Working Class," and "Skilled Workers and Collective Action: Milan, 1870–1898," Center for Western European Studies, University of Michigan, 1976.

59. Società Umanitaria, Milan, *Origini, vicende e conquiste della organizzazioni operaie aderenti alla Camera del Lavoro in Milano*, 1909, 11–12.

60. Lequin, *Les ouvriers*, vol. 2, p. 474.

7

Images of the Peasant in the Consciousness of the Venezuelan Proletariat

William Roseberry

In an influential and controversial book, James Scott has suggested that peasants have a "moral economy" by which they evaluate the destructive effects of capitalist expansion and the increasing exactions of the state. Based on a subsistence ethic, the moral economy demands that those who appropriate peasant surpluses offer guarantees for the continued survival of the peasant household. Although precapitalist orders may be seen as exploitative in a Marxist sense, they may be based on patron-client relations that offer survival guarantees and may not be perceived as exploitative by the peasants who enjoy the guarantees. The intrusion of capitalism or the formation of a colonial state may break the social ties of the old moral economy, erode survival guarantees, appear exploitative to the peasantry, and provoke rebellion.[1]

Scott's analysis of peasant politics in Southeast Asia explicitly draws upon the work of E. P. Thompson and others who have emphasized the moral economy of peasants, artisans, and proletarians in eighteenth- and nineteenth-century England and France. This literature has emphasized the active presence of precapitalist traditions, values, and communities in the early working class—traditions that were transformed with the Industrial Revolution and in terms of which the industrial experience was evaluated, criticized, and resisted.[2] The literature has served an important corrective function with relation to Marxist and non-Marxist economic history, in which the history of capitalism is often considered the history of the capitalists, the history of those who won. Even more important than its recapturing of the history of those who lost, however, the moral economy literature has created the basis for a new theory of consciousness. It has renewed the notion of tradition, not as the dead weight of the past, but as the active, shaping force of the past in the present.

Although the moral economy literature, particularly that dealing with the European experience, must be regarded as advancing our historical understanding, there is an unfortunate tendency to treat the peasant or artisan past in unambiguous, uncritical terms. For example, when Thompson analyzes traditional notions of time in his essay "Time, Work-Discipline, and Industrial Capitalism," he freely draws on examples from the Nuer and other primitive societies without carefully distinguishing among these societies, the nature of their traditions, values, experiences, and communities, and the traditions of the peasants and artisans who were to experience the Industrial Revolution in England. In *Work, Culture and Society in Industrializing America*, Herbert Gutman lumps together under the single label "pre-industrial" a wide variety of peasant and artisan traditions from different parts of Europe and North America and at different historical moments. James Scott has a tendency to overstate his case, romanticizing the precapitalist past and ignoring the forces of disorder and exploitation that preceded capitalism and the colonial state.[3]

One must then question the distance from modernization theory traveled by these theorists. Although they adopt a much more critical stance toward the capitalist transformation than do the classical theorists of modernization, they have remarkably similar starting points for their historical trajectories—a relatively homogeneous, undifferentiated traditional order. More important for our purposes, this weakness has unfortunate consequences for their understanding of consciousness. Although they are correct to point to the active force of the past in the present, their uncritical approaches to the past leave them in poor positions to understand the contradictory images, values, and feelings presented to the emerging proletarian.

In *The Country and the City*, Raymond Williams notes the difficulty in dating the disappearance of an idyllic rural past. For whatever century, it always seems to have recently disappeared or to be in the process of disappearing. In a passage that has special relevance to the moral economy literature, he then observes:

Take first the idealisation of a "natural" or "moral" economy on which so many have relied, as a contrast to the thrusting ruthlessness of the new capitalism. There was very little that was moral or natural about it. In the simplest technical sense, that it was a "natural" subsistence agriculture, as yet unaffected by the drives of a market economy, it is already doubtful and subject to many exceptions; though part of this emphasis can be readily accepted. But the social order within which this agriculture was practiced was as hard and as brutal as anything later experienced. Even if we exclude the wars and brigandage to which it was commonly subject, the uncountable thousands who grew crops and reared beasts only to be looted and burned and led away with tied wrists, this economy, even at peace, was an order of exploitation of a most thoroughgoing kind: a property in men as well as in land; a reduction of most men to working animals, tied by forced tribute, forced labour, or "bought and sold like beasts"; "protected" by law and custom only as animals and streams are protected, to yield more labour, more food, more blood; an economy directed, in all its working relations, to a physical and economic domination of a significantly total kind.

But, some might argue, the "moral economy" need not have existed in the past; it may be simply *perceived* in the past from the perspective of a disordered present. But Williams notes that the perceptions of the past will depend upon the relative positions of the perceivers; different ideal-izations and evaluations will emerge depending on distinct experiences of a "physical and economic domination of a significantly total kind."[4]

In a commentary on Frank R. Leavis and Denys Thompson's *Culture and Environment*, Williams turned this point about the past toward an evaluation of consciousness in the present:

What is true, I would argue, is that a number of new kinds of unsatisfying work have come into existence; a number of new kinds of cheap entertainment, and a number of new kinds of social division. Against these must be set a number of new kinds of satisfying work; certain new kinds of social organization. Between all these and other factors, the balance has to be more finely drawn than the myth allows.[5]

In pointing to these passages, I do not mean to suggest, just as Williams does not mean to suggest, that the industrial capitalist order represented, on balance, progress for humankind and advances for workers. My point has to do with our approach to consciousness. Too often moral economy theorists, while pointing out the importance of the past in the present, analyze a relatively unambiguous transition from an ordered past to a disordered present. We instead need to view a movement from a dis-ordered past to a disordered present. With such a starting point we can assess the contradictions inherent in the development of working-class consciousness and appreciate that the past provides both experiences that may make the transition seem positive and experiences that may make it seem negative. Only then can we see the moral economy as a source for protest and accommodation, despair and hope.

With this in mind, I turn to Venezuelan social history. This chapter has relatively less to say about the proletariat and relatively more to say about the peasantry than most of the contributions in this volume. Also, unlike most of the other cases in this volume, the peasantry I examine has relatively shallow historical roots. It formed in the nineteenth century with the emergence of a coffee economy and underwent a proletarian-ization process in the twentieth century with the rise of Venezuela's petroleum economy. This short historical existence, intimately related to the cyclical development of the world market, corresponds to another basic point of *The Country and the City*: that both country and city (and I would add peasant and proletarian) are ever changing qualities and, as qualities, are to be understood in terms of capitalist history.[6]

Before analyzing the Venezuelan case, I offer some introductory comments. First, although I concentrate on peasants rather than proletarians, I do not pretend to analyze the Venezuelan peasantry as a whole. The Venezuelan peasantry never existed as an identifiable whole but only in its regionally differentiated parts. I concentrate on the coffee-producing peasantry of the Andes, which exhibits a number of unique features. My own personal knowledge of the Andean peasantry is dependent on field research in a smaller, specialized region—the Boconó district of Trujillo state. Second, despite such limitation, I do not give a detailed account of the peasantry's history. Such detail can be found elsewhere. Here I simply summarize those aspects of its history that are necessary for cultural analysis. Third, my analysis of peasant and proletarian consciousness is not based upon my presentation of ideas, opinions, or conceptions that were expressed to me by individuals; nor is it based upon the behavior of peasants and proletarians in elections, unions, or related political events and movements. This is, rather, an attempt to outline the cultural possibilities presented to Venezuelan peasants and proletarians in their social history—the constitutive elements of political consciousness.[7]

I examine these cultural possibilities with four symbolic sets that, in deference to a fashion in cultural analysis, are presented as opposed pairs: coffee and petroleum, backwardness and development, country and city, and dictatorship and democracy. This is hardly an esoteric group of images, but the meanings attached to them constitute political consciousness. In discussing each set, I first trace the political and economic history that produces and connects the images. I then concentrate on the images themselves and discuss how they are presented to the Venezuelans, without distinguishing among different class perceptions. In the process, I attempt to outline the raw materials available for cultural analysis.

COFFEE AND PETROLEUM

The Andean peasantry emerged in the nineteenth century with the growth of a coffee economy. At independence, the Andes were not central to Venezuela's economy, which was based on lowland plantation production of cacao for export. Cacao-producing areas were devastated by the War of Independence, and coffee soon displaced cacao as Venezuela's principal export. Such a shift did not immediately involve major political, economic, or demographic upheavals. Plantation owners in the central and coastal lowlands could expand their holdings into surrounding highlands, planting coffee and displacing the garden plots (*conucos*) of their dependent tenants and slaves. Only in the late nineteenth century did the Andes—which had been relatively depopulated and which produced primarily for regional markets during the colonial period—emerge as an important coffee-producing region. By the end of the century, Maracaibo, which serviced the Andes, was a major port, the Andes produced more than half of Venezuela's coffee exports, and Andeans captured national power in Caracas.[8]

Because the Andes were not densely populated during the colonial period, the formation of the coffee economy could not proceed without an intense migration process. Peasants and merchants from other parts of Venezuela (especially the cattle-producing *llanos* to the south, in decline throughout the nineteenth century), as well as migrants from southern Europe, settled on vacant national lands or in the new towns and cities in the temperate zone where coffee was planted. The migrants entered some areas that were virtually unpopulated and other areas that had a long colonial history. The interaction of migrant and resident, coffee economy and colonial economy, is important for understanding regional differentiation in the Andes and the nineteenth-century political battles between liberals and conservatives. Such detail is, however, not crucial for this analysis. More important is the fact of relative small-scale production throughout most of the temperate coffee-producing zone. Regional differentiation must be stressed here as well, but with the dissolution of colonial forms of landed property, a property-owning peasantry was created. These property-owning peasants, along with those who owned no property but occupied national lands, became the principal coffee producers. For the most part, they entered into direct relations with merchants who loaned them the funds necessary to start a coffee farm and to maintain themselves until the first harvest, and who thus established a claim to most of the product of the coffee farms. The Andean peasantry was therefore unique in many respects. Unlike other parts of Venezuela, where large farms and dependent tenants predominated, a relatively independent peasantry was established in the Andes. Unlike other regions, where landlords were politically and economically dominant, merchants controlled the coffee-producing Andes. This is not to say that landlords were non-existent; it is to say that the merchant-peasant relationship defined the Andean economy.[9]

The bright historical possibilities that faced pioneers who established their own farms and passed them on to their children began to dim in the twentieth century. The coffee economy reached its spatial limits around the turn of the century. Indebtedness became a problem, especially during periodic world market depressions, for example, in its virtual closure during World War I and especially during the 1930 crisis. The depression could be seen as one of a series of cyclical crises in the coffee economy. Two aspects of the Venezuelan situation made the 1930s unique, however. First, the fact that the spatial limits to coffee production had been reached meant that the favored response to crisis—increased production through spatial expansion—was available only by expanding on to less productive land. Second, by the 1930s coffee had been displaced by petroleum as the dominant Venezuelan export. Economic displacement was accompanied by political displacement, even while Andeans continued to hold formal positions of state power. Farmers and merchants facing foreclosure, poverty, and in some cases starvation abandoned the coffee economy. Nearby petroleum camps in the Maracaibo basin attracted some Andean migrants, but most of them went to cities such as Caracas and Maracaibo to participate in the commercial and governmental expansion accompanying Venezuela's transformation. This is not to say that the coffee economy disappeared. Indeed, land area planted with coffee increased in the Andes during the decades following the crisis, even as productivity and total production declined, indicating expansion on to less and less favorable land. Except for growing urban centers in the Andes that participated in Venezuela's commercial and governmental expansion, however, most Andean districts either lost population from one census to the next or maintained extremely low levels of population growth. Sons and daughters left the area, aggravating the situation for those coffee farmers who remained.

The nature of the petroleum transformation is discussed in the next section. Here I concentrate on the coffee economy, the peasantry that characterized it, and the images it presented for a moral economy. First, the relative independence of the Andean coffee-producing peasantry must be stressed. Yet it is remarkable to note the disappearance of this peasantry from the political consciousness of contemporary Venezuela. In both the official version of Venezuelan history and alternative left-wing versions, the rural landscape had been reduced to relatively undifferentiated opposition between landlords and dependent tenants, with a peonage relationship defining the social existence of the peasantry. There is some debate about the relative importance of latifundia in the Andes, in part due to a tendency to ignore regional differentiation and to aggregate state-level statistics.[10] Nevertheless, one would think that the coffee-farming peasant of the nineteenth century would serve as one basis for the construction of a moral economy pointing to an ordered past. A number of factors operate against this alternative historical memory, but I mention only those directly related to the coffee economy and the peasantry. The most important is the process of development of the coffee economy. The expansion and hopes of the late nineteenth century gave way to relative stasis in the early twentieth century and finally to the crisis and collapse of the 1930s. During a price crisis in the early twentieth century, a local Andean newspaper struck a note of despair:

With rare exceptions, what is the capital which has been formed among coffee producers, even when prices were as high as thirty-six or forty pesos for one hundred kilos? None. And when the market presented low prices, our fields were inexplicably and painfully neglected. Many of our *hacendados* had to abandon their farms to go look for another way to survive; others stay on their *haciendas* in a languid, heavy life, with no strength to move themselves.[11]

The people who experienced the years of collapse were the sons and daughters, grandsons and granddaughters of the nineteenth-century pioneers. During the years of crisis, their debt obligations were leading to foreclosures. Their consciousness and memories would not be of independence but of abject dependence.

This leads us to the crucial characteristic of the Andean peasantry that separates it from those peasantries analyzed in the moral economy literature. The moral economists consider peasantries that have deep historical roots. Capitalist development or colonialism intrudes upon that peasantry and disrupts its traditions and forms of organization. There is no sense, however, in which the Andean peasantry was precapitalist. Rather, it emerged in the nineteenth century as the region was incorporated into the world market. It was not oriented toward subsistence but toward commodity production. Its fate was tied from the beginning to the cyclical development of the world market. Because of internal differentiation within the peasantry, some producers could prosper, take advantage of periods of high prices, establish debt relations with poorer farmers, and create a protective cushion to absorb the shock of periods of low prices. Their less fortunate fellows could get by during periods of high prices but suffered at other times. Given their relations with merchants—relations that were essential if the family was to grow coffee—their establishment as a peasantry was simultaneously the establishment of a relationship with a form of capital. While one might argue about whether that relationship was capitalist or noncapitalist, there is little sense in labeling it precapitalist. The coffee economy presented some raw material for a moral economy that could point to an ordered past, but it also presented raw material for a consciousness that could point to a disordered past.

BACKWARDNESS AND DEVELOPMENT

Were it not for petroleum, Venezuela would have fit the stereotypic model of an underdeveloped country—exporting one or two agricultural raw materials and importing manufactured products. At one level, petroleum extraction and export simply replaced an agricultural by a mineral raw material without affecting the basic import-export model. Indeed, Venezuela became more dependent on a single product than it ever had with coffee or cacao. A number of things were, however, different about petroleum. In the first place, it brought in far greater returns than were possible with agricultural products. During the decade in which petroleum replaced coffee as the principal export, the portion of total export value to which coffee contributed dropped to a miniscule level *before* actual production declined. Second, unlike agricultural and most other mineral products, petroleum was less subject to cyclical fluctuations in demand and price on the world market. Finally, as became evident with the effectiveness of the Organization of Petroleum Exporting Countries (OPEC) after 1973, it was a resource on which the developed world was so dependent that producing countries could exercise some pressure and control in the international market. In short, more things became possible with petroleum than would have been possible with coffee.

While petroleum extraction made an escape from typical forms of underdevelopment possible, it would be a mistake to automatically link coffee to backwardness and petroleum to development. The petroleum economy simultaneously symbolizes Venezuela's backwardness and its development. The coffee economy was never under foreign control. Import-export houses in port cities were owned by resident foreigners— Germans and English—and their Venezuelan-born children, but local production rested in Venezuelan hands. Even when a foreigner controlled some aspect of production or marketing, the foreigner was not a corporation; the Venezuelan patrimony had not been sold. In contrast, the granting of concessions to Anglo-Dutch Shell or the Standard Oil Corporation introduced a wholly new chapter in Venezuela's underdevelopment. The early laws governing the concessions were written by representatives of the companies themselves and called for a modest royalty to be paid to the Venezuelan government, but the vast majority of the oil wealth was extracted by foreign companies to feed foreign capital accumulation. In short, the rise of the petroleum economy meant the insertion of Venezuela within the imperialist system.

A kind of development nevertheless occurred in Venezuela. In the previous section, I referred to the "commercial and governmental expansion" of Venezuela's economy. We must now give some content to that phrase. Venezuela's oil wealth has been distributed primarily by the state. Even in the early years, when foreign companies paid modest royalties to the state, the sums generated allowed for an enormous expansion of the government apparatus. As production and the percentage of royalties owed to the state increased over the decades, this apparatus grew even larger. To serve the members of the growing bureaucracy

and their families, merchants of consumer goods proliferated. One remarkable result of the petroleum transformation, then, was the growth
of an urban middle class, dependent on incomes from government or
commerce. Venezuela's industrial structure, however, was weak. It was
only with efforts starting in the 1940s to "sow the petroleum" that the
growing state began to turn its resources toward stimulating diversified
production. Industrial investment and development were promoted by
import-substitution policies starting in 1959. The state began in 1974 to
encourage basic industry (e.g., petrochemicals) in public and mixed public and private enterprises. But even with these recent attempts to stimulate industrial development, Venezuela has become an urban, essentially
non-industrial country.[12]

This is reflected in statistics on the distribution of gross national product (GNP) and population among primary (agriculture, mining), secondary (manufacture, construction, utilities), and tertiary (commerce,
transportation, service) sectors. Distribution of GNP among sectors has
been relatively stable because of the importance of petroleum earnings
in the primary sector. From 1950 to 1969, nevertheless, there was significant slippage in the primary sector (down from 38 to 28 percent of
GNP), a minor proportional increase in the secondary sector (up from
17 to 20 percent), and a larger proportional increase in the tertiary sector
(up from 45 to 52 percent). If we divide the economically active population among these same sectors, however, a more dramatic change appears. In 1950, 46 percent were working in the primary sector; by 1971,
only 22 percent were. The secondary sector has remained relatively
stable (rising from 17 to 20 percent), and the percentage of the population working in the tertiary sector increased from 34 to 42 percent.
The major increase was in a group that confounded the census takers
and that will be discussed later. The residual "others" increased from 3
to 16 percent. The decline in the percentage of people engaged in the
primary sector can be explained by the decline in the agricultural sector,
which dropped from 43.0 to 20.3 percent of the economically active
population.[13]

The statistics tell us that a dramatic change has occurred in the structure of the Venezuelan population; one aspect of that change is discussed
in the next section. Statistics also indicate the skewed structure of Venezuela's economy—the overwhelming weight of petroleum in the primary sector and of government services and commerce in the tertiary
sector. They can only hint, however, at the quality of life that allows
Darcy Ribeiro to write of the "Puerto Ricanization of Venezuela."[14] He
refers in part to the historical importance of the petroleum companies
and in part to the increased importance of multinationals in Venezuelan
industry and commerce since 1959. He refers as well to a cultural trans-

formation that—especially in urban areas such as Caracas and Mara-caibo—affects language, dress, social relations, art, cinema, and other cultural manifestations.

The sketch of economic evolution in this century and of macro-level statistics also does not indicate the struggles that have been waged around the petroleum sector. Efforts to "sow" the petroleum in the 1940s, increased royalties assessed by the state, import substitution and industrialization in the 1960s and 1970s and, finally, the nationalization of the petroleum companies in 1976, are associated with a series of political movements that are best assessed in our discussion of dictatorship and democracy. These struggles give social content to images of backwardness and development. Venezuela has been defined as a petroleum economy for most of this century. In the selling of Venezuela's patrimony, in the dominance of multinationals, in the cultural influence of New York, Miami or Paris, the petroleum sector stands for Venezuela's backwardness. In the early labor struggles in the petroleum camps, in the attempts to redefine the relationship between the state and the corporation, in the nationalization of iron and petroleum, in the attempt to promote industrial development, and in the attempt to create and maintain democracy, the petroleum sector is made to stand for the possibility of Venezuela's development. With petroleum embodying both development and backwardness, coffee and the agricultural past occupy an ambiguous position. They are relegated to a relatively ahistorical tradition, largely devoid of social content and the positive and negative valuations that are placed on petroleum. This allows rather contradictory attitudes toward the countryside.

COUNTRY AND CITY

There is perhaps no more visible marker of Venezuela's transformation than urbanization. In 1936, 35 percent of all Venezuelans lived in urban areas; by 1971, the figure was 77 percent. Much of the urban concentration has been in Caracas, but the phenomenon is not limited to the capital. Even the Andean states, once predominantly rural and one of many sources of migrants for Caracas and other urban centers have become primarily urban. Although the Andean states have been major sources of migrants, they are not the only sources. Migrants to the city come from various regions and a variety of rural experiences.[15] One factor in the urbanization process has been the stagnation of the rural sector, of which the coffee economy is only the most visible example. Another factor concerns the transformation of Venezuela's political economy and the expansion of government services and commerce mentioned earlier.

People who move from rural areas to the city may move into these growing spheres. This is less true for peasants and their sons and daughters than it is for the sons and daughters of the middle class from towns and cities in the interior. Such opportunities are not, however, entirely closed to the peasant. The first urban experience for such a person may be living with a relative in a provincial center while attending secondary school. This can open doors in the educational establishment or for low-level positions elsewhere in the bureaucracy, as a person with a high school degree and modest political connections can become a grade school teacher. For a young daughter, the first urban experience may, however, be living in a provincial center or in Caracas with a family that has hired her as a domestic servant. Or the move for a young man may involve a series of stays with relatives and searches for work during the agricultural dead season. He may eventually stay in the city. The work he finds, if he finds it, probably will not be in industry. It may be in commerce; it may be in petty trades servicing the growing urban population of unemployed and underemployed; it may be a series of short jobs in construction, commerce, and petty trades. This last group makes up the "other" category that so confuses the census takers. A growing literature on these migrants in other parts of Latin America tells us that their "marginality" is a myth. This is particularly clear as we pay more attention to the petty trades that elude macro-level statistics. If we do not say that they are "marginal," however, we must also not say that they are "proletarian," in the sense that they are integrated within an industrial economy. The move from country to city is not, in most cases, a move from peasant to industrial proletarian but from peasant to "other." The industrial sector is too constricted to absorb the working population, and the portion of the population it absorbs is not, again for the most part, right off the farm.[16]

Physical evidence of unemployment and underemployment of migrants can be found in the *ranchos* or slums that climb the hillsides and cling to the walls of riverbeds in towns of modest size and in major cities. The existence of *ranchos* is not to be understood solely in terms of the economic condition of their residents. Some have a rather long existence. With time, the cardboard houses give way to concrete tiles and zinc roofs; with time, water and electrical services, as well as public health and educational facilities, may be introduced. (Or the *rancho* may be displaced by a government-sponsored housing project that *rancho* dwellers cannot afford to move into.) In addition to offering evidence of unemployment and underemployment, then, the *rancho* is also indicative of disordered urban growth. More migrants arrive than a city can absorb, and they find a place by creating one. City services follow at a slower pace and are constantly stretched beyond their capacity.

Even so, no discussion of a city like Caracas is adequate unless one mentions that it is an exciting place. This is obviously true for those who can afford to enjoy its restaurants and clubs, who can buy the latest New York or Paris fashions, or who can while away an afternoon discussing Marxism at a sidewalk *cafetín*—but these people and their historical memories are not central to our analysis. The city can also be an exciting place for one whose possibilites are more limited. Even if urban employment is limited, there is always a chance one will get a job. That chance may not exist in a stagnating countryside. Moreover, the petty trades can offer some opportunity for modest wealth. The city also offers other opportunities. For example, a young woman may find schooling in a place like Barquisimeto or Caracas a necessary step in liberating herself from her family of orientation without getting married.

This brief discussion has indicated something of the contradictory images presented by notions of country and city. In the section on coffee and petroleum, I indicated that the image of the peasant and countryside emerging from the coffee economy is that of a disordered past, but the migrant moves from a disordered countryside to a disordered city. The city that presents itself as a symbol of modern Venezuela also creates its critical opposite: the pastoral countryside. Coffee, the countryside, and the peasant, which serve as symbols of an agricultural past, are also countersymbols to the present. They evoke a half-remembered pre-petroleum, pre-urban, pre-modern Venezuela. This symbol is less effective for the recent migrant for whom the backwardness of the countryside is part of his or her lived experience. For one born in the city, perhaps with parents who grew up in the countryside, or for someone who has lived in the city for a number of years, however, the country may be given a positive valuation. The countryside is able to carry this weight because, as noted previously, petroleum and the city that is a product of the petroleum economy simultaneously symbolize backwardness and development. The countryside, purged of its own history, comes to represent the true Venezuela.

This is evident in Venezuelan popular music. Protest music seldom celebrates the city. When it refers to the city at all, it is to the *ranchos*, the "houses of cardboard." The city is an object of protest along with imperialism, the petroleum economy in general, the state, and similar institutions. The countryside, however, has numerous referents. It too may be the object of protest, as songs call attention to the exploited position of the peasant, in the past and in the present, but it can also serve as a counterpoint to the present with the evocation of the simplicity of peasant life, the positive virtues of agricultural labor and the daily life and interactions of the family. In addition to protest music, the production of folklore as an industrial commodity recalls the rural past as well. Recent folk music may nostalgically recall the "streets of my childhood." More important, traditional themes of folk-music—love, nature, and the family—are placed in a rural setting and are presented in distinctive regional styles—such as the *tonada* (tone poem) of the *llanos* and the waltz of the Andes. On record albums or on television programs they celebrate a past when the regions mattered. In one sense, disordered ubanization creates an image of a homogenized countryside stripped of history and regional differentiation. In another sense, especially in popular music, regional affiliations are reasserted as differences in style and temperament.

I do not mean to enter into an extended discussion of popular music in Venezuela, but simply to indicate that the disordered nature of Venezuelan development, including the urban disorder of Caracas, calls up the image of a Venezuelan past without disorder. This image can gain expression because most urbanites have some connections with the countryside where they or their parents grew up. Kinship ties connect them with rural regions, and they return to their or their parents' childhood home for Christmas or Holy Week. Some provincial towns organize reunions in which former residents are asked to return for a day-long celebration. While there, the urban resident can go to a country house for a *paseo* (picnic), where a *sancocho* (soup) is prepared, much rum is drunk, and the ideal of rural order is confirmed.

DICTATORSHIP AND DEMOCRACY

The final symbolic pair requires that we move in a different direction from that implied by our discussion of country and city. It is an essential direction, however, if we are to tie together the various threads of this discussion. The main lines of twentieth-century Venezuelan political history are fairly well known and can be widely found in literature available in North America. I simply indicate a few key features and draw some conclusions important for our cultural analysis.[17]

Coffee was displaced by petroleum during the dictatorship of Juan Vicente Gómez, who ruled from 1908 to 1935 and who, paradoxically, first came to prominence as a coffee grower in the Andean state of Táchira. He oversaw the transformation that removed coffee from its privileged position in the economy. Despite the fact that Andeans held positions of authority in the army or the administration, the entire period of Andean rule represents a progressive loss of political and economic power by Andeans and the coffee economy. The transformation, and the emergent middle class that accompanied it, created an incipient democratic movement. Its first expression was in student protests at the Central University, the most famous of which occurred in 1928 and was led by men who later founded the social democratic party Acción Democrática (AD), which later became the dorminant political party. A series of political parties emerged after Gómez's death, although political power continued until 1945 to rest with Andeans, who granted more democratic freedoms that did Gómez. Acción Democrática came to power in a coup that members continue to refer to as the Revolution of '45. The party then organized the first Venezuelan presidential election based on universal suffrage, from which the novelist Rómulo Gallegos emerged victorious. His administration was overthrown by a military coup in 1948, shortly after a number of progressive measures were passed—among them a series of agrarian reform laws and a law requiring the petroleum companies to pay 50 percent royalties. Pérez Jimenez eventually became the strong man of the junta until massive demonstrations in 1958 forced him to flee and ushered in a democratic period that has lasted until the present.

Acción Democrática has dominated this period, although in recent years the two major parties—AD and the Christian democratic COPEI (Committee for Political Organization and Independent Elections)—have exchanged positions every five years in general elections. When AD came to power in 1959, many in its top leadership maintained their commitment to democracy, but they had abandoned the radical perspectives of their youth. Rómulo Betancourt and his followers defined their project in nationalist terms. They would exact ever greater royalties from the petroleum companies—from 60 to 80 percent during the 1960s—and would assume control of the petroleum sector by a series of steps that would culminate in 1976 with nationalization. They would initiate and participate in the formation of OPEC. They would institute import substitution policies to stimulate industrialization. Diversification—"sowing the petroleum"—had been a concern of AD since the mid-1940s, but diversification and industrialization did not exclude participation by multinationals. The direction of new foreign investment changed dramatically from petroleum and iron extraction to industry and commerce after 1959. AD welcomed foreign investment as part of its attempt to alter the course of Venezuelan development.

A number of participants in Acción Democrática, as well as members of other parties including the Communist party, were disillusioned with AD's project and initiated a guerilla movement in the countryside during the 1960s. The movement never attracted much support. One reason was that it romanticized and attempted to organize the peasantry during a decade when it was disappearing. By the end of the 1960s, the economically active population engaged in agriculture was only 20 percent of all Venezuelans. More important, however, peasants were sympathetic to AD. This brings us to a point crucial to understanding Venezuelan culture and politics. AD's initial strength was in popular organizations of peasants, workers, and others without representation in a backward, dictatorial Venezuela. There were two aspects of this. AD owed its existence and support to such organizations, and peasants and workers were first organized and first acted politically through Acción Democrática. These bases of support were not ignored by AD, even if they were not always well served. One of the first measures passed when AD came to power, after Pérez Jimenez was an agrarian reform law. It was weak but was nonetheless an apparent reform.

There is in the formation of Acción Democrática and the political history of which it is a part an aspect that too often eludes those on the left who deride Venezuela's democracy. Three movements were symbolically united in AD: development, democracy , and the organization of working people. AD gave particular definitions to development and democracy, and it was able to impose those definitions through its organizations. Images of backwardness and development in the petroleum economy are associated with the images of dictatorship and democracy. The backwardness of the petroleum economy is a legacy of the past, of the dictators who sold the Venezuelan patrimony and who, as it happens, were also associated with the coffee economy. The struggle for development was simultaneously a struggle for democracy.

This symbolic association has exercised enormous power in the political consciousness of Venezuelan peasants, proletarians, and "others," but there are two sorts of weakness in that association that require elaboration—the potential failure of development and the potential failure of democracy. Given the fact that the democratic period has lasted over two decades, both sources of weakness have become apparent and have given greater space to movements of the left and right than existed in the early 1960s. The failure of development results in part from the fact that th political leaders and spokesmen for AD and other parties often pursue individual aims and individual careers. Parties or factions of parties may pursue their own projects and candidacies by endlessly debating relatively trivial matters in Congress. There is a tremendous dissipation of energy in Venezuela's democracy, and during periods of economic crisis, when the country's development seems imperiled, "democracy" can seem a nonessential luxury. The failure by leaders pursuing their own goals to aim for development calls democracy into question and gives organizational space to the right, as demonstrated by support expressed for Pérez Jiminez in the 1968 elections or in persistent rumors of a military coup.

The failure of democracy results in part from the fact that multiclass democratic political parties like AD are nonetheless pursuing class projects. AD's class project is associated with an incipient industrial bourgeoisie. The form of development they advocate closely approximates F. H. Cardoso's notion of associated dependent development—linkage between sectors of local capital, state capital, and multinational capital in the diversification and industrialization of the Venezuelan economy. Unlike other examples of this model, the linkage between development and democracy is more than a symbol, and Venezuela has so far escaped the

more authoritarian forms of government usually associated with this
model. Much of the explanation for this rests with the petroleum sector.
As indicated, petroleum wealth has been channeled by the state into the
tertiary sector, and part of that expansion has been an expansion of
social services, subsidies for agricultural producers, marketing organizations, and housing projects. The democrats therefore are simultaneously able to promote dependent development and to incorporate
significant segments of the Venezuelan population into the state through
social services. However, as the attempt to promote basic industry has
in recent years encountered declining petroleum revenues, the state has
diverted funds from social services. The results for the fortunes of the
two major parties of this diversion are not yet clear. A class project may
no longer be coterminous with a democratic project. Acción Democrática
has lost much popular support in recent years, and its old linkage of
democracy and development seems imperiled. Its weakness gives organizational space to both the left and the right.[18]

Can we put these shifting and contradictory images of Venezuela's
past, present, and future into a coherent picture? To address this question, I turn to the cultural analysis suggested by Raymond Williams in
Marxism and Literature. Unlike an older anthropology, Williams's notion
of culture cannot be separated from political economy. Elaborating Antonio Gramsci's notion of hegemony, Williams points to the construction
of a "dominant culture" that is not a coherent integrated system or
structure but a rather inchoate set of lived experiences, feelings, and
relationships within a political and economic order of domination. Because it is not a closed system, as might be a "ruling ideology," it is in a
constant process of construction, reconstruction, and, to use a popular
word, deconstruction. Although many elements could be considered
constitutive of a dominant culture, one that Wiliams points to is of particular relevance to the moral economy literature: tradition as a *selective*
tradition—a version (indeed, the ruling version) of a people's history.
Tradition as selective tradition is important when we consider one of
Williams's central points about dominant culture—that no order of domination is total. There are always sets of relationships and experiences
that are excluded and that may serve as points around which alternative,
perhaps oppositional, cultural forms can emerge. With the creation of
an alternative culture, a basic element must be an alternative tradition—
a reinterpretation and rewriting of history, concentrating on events and
relationships excluded from the ruling version and pointing to a different set of historical possibilities.[19]

Williams is clearly suggesting a cultural analysis that goes beyond such
simplistic notions as "Venezuelan culture" or "national character." He
has tied his notion of culture to a historical process and to class structures
and relationships. Nevertheless, there is no sense in which dominant and

emergent culture are coterminous with particular class positions. The images of Venezuela's tradition that have been discussed in this essay are not class specific. A class culture or class discourse is never given; it must be constructed from the cultural raw material presented by history, from the "tradition" that is used to construct both dominant and emergent forms of culture. It is in this sense that I refer in the title to the consciousness of a proletariat. I cannot pretend to trace *the* consciousness of Venezuela's proletariat. I can, by analysis of Venezuela's history, indicate the kinds of images that have been used to create a hegemonic order or dominant culture. I can also indicate the kinds of images that are available for a counterhegemony. In both cases, cultural creation and the formation of consciousness are political processes. An emergent culture must be created by using elements of past and present that have been excluded in the dominant culture or by giving new meanings to elements that have not been excluded.

Thus the first point to be made about the dominant culture in Venezuela is that it is political. The linkage between development and democracy created by Acción Democrática is so profound that it sets the terms for all political debate. The principal opposition party, COPEI, accepts the linkage and contests particular policies. Most socialist parties also accept the linkage but argue that the dominant parties are not *really* democratic or that their form of development is not *really* development. To a certain extent, this linkage and associated aspects of dominant culture are consciously promoted and can be seen as constitutive of a ruling ideology. Professors of history sympathetic to AD write histories of Venezuela showing a movement from degradation to democracy and from backwardness to development. All history is a movement toward the progress enjoyed in the present. There is also a constant manipulation of emotions in the use of television, public rallies, and state occasions. For example, the contradictory images of the peasant and the countryside—images that stress an exploited past or that stress pastoral calm and independence—can be simultaneously expressed and played against each other. Official celebrations of the anniversary of the agrarian reform law romanticize the Venezuelan peasant even as they emphasize the exploitative past. The dominant culture cannot, however, simply be dismissed as conscious manipulation or ruling-class ideology. When these histories are written, or when the past is unfavorably compared with the present, the ideologues are touching on one aspect of the lived experiences of peasants and proletarians. The move from country to city, from peasant to proletarian or "other," or from backwardness to development can be experienced as progress.[20]

Given the contradictory nature of Venezuela's development, the dominant culture can only touch on one aspect of that experience. It can point to Venezuela's progress; it cannot point to all that is troubling and contradictory in that disordered progress. To what extent does the past provide raw material for an emergent culture, a moral economy of protest? The past is certainly available, most obviously in the everyday comparison of present basic consumption goods prices with those in effect a generation, a year, or even a month ago. By examining the symbols of coffee and petroleum, backwardness and development, country and city, I have traced the emergence of an image of an ordered rural past that serves as critical counterpoint to the disordered present. Can this image serve as the basis for an alternative emergent tradition? I think not. It represents not historical memory, but historical nostalgia. It has no connection with the lived experience of most peasants or even most proletarians. It simply calls up an idealized past, and as an ideal it can support the present order or, in the event of the failure of Venezuela's models of development and democracy, a fascist turn. Here it is interesting to note that most socialist historians do not fundamentally differ from AD historians on large segments of Venezuela's past. Both stress the dependence and backwardness of the early petroleum economy. They differ on their interpretations of the present and on some of the labels they give to past and present. They differ, in short, in their valuations of Venezuelan forms of development and democracy.[21]

The construction of an emergent culture that can serve a proletarian consciousness, then, cannot turn to an idealized past but must begin with the life experiences of Venezuelan proletarians. The starting point is the very linkage that proved so powerful for the dominant culture—development and democracy. It must recognize and celebrate those aspects of progress in Venezuela's twentieth century that represent historic gains: the emergence of forms of organization of popular masses, the struggle to gain control over petroleum resources and to turn the wealth created by the petroleum sector toward national development, and the struggle for democracy. Because these achievements have been progressive and because historically they are associated with Acción Democrática, they have served as constitutive elements of the dominant culture, but the contradictions inherent in the dominant parties' approach to development mean that these same achievements can be turned into constitutive elements of an emergent culture. Development and democracy may still serve as the basis for working-class consciousness, but the terms may be given fuller, more critical, more demanding meanings. Workers may demand forms of organization they control, forms of development that exclude multinationals, forms of democracy that give them greater control over their own destiny. The construction of this emergent culture takes us beyond the task and potential of an interpretive essay.

The moral economists argue that a first-generation proletarian or a peasantry first confronted with capitalist development looks backward for its forms of response at the same time that it looks forward. This is true in Venezuela; a less anthropologically inclined writer might argue that it is universally true. When Venezuelan peasants and proletarians look back, their view is not clear. Venezuelan peasants and proletarians are confronted with a disordered past that has given way to a disordered present. Their political and cultural task is to take aspects of the past and of the present that have offered promise and turn them into demands for the future.

NOTES

My understanding of Venezuela began with fieldwork conducted from 1974 to 1976 with the institutional support of the Instituto Venezolano de Investigaciones Científicas and the financial support of a National Science Foundation (NSF) Graduate Fellowship, an NSF Dissertation Improvement Grant (SOC 75–18655), and a Doherty Fellowship. This essay, however, raises many questions that I was not asking when the original research was conducted. I thank Richard Blot, Scott Cook, Mary Fallica, Michael Hanagan, Thomas Hardy, Francine Moccio, and Jim Wessman for criticizing an early version of this essay.

1. James Scott, *The Moral Economy of the Peasant* (New Haven, 1976); James Scott, "Protest and Profanation: Agrarian Revolt and the Little Tradition," *Theory and Society*, 4 (1977), pp. 1–38, 211–246. See also Samuel Popkin, *The Rational Peasant* (Berkeley, 1979); and especially Michael Adas, " 'Moral Economy' or 'Contest State'? Elite Demands and the Origins of Peasant Protest in Southeast Asia," *Journal of Social History*, 13 (1980), pp. 521–546.

2. E. P. Thompson, *The Making of the English Working Class* (New York, 1963), p. 63; E. P. Thompson, "The Moral Economy of the English Crowd in the Eighteenth Century," *Past and Present*, 50 (1971), pp. 76–136. See as well Eric Hobsbawm, *Primitive Rebels* (New York, 1959); and George Rudé, *The Crowd in History* (New York, 1964).

3. E. P. Thompson, "Time, Work-Discipline, and Industrial Capitalism," *Past and Present*, 38 (1967), pp. 56–97; Herbert Gutman, *Work, Culture and Society in Industrializing America* (New York, 1976); Scott, *Moral Economy*.

4. Raymond Williams, *The Country and the City* (Oxford, 1973), pp. 37–38 et passim.

5. Raymond Williams, *Culture and Society* (New York, 1960), p. 279; cf. Frank R. Leavis and Denys Thompson, *Culture and Environment* (Westport, Connecticut, 1977 reprint) [originally published 1959].

6. Williams, *Country and City*, p. 302 et passim.

7. A more detailed account that concentrates on one region in the nineteenth and twentieth centuries can be found in William Roseberry, *Coffee and Capitalism in the Venezuelan Andes* (Austin, 1983).

8. See John Lombardi and James Hanson, "The First Venezuelan Coffee Cycle, 1830–1855," *Agricultural History*, 44 (1970), pp. 355–367; Gastón Carvallo and Josefina Ríos de Hernandez, "Economía Cafetalera y Clase Dominante en Venezuela (1830–1920)," in *Agricultura y Sociedad: Tres Ensayos Históricos*, Equipo Sociohistórico (Caracas, 1979); Domingo Alberto Rangel, *El Proceso del Capitalismo*

Contemporaneo en Venezuela (Caracas, 1968); Rangel, *Capital y Desarrollo: La Venezuela Agraria* (Caracas, 1969).

9. Rangel, *Proceso*; Rangel, *Capital y Desarrollo: La Venezuela Agraria*; William Roseberry, "Capital and Class in Nineteenth Century Boconó, Venezuela," *Antropológica*, 54 (1980), pp. 139–166; Roseberry, *Coffee and Capitalism*.

10. For a different account of the agrarian structure of the Andes in the 1930s, when the coffee economy was in crisis but still dominated the region, see Federico Brito Figueroa, *Historia Económica y Social de Venezuela*, vol. 2 (Caracas, 1966), p. 490. Note, however, that he constructs his argument against those who deny the dominance of *latifundia* in Trujillo state by taking the total rural population and subtracting it from the number of farms. This allows him to claim that the vast majority of the rural population was landless. The landless, according to this method, would include wives, children, and the aged within particular households.

11. *El Renacimiento* (Boconó newspaper), March 4, 1904.

12. See, for example, Loring Allen, *Venezuelan Economic Development* (Greenwich, Connecticut, 1977); Brito Figueroa, *Historia*; Armando Córdova, *Inversiones Extranjeras y Subdesarrollo* (Caracas, 1973); Hector Malavé Mata, "Formación Histórica del Antidessarrollo de Venezuela," in *Venezuela: Crecimiento sin Desarrollo*, D. F. Maza Zavala, et al. (Mexico, D. F., 1974); Domingo Alberto Rangel, *Capital y Desarrollo: El Rey Petroleo* (Caracas, 1970); Jorge Salazar, *Oil in the Economic Development of Venezuela* (New York, 1976); and Franklin Tugwell, *The Politics of Oil in Venezuela* (Stanford, 1975), for more detailed presentations of the transformation outlined here.

13. Venezuela, Banco Central, *La Economía Venezolana en los Últimos Treinta Anos* (Caracas, 1971); Ministerio de Fomento, *X Censo de Población y Vivienda: Resumen General* (Caracas, 1971).

14. Darcy Ribeiro, *The Americas and Civilization* (New York, 1972), p. 288.

15. Ministerio de Fomento, *Censo*; Julio Paez Celis, *Ensayo sobre Demografía Economica de Venezuela* (Caracas, 1975); María Matilde Suárez and R. Torrealba, "Internal Migration in Venezuela," *Urban Anthropology*, 8 (1979), pp. 291–311.

16. See, for example, Janice Perlman, *The Myth of Marginality* (Berkeley, 1976); Larissa Lomnitz, *Networks and Marginality* (New York, 1977); for Venezuela, Talton Ray, *The Politics of the Barrios of Venezuela* (Berkeley, 1969); and Luise Margolies, ed., *The Venezuelan Peasant in Country and City* (Caracas, 1979).

17. See, for example, Enrique Baloyra and John Martz, "Culture, Regionalism, and Political Opinion in Venezuela," *Canadian Journal of Political Science*, 10 (1977), pp. 527–572; Enrique Baloyra and John Martz, *Political Attitudes in Venezuela* (Austin, 1979); Frank Bonilla, *The Failure of Elites* (Cambridge, Mass., 1970); Frank Bonilla and Jose A. Silva Michelena, *A Strategy for Research on Social Policy* (Cambridge, Mass., 1967); Steven Ellner, "Political Party Dynamics in Venezuela and the Outbreak of Revolutionary Warfare," *Interamerican Economic Affairs*, 34:2 (1980), pp. 3–24; Steve Ellner, "Factionalism in the Venezuelan Communist Movement, 1937–1948," *Science and Society* 45 (1981), pp. 52–70; Daniel Levine, *Conflict and Political Change in Venezuela* (Princeton, 1973); Daniel Levine, *The Church and Politics in Latin America* (Princeton, 1981); John Martz, *Acción Democrática: Evolution of a Modern Political Party* (Princeton, 1966); John Martz, ed., *Venezuela: The Democratic Experience* (New York, 1977); Humberto

Njaim et al., *El Sistema Político Venezolano* (Caracas, 1975); James Petras, Morris Morley, and Steven Smith, *The Nationalization of Venezuelan Oil* (New York, 1977); John Duncan Powell, *The Political Mobilization of the Venezuelan Peasant* (Cambridge, Mass., 1971).

18. Fernando Henrique Cardoso, "Associated Dependent Development: Theoretical and Practical Implications," in *Authoritarian Brazil*, ed. Alfred Stepan (New Haven, 1973); Fernando Henrique Cardoso and Enzo Faletto, *Dependency and Development in Latin America* (Berkeley, 1979).

19. Raymond Williams, *Marxism and Literature* (Oxford, 1977), pp. 108–127 et passim.

20. For a representative AD history, see J. L. Salcedo Bastardo, *Historia Fundamental de Venezuela*(Caracas, 1972). When I refer to COPEI as an opposition party, I am aware that they are currently in power. Throughout the period since 1958, however, AD has been the dominant party, even when not in power. COPEI has been an opposition party par excellence.

21. For a representative leftist history, see Malavé Mata, "Formación Histórica."

8
Migrants and Working-Class Consciousness in Kenya

Sharon Stichter

The pattern of early industrial development in Kenya, and indeed in Africa as a whole, produced a wage-labor force that was in large part migrant, traveling long or short distances to the work site, remaining there for a month, six months, or several years, and then returning to the rural areas. Although writers on Africa have often viewed migrant labor as a phenomenon peculiar to that continent, in fact it is not at all unique. Various forms of partial and temporary proletarianization have been common features of early industrialization in many parts of the world. What is peculiar to Africa is that in the early years of industrialization nearly the whole of the work force was migrant, and migrancy persisted over a lengthy period—from the turn of the century until the mid-1950s in some areas, in other areas up to the present day.

The question of what kinds of working-class consciousness and collective action can be expected from migrant or partly proletarianized workers is clearly important. Migrant labor as it evolved in Kenya is an example of a distinct variety of labor system, a particular form of low-wage, low-skill, labor-intensive production used here in agriculture on coffee, tea, and sisal estates. Coexisting peasant or subsistence economies supplied the labor and subsidized a good part of the worker's wage, providing subsistence for his wife and children and for the worker himself in old age, thus insuring the reproduction of the labor force. In this system laborers experienced a particular set of class relationships and evolved appropriate strategies of collective protest and labor market action. I will

The author is grateful to Longman Group Ltd., London, for permission to use, in somewhat revised form, material from Sharon Stichter, *Migrant Labour in Kenya: Capitalism and African Response, 1895–1975*, London, 1982.

present here an overview of labor actions typical of the migrant workers in Kenya, both when the migrant system was at its height in the years before 1945, and when it became more fully proletarianized.

One key point is that migrant labor action—and by extension, labor consciousness—requires interpretation in the context of production relations in both the wage labor sector *and* the peasant sector. As Charles Perrings put it in relation to Northern Rhodesian mineworkers in the 1930s, the "structural migrancy of labor" is the totality of the African worker's experience, and must remain the point of departure for any inquiry into worker consciousness.[1] In colonial Kenya, the various forms of labor action depended greatly on the articulation of the estate and peasant sectors. In addition to this consideration, we also emphasize the role of other factors such as urbanization, the skill structure of the labor force, and government policy in the development of labor action.

In the early years, migrant labor protest consisted mainly of avoiding recruitment and desertion from employment, both attempts to maintain flexibility in the labor market or between the labor market and household commodity production under conditions of labor scarcity. Later, strikes and mass labor actions were facilitated by increasing dependence on the labor market and by urbanization of the workforce, while the growth of formal organizations was aided by the emergence of a stratum of more skilled workers. The increasing militance of urban migrant workers in the late 1940s centered on the classic issues of wages, housing, and cost of living, mixed with the growing general sentiment of anti-colonial nationalism. Tactics included organizational development, large and small strikes, and boycotts. By 1952, however, the combined forces of government repression and growing unrest in the countryside led the labor movement into an alliance with the peasant and squatter oathing activities and into the Mau Mau rebellion. In this episode we see again the important impact of conditions in the peasant sector on the direction taken by the labor movement.

THE FORMATION OF THE WORKING CLASS: AN OVERVIEW

Virtually all Kenyan workers were recruited directly from lineage-based subsistence or peasant societies, either in Africa or in India. Unlike Western Europe or North America, Kenya had no long period of guild or artisanal production preceding industrial development and did not have even a small independent artisan class to experience proletarianization as a decline in status.[2] Rather, industrialization, already advanced in the West, was introduced into precapitalist subsistence societies, and it was the "young men" within these societies who experienced a change in status.

Nineteenth-century Mombasa, the main coastal town that predated colonial conquest, had been a center for the East Indian commerce in slaves, ivory, sesame, cowries, and coconuts. Here there were tradesmen, artisans, and workers of various sorts, but they usually did not work full-time for wages. Often they were paid by the job, and many were slaves of Arab overlords. These townsmen and some other immigrants provided the first source of labor for the British conquest of the interior, working as porters, soldiers, and artisans. British abolition of Arab slave-holding made ex-slaves another small source; yet a third source was the over 32,000 Indians imported to construct the Kenya-Uganda railway in the absence of sufficient African labor. About one-fifth of the Indians elected to remain in the colony when their contracts ended. Many of them advanced to skilled positions on the railway or went into independent commercial activities.

The great majority of workers who made possible the development of export agriculture, small-scale industry, and associated commercial activity in the colony were recruited from the independent African societies of the interior, of which the largest were the Kikuyu, the Luo, the Maasai, the Kamba, and the Luyia. The first two together accounted for perhaps half the total African population in Kenya, and both participated heavily in wage labor. The Kamba and especially the Kikuyu were centrally located around the capital city of Nairobi, whereas the Luo and Luyia were further away in western Kenya and had to travel longer distances to work sites.

These African societies had various traditions of craftsmanship, but craftsmen as a group were not highly differentiated. In any case, arriving British entrepreneurs introduced Western technology, bypassing African crafts and craftsmen. The major social divisions in African societies were between men and woman and between young men and elders. African and European customs combined to ensure that it would be the young men who experienced the burden, or in some cases the opportunity, of wage earning.

In contrast to Western Europe and North America, wage earning in Kenya was brought about in the first instance by government intervention and coercion. Beginning in 1903, land was expropriated from the Kikuyu and to a lesser extent from other African societies and granted to British settlers for "estate" agriculture, which relied on migrant and "squatter" labor to grow coffee, tea, sisal, maize, and beef and dairy cattle for export. The land expropriations from the Kikuyu created the semi-proletarianized squatters who, in return for a given amount of labor on the estate, received use rights to land. The "reserves" policy, the confining of the remaining African populations to a limited land area, created a "voluntary" outflow of wage laborers by the late 1920s and 1930s, when populations began to increase. But a very large growth in African wage earning took place before that time and was brought about largely by administrative coercion and more or less forced recruitment, aided by the imposition of cash taxation.

Coercion of African young men was undertaken by government-appointed chiefs and sometimes by private recruiters. Chiefs were pressed by the colonial district commissioners to provide labor, but in theory no force was to be used. The extensive evidence given the 1912 Native Labour Commission, however, documents the widespread use of coercion. One chief supplied workmen for the Magadi Railway by "sending out his spearmen and asking for volunteers."[3] Another testified that if the district commissioner required men "he would at once turn them out for him and if one refused he would choose another in his place."[4] It was reported that in Chief Kinyanjui's area of Kikuyuland, "those Kikuyu who refused to go were fined a goat in order to pay for a substitute and in certain cases were flogged for disobedience to Kinyanjui's orders."[5]

In 1908, a formal ban on official recruiting led to the rise of professional labor recruiters, both African and European. Labor recruiting was common in central Kenya in the early years and flourished in western Kenya among the Luo and Luyia peoples through the 1920s. There, recruitment was associated with the institution of the "long contract" of one or even two years, and was used largely for work on downcountry sisal plantations, railway construction, soda ash mining, and other less skilled employment. Many recruiters employed force or stratagems such as masquerading as government agents to secure labor. The practice of inducing workers with an advance of up to a month's wages was also common, but the results were not as drastic as in the more developed Latin American form of debt-bondage.

In the Kenyan context, labor recruitment was mainly a response to the problem of scarce supply. Labor recruiters usually did not take part in the organization of production and the management of labor, as they did in the more extensive "contract" systems in China, India, and elsewhere.[6] But at least one exception to this rule can be found in the quarrying industry outside Nairobi, where subcontractors recruited and supervised gangs of stone cutters, dressers, and laborers, paying their wages after selling the finished stone to Indian quarry owners.[7]

Labor recruiting in Kenya declined by the end of the twenties, however, as economic pressures including land shortage, rising populations, stagnation of peasant agriculture due to government restrictions, and rising consumption desires, combined to produce a growing "voluntary" supply. By the end of the decade, employers no longer complained of supply problems, and the era of shortage was over. The pattern of predominantly part-time and migrant wage work lasted until the mid-1950s. European-owned estates in the "White Highlands," the Rift Valley and Uasin Gishu dominated the lucrative export market; on the domestic market they competed with African peasants and pastoralists who produced maize, vegetables, and dairy products. Many African subsistence economies became more or less rapidly transformed into peasant economies, at the same time exporting increasing numbers of migrant laborers.

THE RESPONSES OF MIGRANT LABORERS

The reaction of Africans to the burden of coerced migrant labor may be seen in the high rates of avoidance of recruitment, "desertion" from employment, and work inefficiency that plagued settlers and government throughout the early years. These forms of resistance are characteristic of migrant workers. In general migrants sought to control the extent of their commitment to the labor market and to maximize their flexibility to leave it. The earliest employers, for example the Uganda Railway, thus could not get Africans to work for long periods of time nor very far from their homes. One European complained in exasperation: "No man can run a farm with monthly relays of raw labour; such labour is capricious and always likes to desert."[8]

Forced labor, labor recruiting, the contract system, and laws prohibiting "desertion" from employment were the main strategies by which employers attempted to control African mobility in the market. Forced or not, recruiting bound workers to contracts for specific lengths of time according to employers' needs; coffee farmers worked on a month-to-month basis because labor needs fluctuated; workers on the coastal sisal estates tended to be on six-month contracts; while those in the railway ballast-breaking camps were on a one- or two-year basis. It was the practice to put all labor on contract, even if only monthly. Breaking contract then became illegal. The Masters and Servants Ordinance, introduced in 1910, made "desertion" from employment a criminal offense.

Resistance to forced recruitment occurred in every major African society in the early years. The very necessity of resorting to force, common to all areas, testifies to the spirit of opposition in the African population. Even today among the Luo and Luyia, the period of forced labor is remembered as oppressive.[9] The Giriama area, where the whole able-bodied male population of one township "took refuge in the bush" when recruiting officers approached, was only the most extreme case.[10] Another form of resistance, for those who could afford it, was bribery of chiefs to avoid the work, or payments to a substitute. Failing this, some workers feigned illness in order to fail the medical examination. The commonest response, perhaps, was desertion—simply to run off after recruitment at the first available opportunity.

But as economic incentives to enter the labor market increased, as travel routes and prospective employers became more familiar, and as more Africans could afford transport costs themselves, they took matters into their own hands and began going out voluntarily. Before World War I, almost all labor in western Kenya leaving the province went out on long contract, but by 1922 in the north and central districts "by far the greater number of men out at work . . . engaged themselves as volunteers," preferring this to the six-month written contract offered by recruiters. "Expense and delay is saved the employer by this method and labour comes to him more freely, as a long contract is not liked by the native."[11]

Desertion could be a response to forced recruitment or to conditions at the workplace. Often sickness, harsh treatment, or poor diet prompted desertions. Even jobs that appeared particularly difficult or distasteful could cause desertions. Kamba labor was impossible to obtain in 1912 for transporting poles across the hot, dusty plains for the Magadi-Machakos telegraph lines, and the "Nairobi Akikuyu bolted almost immediately."[12] For the Magadi Railway, recruiters obtained a considerable number of Kamba, but most of them ran off on arrival. The commissioner reported that "fortunately the Nzamas [councils of elders] in some cases have had the sense to assist in the return of the deserters, some 95 having been recently sent back to work."[13]

The situation in the peasant economy always had an important bearing on African labor action. At first, when peasant production offered greater opportunities relative to wage labor, desertions were most frequent. Deserters went back to the peasant economy rather than to wage work elsewhere. The seasonal pattern of labor flows was another spontaneous African strategy. When they could, Africans chose to let the requirements of production on their own shambas [farms] set the limits of their participation in wage earning. In the period of labor shortage before 1925, desertion to the reserves, seasonal work, resistance to recruitment, and avoidance of "bad" employers were the most important and effective strategies of resistance by migrant laborers.

But as the terms of the labor market shifted in the late 1920s, so did migrant laborers' strategies. The peasant economy held out fewer opportunities, escape from wage earning became less possible and desirable, and migrants of necessity turned to strategies within the wage labor sector rather than outside it. African economies experienced drought, competition, and government neglect as European agriculture predominated. The era of labor shortage was over. By the 1930s, population pressure in some reserves had become acute, contributing to soil erosion and further emigration.

As dependence on wage labor increased, the frequency of desertions decreased. Reported desertions—a small fraction of actual desertions—declined from 3,544 in 1923 to 312 in 1928.[14] Rather than indicating a return to the peasant sector, desertion was now a strategy for moving from jobs with inadequate pay and poor conditions to areas that offered better opportunities. In the late 1920s, for example, recruiters complained that workers would sign on for one to two years' work on the coastal sisal estates, obtain free rail passage downcountry, and then immediately desert to higher-paid work in the port city of Mombasa.[15]

Informal labor protest on the job was a pervasive characteristic of the migrant labor economy. Employers, especially settlers, constantly complained of inefficiency and dishonesty on the part of their laborers. From the workers' point of view, laziness, theft, and minor deceptions were often the only way to gain a measure of freedom or personal dignity, or to protest low wages, late payment of wages, or deductions from wages. On the tea estates in the 1920s and 1930s, in response to deteriorating conditions, instances of dodging work, drinking beer on the job, and theft of pruning knives, hoes, pangas, and axes (all of which could be used on the farm at home) were common. At times the management imposed collective fines for thefts, but this usually meant punishing the innocent since those who had stolen had already run off. Protests against harsh *nyaparas* [gang headmen]—cursing them or shouting them down— also took place.[16]

It is but a short step from those informal labor actions to the open withdrawal of labor with the aim of negotiation with the employer. A few strikes by African "long contract" workers in Mombasa, who could not easily desert and return home, are reported as early as 1910, 1913, and 1916.[17] By the late 1920s, such organized collective action had become more common. In times of economic expansion, when African labor was in high demand, strikes could be successful. Hence in the late 1920s, the late 1930s, and during the war, there were notable increases in the number of strikes. In the large but isolated ballast-breaking camps and relaying gangs along the railway there were strikes of two and three hundred men in 1925, 1927, and 1928, large numbers of desertions, and "constant agitations." At times compulsory labor had to be brought in for lack of voluntary labor. Health and food conditions in these camps were exceptionally bad, work was arduous, and Indian employers operating on small profit margins often defaulted on wages. Workers were mostly Luo and Luyia.[18]

During the Depression of the 1930s, however, strikes virtually ceased. Then, with the upturn in the labor market after the Depression, the number of strikes markedly increased, both on rural estates and in towns. The conjuncture of rising peasant incomes with stagnant wages but rising demand for labor produced a number of important rural strikes in the mid-1930s among coffee and sisal workers and African fishermen.

Migrant workers had a certain advantage over full-time ones with respect to strikes; they had some means of subsistence from family *shambas* should the walkout be long. But the barriers to successful strike action probably outweighed the advantages. Most migrant workers were unskilled and could easily be replaced unless there was a labor shortage. Thus the most successful early strikes were by the more skilled. Government control of compulsory labor made it possible to undercut protests by the unskilled, as occurred in the ballast camps in the late 1920s.

Migrant laborers in agriculture were scattered on many small estates over the countryside, making it difficult to organize on a large scale. Labor action among agricultural workers was also inhibited by the close personal supervision many farmers gave their labor force and the paternal relationships that sometimes were built up. Also, the settler's or manager's close control of the premises made labor organizing by outsiders very difficult.

The migrant worker's part-time status in the labor force provided only a temporary sense of community with co-workers. Some work groups were families, for example among squatters and on sisal estates, but the majority were composed only of young men. Concerted action had to draw first upon ties from communities of residence and reproduction—upon ethnic and village ties. Very often work groups in rural areas were composed of the same ethnic group because of the location of the work site or the operation of the recruiting system, or because employers found that they worked better that way. Early labor actions thus tended to be carried out by members of the same ethnic group, but this does not mean that they depended on "traditional" leadership or aimed at "traditional" goals.

THE STRAINS OF GROWTH: URBANIZATION, DIFFERENTIATION, AND PROTEST

Two key processes of socioeconomic change were introduced in the late 1930s: urbanization and upward social mobility for some African wage earners. Both these trends increased markedly during the war years. Urban areas had always been the high-wage pole of the export economy and had attracted workseekers from the beginning. Now migration to the towns increased; urban employment grew, but so did unemployment. In Nairobi District employment grew from 17,027 in October 1936 to 22,584 in December 1941, a 33 percent increase; Mombasa District exprienced a 28 percent increase.[19] By 1941 a majority (56 percent) of African workers were employed outside agriculture, either in public services or in industry and commerce.[20]

Urban migrants often stayed in employment for longer lengths of time than rural migrants, especially if they were long-distance migrants who had invested time and money in transportation. Urban workers were also temporarily more dependent on purchased items for subsistence; they regularly bought such items as maize meal, ghee, khaki drill cloth, sugar, and tea, and were sensitive to price rises in these basic commodities. Some urban workers also paid rent if housing was not supplied by the employer. Finally, urbanization congregated large groups of workers at both work sites and residential areas; here news traveled quickly, the scale of protest actions enlarged, and strikes became more common. The unemployed were also volatile, joining in many mass protests. Strikes always had the potential of becoming citywide; mass urban strikes were a prominent feature of labor protest in Kenya, occurring in 1939, 1947, 1956, and 1957 in Mombasa, and in 1950 in Nairobi.

When Africans left the peasant economy, they entered a wage labor economy hierarchically structured by the property distinction between capitalist and worker, and by technically defined occupational divisions. Until World War II, the occupational structure did not change much in itself; rather, Africans worked their way up against great odds, slowly acquiring literacy and skills and increased ability to remain permanently in the labor force. It was this process rather than the lack of it—the process of upward mobility begun but held in check—that proved to be a second major force behind labor protest.

The migrant labor economy offered a very limited range of skilled positions in agriculture since mechanization was not widespread. The non-agricultural sectors offered larger scope for educated and skilled work, yet initially these middle-level positions went to full-time workers from India or Goa. African advance was restricted by their part-time relationship to the labor force, by inadequate education and training facilities, by racial discrimination, and by legalized differential pay systems such as the racial "grades" on the railway and in the civil service. Gradually, however, the logic of the market pushed employers into training the cheaper African labor. The two most important and best-paid categories of skilled workers during the colonial era were clerks and teachers, and skilled manual workers; the most numerous semi-skilled categories were domestic workers and shop assistants.

Clerks and other white-collar workers rapidly became the segment of the work force most stabilized in employment. While many owned or purchased land and were active in agricultural enterprise, they also tended to remain in full-time employment until retirement. Many, for example, contributed to provident funds. They were the earliest group of workers to form staff associations and to experience the social "color bar" which restricted African advancement. The Kenya African Civil Service Association was formed about 1930, the Kenya African Teachers' Union about 1934, the Railway African Staff Association (mainly white-collar) about 1940, and the Nairobi African Local Government Staff Association by 1941.[21]

Skilled manual workers were likewise a small but growing stratum. Training programs for small numbers of Africans began early on the railway and in the Public Works Department; the railway's formal apprenticeship scheme began in 1923. Many mission schools put great emphasis on craft instruction, and by about 1925 there was a government industrial school at Kabete known as the Native Industrial Training Depot. Many Africans, though, learned important skills on the job, often through surreptitious observation, particularly in the construction, quarrying, and machinery repair industries.

The demand for African skilled labor increased significantly in the late 1930s. One factor was the opening of gold fields in west Kenya which, though short-lived, created a demand for African carpenters, blacksmiths, brickworkers, engine drivers, and shaft hoist operators. In urban areas the general prosperity was a factor, as well as the stiff competition between European and Indian employers in the building trades and the growth of trade unionism among Asian artisans. European building contractors turned increasingly to African skilled labor in order to compete with Asians. As a result of the long strike by Asian artisans in Nairobi in 1937, more African artisans were hired.

An African who started as an assistant or trainee often had to work his way up by moving from job to job. Many African carpenters, painters, and bricklayers became self-employed, working on daily rates for the duration of a job. Many barbers and cobblers were self-employed. Some tailors worked for small Indian-owned shops, but many worked on their own in African marketplaces in towns and reserves, using small, rickety sewing machines. Some African taxi drivers were self-employed, but most worked on commission from Indian or European fleet owners. African mechanics and bus and lorry drivers worked for a variety of employers.

Larger employers of African skilled labor included the Railway Marine Workshops at Kisumu, Mombasa port landing and shipping companies, the Public Works Department, the Medical Department, and the Post Office. By far the largest employer of African skilled labor was the railway. Africans worked as engine drivers, fireman, shunters, signallers, station masters, telegraphists, crane drivers, pointsmen, fitters, carpenters, riveters, supervisors, inspectors, and foremen. In 1936 the railway employed a monthly average of 14,350 Africans; of these only about 14 percent were skilled or semi-skilled, but by 1945 the railway employed 17,144 Africans, of whom 34 percent were above the unskilled level, indicating a great deal of African advancement during these years.[22]

The expansion of secondary industry during and after the war, and accelerated training programs undertaken in the defense forces and elsewhere, meant that the numbers of African skilled workers increased rapidly after the war. Wages increased as well; whereas in 1936 they averaged Shs. (Shillings) 24 to Shs. 29 a month colony-wide, by the end of the war the average montly cash wage of carpenters was Shs. 79, of drivers Shs. 77, of masons Shs. 60, and of mechanics Shs. 57. These rates were equal to or higher than the average clerk's wage and about four times the wage of agricultural laborers.[23] Domestic workers and shop assistants, whose numbers also increased during the war, made somewhat lower wages.

Many of the earliest and most successful strikes were undertaken by these skilled workers. In Nairobi there were strikes by stonemasons in the quarries in May 1937, by drivers and conductors for the Kenya Bus Company in 1938, and by railway apprentices in June 1939. The first two were successful; the masons received a wage increase and so did the drivers and conductors, despite the fact that they already earned relatively high wages of Shs. 70 and 50 a month.[24] But apprentices were not in nearly so strategic a position. Sixty-four of them, all Luo, went on strike because their "taking-on" pay after training had been reduced two years earlier from Shs. 40 to Shs. 30 a month. The railway wondered why they had waited so long to present their grievance (doubtless in order to benefit from the training) and in a tough response laid them all off.[25]

The urban strikes of the late 1930s and the war years were fueled by the rising cost of living and wages that did not keep pace. In Mombasa, the stevedores and port workers for the Kenya Landing and Shipping Company successfully struck in July 1934 to prevent a proposed wage reduction. They struck again in 1936, as did the Shell Company employees in 1937 and 1938. Stevedores and those on monthly contracts were among the most skilled and experienced manual port workers, but by 1939 unrest had spread to the large number of unskilled daily paid workers at the port; in the 1939 and 1947 general strikes in Mombasa, these workers were the first to act, though the strike then spread quickly to nearly all town and port workers. Though the late 1930s also saw riots between competing ethnic groups in Mombasa, the labor actions began to overcome inter-ethnic hostility. In the two general strikes, as well as in several smaller strikes in 1942, workers of many different ethnic groups cooperated.

During the war in Nairobi, barbers, taxi drivers, painters, carpenters, and cobblers all formed craft associations. Shop workers and messengers, night watchmen, and domestic workers soon followed. Perhaps the earliest formal organization among skilled African manual workers was created by stonemasons in the quarry areas after their 1937 strike. Many of these were also small employers, however, and their association was disbanded by the Labour Department on charges of levying arbitrary fees on stone workers.[26]

The context of rising demand for African skilled labor and short supply made the war years propitious. The building industry was booming, and domestic workers were in especially high demand because of the increase of Europeans in uniform. Labor officers reported that domestic workers were "exploiting" the shortage situation by setting strict limits to the tasks they would do and by being "fastidious" in their choice of employer. Those looking for work would only accept it at "considerably enhanced" wages.[27] This sort of spontaneous individual protest was a forerunner to group efforts. By 1945 a largely Kikuyu Houseboys Association had been formed; it protested the low wages of domestic workers and the Domestic Servants' Red Book they had to carry at all times. The association asked that wives be allowed to stay with the men and that servants get more time off; it attempted to combat prostitution among Kikuyu women and the flow of young Kikuyu girls into town. There was also another group known as the Jaluo Houseboys Association, as well as an association of Houseboys of Indians and Goans.[28]

The imposition of pass laws regulating the entry of Africans into Nairobi provided another impetus to the formation of organizations. This was the case among painters, whose union was formed in 1944, and among barbers, cobblers, masons, and carpenters. Since they were self-employed they lacked the proper evidence of employment, a signed registration certificate or *kipande*. The unions were formed to serve as authenticating agencies, as well as to help members get residents' permits and ration cards. The Painters' Union also attempted to raise wages by the novel method of advertising in the Swahili newspaper *Mwalimu* that no painter should accept less than Shs. 5 per day. The previous rate had been Shs. 2. The union also attempted to get its members trade-tested to improve skill and marketability in the program set up by the Labour Department at Kabete.[29]

Attempts by the government to license or otherwise regulate occupations during the war led to more protests and organizing efforts. Stringent licensing laws introduced by the municipality led to the formation of the Nairobi African Taxi Drivers' Union and eventually to a transport strike in 1949. In the quarries outside Nairobi, more government regulation was attempted. The price of building stone was rising, and increasing members were employed in the quarries. Labour Department officials felt that the large number of African subcontractors and sub-subcontractors was uneconomic and driving up the price of stone. Efficiency was thought to be low since cutters and dressers seldom worked more than 18 days a month. They therefore limited the numbers employed in each quarry and attempted to abolish African subcontracting, but with little success. Postwar controls on the quality of stone accepted in Nairobi meant financial hardship for quarry owners, who tried to pass the loss on to the subcontractors. In 1947 it was reported that a great number of African subcontractors made a loss every month. These events led to the renewed formation of unions by African subcontractors in 1948. The objectives of their association were mutual help in case of sickness or death, temporary loans to subcontractors who incurred debts, and "to amass such an amount of money as would make them rich enough to become owners of a quarry." The Labour Department, however, insisted that any union must include all categories of quarry workers, as well as other masons in the building trades. The Nairobi Stone Masons Association, first formed in 1944 to represent masons in town, eventually amalgamated with the quarry groups at Labour Department suggestion, to form the African Stone Workers Union.[30]

MIGRANTS AND MILITANT LABOR ACTION

The war and postwar years in Kenya saw not only the beginnings of labor organizing among urban skilled workers, but also an upsurge of labor unrest including several general strikes and the formation of organizations to represent the whole of the working class. This militant activity in a still largely semi-proletarianized labor force may be understood by reference to three broad factors: (1) socio-economic changes in the workforce itself; (2) government repression of the workers' movements; and (3) rebellion by land-hungry Kikuyu peasants and dispossessed squatters in the countryside. In a situation where most workers still had some ties to the land, the link between urban and rural protest was strong.

From the perspective of the system as a whole, the 1940s and 1950s were a period of strain and contradiction in the migrant labor economy. The delicate balance between peasant and industrial conditions that had supported the migrant labor system was beginning to break down under the pressures of development. On one hand, population pressure and peasant development in the main African reserves were producing an ever-growing supply of partly proletarianized unskilled labor. On the other, the limited industrialization of the war and postwar years and the influx of foreign capital and technology by the 1950s were creating opportunities, not for large numbers of unskilled workers, but for smaller numbers of skilled and semi-skilled ones, resulting in the paradox in urban areas of labor surpluses but persistent shortages of skilled labor. A transition to a new pattern of labor utilization would have to be made, but until then the bottleneck predisposed workers of all sorts to militant action.

Within the workforce, the increasing numbers of employed Africans, the growth of non-agricultural employment, and the increase in skilled labor have already been mentioned. Also important for the rise of labor militance was the increasing length of time Africans spent in wage earning. For many urban workers the pattern of a periodic one- or two-year stint at wage earning, followed by an equally long return to the reserves, began to give way to one in which wage earning occupied almost the whole of the worker's life. The label of "target worker" was no longer applicable to these workers, and they were increasingly dependent on their wage earnings for the majority of their income.[31]

While some groups of workers experienced increasing stability, others, particularly the unskilled, were still short-term migrants. There was a growing difference between the situation of the better-off trained and stabilized workers and the unskilled who were still employed at the statutory minimum wage. Though real wages for skilled workers were undercut by inflation during the war, they rose markedly after it. Between 1948 and 1953 average African earnings in the non-agricultural private sector rose 90 percent, yet the statutory minimum wage rose only 50 percent.[32] The bulk of the increase thus appears to have gone to those above the minimum wage. The situation of unskilled workers was increasingly difficult. As the 1954 Carpenter Committee finally acknowledged, the urban minimum wage provided only the bare essentials of day-to-day living for the single man; it was impossible to support a family on such a wage. The committee estimated that approximately one-half of all urban workers in private industry and one-fourth of those in the public services were receiving wages "insufficient to provide for their basic, essential needs."[33]

The boom conditions of the postwar years activated the struggles of both kinds of workers—of the skilled workers, who were partially benefitting but found further upward mobility blocked, and of the rest of the urban masses, who were excluded from the visible prosperity around them. The rising expectations were met, however, by an alternately repressive and paternalistic government response; the British in Kenya actively tried to shape and manage the emerging labor movement.

The interventionist role of the government, first in the recruiting of labor and then in the manipulation of emerging labor movements, distinguishes African colonies from Europe, America, and other non-colonized regions. With the exception of the railway, Kenya lacked well-capitalized and paternalistic employers like the southern and central African mining companies, so much of the handling of day-to-day labor disputes fell to the Labour Department, which began as a section of the Native Affairs Department in 1919 and became a separate agency in 1940. European settlers in Kenya strongly opposed any form of trade unionism for workers, and under their influence the department adopted a repressive policy until the mid-1930s when, as a result of Indian strikes and organizing, trade unions became legal although subject to control through compulsory registration. Faced with the growth of African organizing and labor unrest during World War II, and under pressure from the Colonial Office and the British Labour government during and after the war, Kenya shifted to a policy of fostering the slow growth of "responsible" and "non-political" unionism, placing primary emphasis in the short run on works committees and staff associations. Most Kenyan officials had misgivings about this policy, and most settlers continued to oppose it. The nearly impossible job of actually fostering African trade unionism in this hostile climate fell to a Trades Union Labour Officer, James Patrick, sent out to Kenya in April 1947.

The far-reaching effects of government policy toward African union-ism can best be seen by a brief review of labor struggles in the postwar years. After the 1939 general strike in Mombasa, there was labor unrest in the city throughout the war years—small strikes and threatened large ones, culminating in the 1947 general strike. On the first day of the strike, the African Workers' Federation (AWF) was formed and aspired to unite all African workers.[34] Similar attempts to form "one big union" can be found in other early industrial situations. As AWF grew, it re-ceived support from nearly all sections of workers in Mombasa, and, indeed, from the unemployed. In some of its statements it spoke for the self-employed as well, and sometimes for Africans as a whole. Chege Kibachia, the federation's leader, traveled throughout the colony urging workers to join; he received support in several cities and on agricultural estates. In Nairobi AWF leaders met with representatives of the various skilled workers' associations, and by July 1947 these associations had decided to amalgamate in a branch of the federation.

The colonial government opposed AWF as too broad, too militant, and too nationalist. After the strike James Patrick, the Trades Union Labour Officer charged with the responsibility of promoting "respon-sible," "non-political," and occupation- and industry-specific unions in Kenya, went to Mombasa to explain the government view to various groups of workers around the city. The response he got gives a rare glimpse into African worker consciousness at this time. He reported that workers "were showing no interest in Trade Unions, in fact they were opposed to everything of a trade union description. All they wanted and all they were interested in was AWF and uniting all Africans in one Union."[35] AWF members opposed both trade unions and staff councils since they were European impositions and were being proposed as sub-stitutes for AWF. At Vacuum Oil Company, they told the Labour Officer:

The European did not come here today but a very long time ago. He has done so many bad things we cannot forget. He now comes to tell us trade unions are good. We are suspicious knowing that a goat and a lion cannot lie down together.

Employees at Shell Company

indicated at the very commencement that they did not wish a trade union as they could not see what good it would do them. They had a long experience of Government and this experience boiled itself down to this; that nothing very tangible had been done in their interests. They had no interest in the present moment other than the further development of African Workers Federation.

When Patrick explained that trade unions (in the government's view) meant negotiating with European employers instead of striking, they informed him that on account of the racial color bar Africans would not be able to negotiate on equal terms with Europeans:

A trade union would mean mixing with and discussing and interviewing the Europeans. How was it possible to mix with the Europeans in such a fashion, when they were not allowed to eat with the European, they were not allowed to smoke with him, nor dance with European ladies. . . . Considering all these things, how could trade unions be a success?

AWF thus challenged not only the wage levels of Africans, but the whole social and political order in Kenya. In its emphasis on African worker unity, it reflected not only the racial divisions of the society, but also the migrant, relatively undifferentiated character of the African workforce. Its potential power was so great that the government acted immediately to arrest and deport its leader, Chege Kibachia. The organization then declined through lack of leadership.

After the enforced demise of AWF, the various workers' associations in Nairobi did try to become official registered trade unions, having little other recourse at this point. But cooperation with the Labour Department proved short-lived; frustration and delay led most unions to turn for advice to Makhan Singh, a left-wing Indian trade unionist who had been attempting to organize an interracial Labour Trade Union of East Africa (LTUEA) since the 1930s. By 1949 the most active and indeed the only legally registered African union, the Transport and Allied Workers' Union (TAWU), an outgrowth of the taxi drivers' union led by Fred Kubai, had agreed to join with Singh's Labour Trade Union to form the East African Trades Union Congress (EATUC). Launched in May 1949, its affiliates also included the predominantly Asian Typographical and Shoemaker Workmen's Unions, and the predominantly African Tailors Union, Domestic Workers Union, and Painters' Union, the latter two as yet unregistered because of Labour Department opposition. The EATUC ran head on into government opposition, as had its predecessor, AWF. Labour Department officials argued that most Africans were not ready for trade unionism, let alone a central federation. They regarded Singh, who had been influenced by South African and Indian communist trade union leaders, as an agitator and troublemaker. One official report even referred to the movement as "subversive and anti-British."[36]

EATUC backed the large taxicab drivers' strike in Nairobi in October 1949, led by TAWU. For several years TAWU had campaigned against the municipal by-laws, which imposed stringent standards of physique and training on licensed cab drivers and threatened to cost many of them their jobs. Now they went out on strike, although unsuccessfully. EATUC also actively pressed for workers' representation on government commissions concerned with labor, and it protested price increases, trade-testing schemes designed to exclude artisans from certain fields, and a bill to force the "voluntarily unemployed" to work. It called for the release of Chege Kibachia, the AWF leader. Its most successful action was a mass boycott of Civic Week celebrations in Nairobi in March 1950, to mark the granting of a Royal Charter to the European-controlled Nairobi City Council. EATUC pointed out that given the crowded and unhealthful slums in the African sections of town, the exclusion of Africans from political power in the city, the high cost of living, the low wages and poor working conditions, the failure of the taxicab strike, and the fears of many Africans about their access to adequate land, the Nairobi masses had little to celebrate.[37] EATUC's articulation of these issues obviously struck a chord of response among Nairobi Africans; the boycott was widespread and successful. Largely as a result, Singh and Kubai were arrested in May 1950 on charges of being officials of an unregistered trade union. This action triggered the large general strike in Nairobi, the only one in that city's history. It lasted nine days and successfully forced an increase in the minimum wage, but did not secure the immediate release of Singh or Kubai. Gradually EATUC declined through lack of leadership.

By moving against both EATUC and AWF, the government effectively discouraged labor organizing on a class-wide or interracial basis in Kenya, insuring instead that unions would remain at the smaller occupational level, moving slowly to the industrial level of a few years later. Also, unions remained racially separated until after national independence. Until 1952, even the occupational associations faced continuing inaction from the Labour Department, which had to approve them as "registered" unions before they could legally collect dues or initiate negotiations with employers. Large-scale citywide strikes were also repressed; they did, however, force the government and private employers to grant wage increases. Labor unrest was also an important factor in persuading the Carpenter Commission of 1954 to recommend, and the government finally to implement, substantial increases in the minimum wage. This endorsement of the concept of a "family minimum wage" rather than a "bachelor minimum" was a watershed in the transition away from the migrant labor system in urban areas.

This history of government repression of the labor movement in Kenya is an important reason why, in the next phase of protest, a large section of the urban labor movement allied itself with Mau Mau, the growing oathing movement, and rebellion in the Kikuyu countryside. A critical turning point came with the release of Fred Kubai from detention in 1951; at that time he decided not to return to fruitless joustings with the Labour Department and employers, but to "bring the force of the African workers into KAU [Kenya African Union]," the umbrella African nationalist movement led by Jomo Kenyatta.[38]

WORKERS AND THE MAU MAU REBELLION

By 1952 the struggles of Kikuyu workers had turned from general strikes and organizing to a phase of participation in the Mau Mau rebellion. A few non-Kikuyu workers also participated; most were passively sympathetic. In order to understand this escalation of tactics on the part of one section of the workforce, one must take into account not only the history of government frustration of union organizing and lack of responsiveness to workers' grievances, but also the situation in the rural economy.

In settler agriculture, wartime price supports and postwar price increases were making possible expansion of production and the fuller use of the land. The increased investment in machinery, in acreage under cultivation, and in the number of European farmers had a particularly unfavorable impact on one section of the farm population, the African squatters, many of whom were Kikuyu. Settlers had less and less need for independent squatters with extensive stock and land requirements. In the late 1930s, a movement began in some areas to restrict squatters' rights and increase their labor time; this was expressed in the Resident Labourers Ordinance of 1937, which limited the amounts of stock and increased labor time. Enforcment of the ordinance, delayed by the war, was begun in 1944. Many squatters refused to consent to the new terms and were forcibly removed from the farms, but the settlers' efforts to divest themselves of surplus labor met one great obstacle: there was no longer any room for returning squatters in the crowded Kikuyu reserve. The very growth and differentiation in the peasant economy had made their return impossible. Thus the squatters' demand became land, and preferably land in the White Highlands. Out of their resistance to enforced proletarianization they developed the oathing movement, which made use of traditional symbols to secure unity against the oppressor.[39]

In the peasant sector, rising produce prices in the postwar years held out the hope of a prosperous peasant life, if only enough land could be obtained. While the well-off peasants or "better farmers" made a reasonable living, further development of their holdings was blocked by market competition from settler agriculture and by discriminatory state policy in many areas, especially with respect to which crops could be grown. But the majority of farmers remained poor and middle peasants, with few resources to protect themselves against population pressure, soil erosion, and falling crop yields. These peasants, the returning squatters, and the traditional tenants would have to turn increasingly to wage labor in order to subsist, yet wage earning did not offer them a real alternative to rural life. These pressures were greatest in the Kikuyu reserve. There economic competition and social differentiation were much greater than elsewhere, and tendencies toward a large landowning class on the one hand and a landless class on the other were increasing. The core of active support for Mau Mau came from the poor and middle peasants whose positions were threatened by these new trends. Those who benefitted—chiefs, large land owners, and educated Christians—held aloof, preferring to air their grievances through more moderate, non-violent political organizations.

The changing conditions in the urban migrant labor sector have been described above. They did not hold out much hope that expanding employment opportunities could solve Kikuyu peasant problems. Migration toward urban areas increased, but so did unemployment. The long-term solution to the peasant problem was to return to Africans the land that had been expropriated from them. This was finally done in the decolonization settlement after Mau Mau, under a policy that supported the middle peasant and attempted to combat both landlessness and the growth of large land owners. The solution to labor unrest in the migrant labor sector was to move to a higher-wage, somewhat more stabilized working class. The price, of course, was a slowing of employment growth and more unemployment.

Meanwhile, peasant and worker discontent matured into social revolution. The actual rebellion was the coalescing of several streams of African struggle, from different sections of the population with somewhat differing aims: nationalist demands were voiced by white-collar workers and by aspiring large farmers; wage demands by skilled and unskilled workers; and demands for more land from peasants and ex-squatters. Thus Mau Mau was not, as it has too often been characterized, simply a "peasant revolt,"[40] nor was it simply a "squatters' revolt,"[41] nor even a revolt of only migrant laborers. Rather, all three of these elements were involved, and it was the combination that made the revolt a large-scale social upheaval.

The rebellion began in the rural areas, first as oathing and mass meetings, then as a series of attacks on cattle, on European farmers, and on unpopular chiefs. Oathing was a traditional custom put to the new use of reaffirming Kikuyu solidarity in the face of European dominance; loyalty to the land and to the founders of the tribe were key themes. Oathing was used selectively by Kikuyu political leaders in the reserves as early as the 1920s, but seems to have reemerged spontaneously among Kikuyu squatters facing eviction from the Rift Valley farms. Returning squatters, notably a group from Olenguruone who had resisted forced resettlement, spread mass oathing and a spirit of resistance throughout the Kikuyu reserves in the early 1950s. Though oathing bound the

Kikuyu to defend their land through violence, organized rebellion did not actually occur until precipitated by the declaration of a state of emergency in October 1952 and the sending in of British troops.

Nairobi, where the urban revolt took place, is situated on the edge of the Kikuyu reserve.[42] Its workforce was predominantly Kikuyu. The underground oathing in the city was organized according to rural territorial units—members were assigned to cells based on their area of origin. The migrant system, the constant shuttling of workers between city and reserve, helped tie the urban rebellion closely to the rural one. Organizers, often recruited in the city, were able to go frequently to rural areas to recruit kinsmen, friends, and neighbors. Waruhiu Itote, an important Mau Mau leader, recalls that he was "a fireman on the Railways by day and a revolutionary by night."[43]

When the emergency was declared, thousands of Kikuyu retreated from farms and cities into the forests to prepare for resistance. In Nairobi much of the Mau Mau leadership was immediately arrested in the first emergency "sweep" known as Operation Jock Scott. But the Kikuyu masses continued the struggle. Many of the unskilled and unemployed provided recruits for the forest fighters. The educated white-collar Kikuyu, however, were much less likely to support the rebellion or participate in the fighting.[44]

Many of those who did not go to the forests continued to organize oathing, collecting funds, and procuring of supplies for the fighters, becoming part of what the administration termed the "passive wing." Mau Mau fighters were greatly dependent on these underground activists and sympathizers. African employees of the police, the Kenya African Rifles, the prisons, government officers, and railways provided Mau Mau activists with such essentials as uniforms (so that they could travel unchallenged), identity papers, guns, ammunition, food, and medical supplies.[45] They also performed important intelligence functions.[46] Stealing from government stores of bottles, explosives, firearms, and metal tubing for homemade guns was common. Domestic employees of high government officials in several notable instances supported Mau Mau activists.[47] Even some African white-collar workers cooperated in the intelligence network.[48] The latrine sweepers employed by the Nairobi City Council were particularly sympathetic.[49]

The unemployed and self-employed were also very important. Kikuyu who ran small independent businesses such as "hoteli," tea kiosks, and garages were helpful in harboring activists.[50] Itinerant traders were carriers of information, money, and supplies. Unemployed youth gangs served as the strong-arm wing.

The government quickly moved to contain the revolt in Nairobi. During 1952 and 1953 there were constant police raids on African residential areas and housing estates. Thousands of Kikuyu who were not in possession of proper papers or who had been implicated by the screening teams of tribal police and elders were sent back to the reserve. Many left of their own accord. Illegal squatter villages on the outskirts of the city were evacuated and destroyed. In the central African residential areas, a policy of ethnic segregation was implemented. A curfew was imposed.

Shooting incidents and armed robberies increased; most were carried out by Mau Mau activists to obtain supplies and money or for political ends. The campaign of terrorism was supplemented by demonstrations. A campaign against drinking European beer was launched, and "sales in Council's beerhalls and African-owned shops dropped to negligible proportions."[51] A bus boycott was staged, and "within two days this was completely effective."[52] There were also boycotts against Asian eating houses, smoking, and wearing hats. A general strike was threatened. These actions give some indication of the extent of support for the underground movement among the mass of Nairobi's African workers. Administrative reports admit that the "vast majority" of Nairobi's Kikuyu supported Mau Mau,[53] and some Kamba and Maasai, as well as several prominent Luo and Luyia were involved.

The main wing of the organized trade union movement also supported the rebellion. The focus of this activity was the TAWU, whose officers, Fred Kubai and John Mungai, moved into the Nairobi branch of KAU and also became leaders in the secret Central Committee, which directed oathing in Nairobi. They continued building up the membership of TAWU, using it as one of a number of vehicles in the spread of oathing. Also on the Central Committee were representatives from the Labour Trade Union of East Africa and from the Clerks Section of that union.

As the emergency progressed, however, the main pro–Mau Mau leadership in the unions was arrested and detained. The many Kikuyu junior officials who remained, especially in the TAWU, the East African Federation of Building and Construction Workers (EAFBCW), the Nightwatchmen, Clerks' and Shopworkers' Union (NCSU), and the Tailors' and Domestic Workers' unions, continued to use their positions as dues collectors and branch leaders to organize oathing and collect money for Mau Mau until near the very end of the emergency. Eventually, at the national and the local levels, all the pro–Mau Mau unions experienced an enforced turnover of leadership in which non-Kikuyu or non–Mau Mau leaders succeeded the Mau Mau ones.

In addition to repressing Mau Mau influence in the unions, the state actively reorganized the entire union movement. In doing this, the Labour Department made a significant about-face in policy. Abandoning the go-slow stance of preceding years, it decided to bring into being a pro-government wing of the movement to counteract the Mau Mau wing. In its search for allies it found some success, playing upon differences in political outlook between different ethnic groups and between white-collar and blue-collar workers.

The department decided to allow the formation of both a new central federation of unions to replace the old EATUC and certain individual unions that it had previously opposed. In this way, both EAFBCW and NCSU emerged as legally registered unions, undercutting the position of the pro–Mau Mau LTUEA, which had been organizing these groups of workers.[54] In the department's view, if the LTUEA eventually had to be banned, this "could only be justified if the people they professed to cater for were absorbed into other unions, even though they had to be created for such a purpose."[55]

New African union leaders, with whom the department could work, were found in Aggrey Minya, a Luyia, and a group of his associates who had been discussing the possibility of forming a new union federation. In May 1952 the department helped draw up the constitution for the Kenya Federation of Registered Trade Unions (KFRTU), supporting Minya as head. Officials promised that if it worked properly and "non-politically," it would be given representation on such important bodies as the Labour Advisory Board.[56] In June 1952 the KFRTU was officially launched, and under Minya it publicly dissociated itself from Mau Mau and denounced violence.[57] Under Minya's successor, Tom Mboya, the federation did resist further government pressure to denounce Mau Mau, and it criticized government handling of the emergency.[58] At the same time, however, it helped suppress a Mau Mau attempt to call a general strike in Nairobi.[59] The department was successful, therefore, in detaching the union movement from Mau Mau, although not from the wider nationalist cause.

CONCLUSION

The worker-peasant alliance in the Mau Mau rebellion was similar to that which produced successful Third World revolutions in countries such as Algeria, China, and Cuba. Mau Mau, however, was on a smaller scale, and was in fact limited to one ethnic group in the colony, though the largest, most central, and most politically active one. Perhaps most important, though, Mau Mau lacked a clear vision of the new form of society to be established after decolonization. Its objectives remained limited to the ouster of the Europeans and the return of Kikuyu lands. The ideology of the trade union leaders in Mau Mau was similarly un-developed. In the course of struggle they came to see the departure of the Europeans as a precondition for any advance by African workers, but their goals for postcolonial society remained uncrystallized.

For these reasons, the outcome of this struggle was different from successful worker-peasant revolutions. Here the rebels lost the war in a military sense, and although they had actually forced the subsequent decolonization of Kenya, they did not share directly in the fruits of power. Instead, power was transferred to the new African bourgeoisie. Likewise in the trade union movement: after the rebellion, the consolidation of the movement took place under new, more moderate leaders, rather than under those who had been involved in rebellion.

A similar fate befell the pro–Mau Mau socialist tendencies within the labor movement. Even though ideas of interracial working-class unity and anti-capitalist struggle were introduced by Makhan Singh and were taken up by some African labor leaders, Singh's organizations were quickly banned by the government. Since these ideological options were so vigorously repressed, it is difficult to know what wider appeal they might have had. What the government could not succeed in eliminating from the movement, however, either by repression or by co-optation, was the strong sense of African unity and anti-colonial nationalism which had been evident in the first large labor organization, the African Workers' Federation. The labor movement was closely allied to the nationalist movement until the achievement of national independence in 1963.

It is clear that over this 50 year period African workers developed a sense of class identity and interests as workers different from that of other sections of the population. The more skilled and stabilized workers were more apt to be involved in ongoing organizational efforts, but all workers, even the most migrant, showed a consciousness of their own interests in the labor market and a willingness to pursue them. It was only the type of action that changed according to the degree of involvement in wage earning.

At the same time, almost all Kenyan workers also retained some interest in the peasant economy, whether it was as the necessary but meager supplement to low-wage, short-term work, or as the sort of entrepreneurial side venture that many of the better-paid workers undertook. Even the best paid and most stabilized workers relied upon their farms for income after retirement in the absence of any social security system or adequate company retirement benefits. Only a few workers, often the very poorest, were completely landless.

NOTES

1. Charles Perrings, "Consciousness, Conflict and Proletarianization: An Assessment of the 1935 Mineworkers' Strike on the Northern Rhodesian Copperbelt," *Journal of Southern African Studies*, 4:1 (October, 1977), p. 32.

2. See, for example, Sean Wilentz, "Artisan Origins of the American Working Class," *International Labor and Working Class History*, 19 (Spring 1981), pp. 1–22.

3. *Report of the Native Labour Commission*, 1912–13, pp. 238–239.

4. Ibid., 1912–13, p. 150.

5. Dagoretti *Political Record Book*, January 1912, p. 75.

6. For example, see Tim Wright, " 'A Method of Evading Management'—Contract Labor in Chinese Coal Mines before 1937," *Comparative Studies in Society and History*, 23:4 (October 1981), pp. 656–678.

7. Kenya National Archives (hereafter cited as KNA), file LAB9/915.

8. Ukamba Province *Annual Report*, 1911–12.

9. J. Dealing, "Politics in Wanga, Kenya, c. 1650–1914," Ph.D. dissertation, Northwestern University, 1974, pp. 333–336; M. Hay, "Economic Change in Luoland: Kowe, 1890–1945," Ph.D. dissertation, University of Wisconsin, 1972, pp. 163–164.

10. Kilifi *Political Record Book*, vol. 3 "Giriama Rising from Takaungu Political Records," 1914.

11. Nyanza Province *Annual Report*, 1922, pp. 28–29.

12. Ukamba Province *Quarterly Report*, March 1912, p. 29.

13. Ibid., p. 5.

14. Native Affairs Department (hereafter cited as NAD) *Annual Report*, Nairobi, 1923, p. 49, and 1928. See also NAD *Annual Report*, 1924, p. 52.

15. NAD *Annual Report*, Labour Section, 1928; 1929; 1931. This same pattern of desertion as a rational strategy for reaching the best markets has been described for Southern Rhodesian migrants in Charles Onselen, *Chibaro: African Mine Labour in Southern Rhodesia, 1900–1933* (London, 1976).

16. J. Osoro, "African Labourers in the Kericho Tea Estates, 1920–1970," Master's thesis, Department of History, University of Nairobi, 1978, pp. 172–184.

17. Karim Janmohamed, "African Labourers in Mombasa, c. 1895–1940," in B. A. Ogot, ed., *Hadith 5* (Nairobi, 1975); K. Janmohamed, "A History of Mombasa, c. 1895–1939," Ph.D. dissertation, Northwestern University, 1977, pp. 465–468.

18. NAD *Annual Report*, Labour Section, 1925–1928.

19. Special Labour Census, 1941, Table 3. Includes a small number of squatters.

20. Ibid.

21. KNA, files DC/C1 8/54/11; LAB 9/934/8–42; and LAB 9/918/1, 5, 26a. Also Nairobi City Council files, March 1947.

22. NAD *Annual Report*, Labour Section, 1936, pp. 179–180; Special Labour Census, 1945, Table 9.

23. East African High Commission, *East African Economic and Statistical Bulletin*, No. 3 (March 1949), Table E6.

24. KNA, file LAB 9/815. NAD *Annual Report*, 1938, p. 110.

25. *East African Standard*, June 28, 1939.

26. NAD *Annual Report*, 1938, p. 109; see also Makhan Singh, *History of Kenya's Trade Union Movement to 1952* (Nairobi, 1969), p. 66.

27. Labour Department, Nairobi, Intelligence Reports for the Months of July, November, and December 1945. KNA file LAB 9/856.

28. KNA file LAB 9/911.

29. KNA file LAB 9/908.

30. KNA file LAB 9/915/1–14; 54, 55.

31. See, for example, Kenya Colony and Protectorate, *Report of the Committee of Inquiry into Labour Unrest in Mombasa* (Phillips Report), 1945, pp. 37, 53.

32. Statistical Abstract, 1955, Table 160; 1956–57, Table 176. Excluding domestic workers.

33. *Report of the Committee on African Wages* (Carpenter Report), 1954, p. 32.

34. More complete accounts of the African Workers' Federation will be found in C. Rosberg and J. Nottingham, *The Myth of Mau Mau: Nationalism in Kenya* (New York: Praeger, 1966), pp. 208–210; R. Stren, "Administration and the Growth of African Politics in Mombasa," University of East Africa Social Sciences Council Conference Papers, 1968; and Singh, *History*, 141–151.

35. This and the following three quotations are from James Patrick, "Trade Union Labour Officer's Report on His Activities in Mombasa, 29 September 1947 to 27 October 1947...." KNA 9/372/107.

36. Labour Department *Annual Report*, 1949, p. 35.

37. Singh, *History*, pp. 253–254.

38. Rosberg and Nottingham, *The Myth of Mau Mau*, p. 269. Report of an interview with Fred Kubai.

39. See Frank Furedi, "The Social Composition of the Mau Mau Movement in the White Highlands," *Journal of Peasant Studies*, 1:4 (July 1974), pp. 486–505.

40. For example, D. Barnett and K. Njama, *Mau Mau from Within: Autobiography and Analysis of Kenya's Peasant Revolt* (New York, 1966).

41. This label was used by A. Clayton and D. Savage, *Government and Labour in Kenya, 1895–1963* (London, 1974).

42. For a fuller discussion of the support given by the workers and trade unions of Nairobi to Mau Mau, see my "Workers, Trade Unions and the Mau Mau Rebellion," *Canadian Journal of African Studies*, 9:2 (1975), pp. 259–275. The following condensed account has been drawn from that source.

43. Barnett and Njama, *Mau Mau*, pp. 55, 61–62; Waruhiu Itote, *"Mau Mau" General* (Nairobi, 1967), pp. 38–41.

44. Barnett and Njama report that the educated were conspicuously absent in the forests and that the "vast majority" of fighters were "illiterate." *Mau Mau*, pp. 151–153.

45. For example, see Itote, *"Mau Mau" General*, pp. 109–119, and Josiah Kariuki, *Mau Mau Detainee* (Baltimore, 1964), p. 68.

46. Itote, *"Mau Mau" General*, pp. 112–113.

47. Ibid.

48. Kariuki, *Mau Mau Detainee*, p. 62.

49. Itote, *"Mau Mau" General*, pp. 114–115.

50. Instances are found in Kariuki, *Mau Mau Detainee*, p. 68, and Itote, *"Mau Mau" General*, p. 115.

51. Nairobi City Council *Annual Report*, 1952, p. 17.

52. Nairobi City Council *Annual Report*, 1953, n.p.

53. For example, Nairobi District *Annual Report*, 1954.

54. KNA file LAB 9/908/70–73, 79, 83; and LAB 9/944/10–12, 24. Also Singh, *History*, p. 315.

55. KNA file LAB 9/908/32. See also folios 87, 88, 91–92, 133.

56. KNA file LAB 9/908/95.

57. Interviews with Aggrey Minya, May 11 and July 24, 1956, by Robert

Gregory; International Confederation of Free Trade Unions, *Report of the Third World Congress Held at Stockholm*, July 4–11, 1953 (Brussels, 1953), pp. 306–310.

58. See Tom Mboya, *Freedom and After* (London, 1963), pp. 36, 44–56; also Tom Mboya, *The Kenya Question: An African Answer* (London, 1956). Most individual African unions also refused to denounce the rebellion despite repeated requests from the government.

59. Kenya Federation of Registered Trade Unions, *Annual Report* presented to the Annual Federation Meeting, 1955, by Tom Mboya, p. 10. KNA LAB 9/990.

9

Labor Migration, Class Formation, and Class Consciousness among Peruvian Miners: The Central Highlands, 1900–1930

Florencia E. Mallon

Between 1900 and 1930, the mining industry in the central highlands of Peru underwent a major transformation similar in many ways to those being experienced by export sectors in other parts of Latin America. As a result of the changing structure of demand on the international market and the increasing tendency for foreign capital to invest directly in production, both of which were because of the Second Industrial Revolution,[1] mining in central Peru developed from a small-scale, technologically primitive operation into a major industrial concern with a reputation for being one of the lowest-cost copper producers in the world. The prime moving force behind this change was the Cerro de Pasco Mining Company, later known as the Cerro de Pasco Corporation, a North American firm which by 1908 controlled the majority of mining claims in the central sierra.[2]

In addition to permanently transforming the region's landscape and economic relations by building railroads, rationalizing mining production, and constructing smelters to process the ore, the company dramatically affected the lives of the area's inhabitants by creating a much larger and more permanent mining labor force. The number of workers employed in mining more than doubled between 1905 and 1912, rising from 4,250 to 10,500 workers in the department of Junin.[3] Equally important, the very nature of mining work changed as larger and larger numbers of workers were concentrated in a single place. One can imagine the effect these changes had on the laborers, most of them recently arrived peasants from nearby communities, as they faced new surroundings, work experiences, and forms of interaction.

Recent studies on the development of a mining labor force in the central highlands have addressed the question of what kind of working class was formed in the mines. Criticizing the earlier analyses of the mining labor force as an archetypal, class-conscious proletariat, scholars have emphasized the imperfect, transitional quality of class formation in areas where workers continued to maintain ties with their villages of origin and migrated back and forth with regularity. One scholar has examined the nature of early political activity in the mines and has found it spontaneous, crowd-like, and "pre-political."[4] Another has focused on the relationship between class formation and community, arguing that constant migration prevented the establishment of a settled community where workers could develop allegiance to their condition as proletarians and discover a commonality of interest with others in the same situation.[5] Yet another has analyzed the "transitional" nature of mine workers in the context of dependent industrialization more generally, suggesting that an alliance between multinational industrial capital and local petty commercial production has tended to "freeze" the process of proletarianization at some intermediate stage, resulting in a workforce that maintains interests and ties in both rural and urban sectors.[6]

A common issue that emerges from these studies is whether industrialization in peripheral or dependent economies can indeed create the kind of integrated, class-conscious proletariat that presumably emerged in the more "classic" regions of capitalist development. In those areas of the world, such as Latin America, where the transition to capitalism did not emerge organically from internal transformations in the rural sector but was brought in more "artificially" through foreign investment or foreign-oriented export production, the formation of a proletariat certainly must have taken a different course. Traditional subsistence or peasant economies were not wiped out, but reorganized or reconstituted in relation to the expanding export sectors, and provided labor and cheap subsistence goods for capitalist expansion. Under these conditions, it is hardly reasonable to expect that workers in the capitalist sector, still rooted spiritually and materially in their traditional villages, could develop a mature proletarian class consciousness.

While these analyses have moved far beyond earlier work on the mining sector by refusing to equate industry with class consciousness in a mechanistic way, it is still necessary to take a hard and critical look at the underlying assumptions about class and class consciousness that have informed much of the work on the subject, whether about Europe or about the Third World. Associated with the Marxist interpretation of the transition to capitalism, the concepts of class formation and class consciousness have been hotly debated and variously understood. Karl Marx himself used class in several contexts to denote vastly distinct aspects of a single phenomenon, and the dichotomy he established between class of itself and class for itself is a good example. Class of itself, used simply to signify a certain relationship to the means of production or mode of surplus extraction, could apply to virtually any society beyond the hunting and gathering stage. By contrast, class for itself, which implies a more self-conscious and politically constituted social group, is a highly selective category that has largely been applied to classes emerging with the development of capitalism. Yet in both cases, the term *class* has been used.[7]

Marx gave us his most extended analysis of classes under capitalism, since his primary concern was to unmask the logic of the capitalist system. Both he and theorists who have followed him have considered that only the capitalist classes—the bourgeoisie and the proletariat—had the capacity to transcend their narrow concerns and to formulate broader national or international projects for social and political transformation. This was true because capitalism, with its tendency to expand, transform, and homogenize all aspects of social and economic life, for the first time created the material conditions under which human beings could see beyond their back porches or their villages. The very logic of capital— its penchant for incorporating and transforming all other relations— seemed inevitably to lead toward the constitution of one integrated, homogeneous, international proletariat, whose members would first and foremost understand their commonality of interest with all others in the same situation throughout the world and who would unite in a vast project to overthrow the class and system responsible for their exploitation.[8]

The extent to which this theoretical potential has been fulfilled in practice has been the focus of much controversy. When viewed from the fourth quarter of the twentieth century, and in particular from the Third World, the logic of capital has turned out to be a great deal more complex, contradictory, and resilient than it seemed to be in the nineteenth century. Capital has proven itself capable of using many different forms and relations of production, moving back and forth among them. It has adapted creatively to repeated crises. Despite its international character, capital has created fragmented and intricate enclaves that often have set the material conditions for the creation of fragmented and partial consciousness.[9] In developed countries, labor-market segmentation and other factors have militated against the creation of homogeneous and unified working class.[10] On the periphery, the stark contrast between working conditions in the capitalist industrial sector and those in the subsistence economy has fomented reformist tendencies among some of those who have become proletarians.[11]

An even more important drawback of the theoretical model of proletarian consciousness is that it tends to rigidify the historical analysis of class. When other classes in society are viewed in relation to the mature proletariat rather than being understood on their own terms, their forms of protest or consciousness are found to be traditional, reactive, or "pre-political."[12] When specific working classes are compared to this larger-than-life stereotype and found wanting, they are said to possess "false consciousness" or to be at an "immature" stage of development.[13] Ultimately, the use of rigid ideal types can become a substitute for the empirical study of the way in which consciousness is formed. It overlooks the fact that the very process of class and consciousness formation might have an important effect on the kind of consciousness that emerges at the other end. And finally, it minimizes the contributions made by unique cultures and human beings to the emergence of classes, masking the reality that consciousness is, after all, a human and historical creation.

With all this in mind, I will analyze historical and empirical data from the central highlands of Peru in order to examine the process of economic transition and class formation in all its complexity. I will focus on the 1900–1930 period, when the first generation of workers confronted proletarianization in the mines and developed cultural and political responses to that experience. During these decades, industrialization was new both for the laborers and for the Cerro de Pasco Corporation. In confrontation with each other, the company and its workforce each developed a particular adaptation and style that colored their relationship for years to come. It is in this sense that we can refer to the first three decades of the twentieth century as the formative years for industrial mining and for the working class in the Peruvian central sierra.

To analyze a process of industrialization, class formation, and the development of class consciousness is an intricate undertaking under any circumstances; it is even more so in a case where the transformations are set into motion by foreign capital. Under these conditions, the impetus for transition comes from the outside and comes up against a local history and native culture that can present distinct and unusual obstacles to the development of capitalism. In this context, a clear understanding of class formation must take into account not only the logic of foreign capital and the constraints placed upon it by the internal and international situation, but also the character of the indigenous village culture from which most workers come, and the ways in which that culture can serve as a weapon of resistance and can be incorporated into the consciousness of the emerging working class.[14]

Given the complexity of the situation in the central highlands, this paper cannot claim to deal with all its relevant aspects. There is, for example, little space dedicated to the relationship between miners' struggles in this early period and the development of national working-class politics, and at any rate this has been dealt with in great detail elsewhere.[15] Nor is the actual evidence on consciousness as concrete and rich as I would have liked. In many, though not all, cases it has been necessary to rely on indirect manifestations of consciousness rather than on "getting inside" the perceptions of the workers themselves. If June

Nash's recent work on Bolivia is any example, however, it should be possible, through careful field work among the miners themselves, to reconstruct consciousness from a more internal perspective.[16] I hope that the issues raised here can stimulate debate and precisely that type of work for the Peruvian case.

Whatever its limitations, the purpose of this paper is to view the emergence of consciousness in the flesh, as human beings actively use, choose among, and seek out cultural alternatives to help them adapt to, deal with, and struggle against the new conditions they face. The form of working-class consciousness that emerges will, it seems, depend on several factors, including the form investment takes, the particular labor relations and conditions experienced by the workforce, the culture the workers bring with them, and the specific course of the struggle or confrontation in the workplace. In at least some respects, then, each working class constructs a historically and culturally unique consciousness. Yet the examination of this uniqueness in one particular instance does not deny the possibility or the value of generalization across a broad variety of cases. Quite the contrary, building a groundwork of case studies should facilitate the task of comparison and generalization by making it richer, more rigorous, and more valuable.

THE FIRST STAGE OF TRANSFORMATION, 1900–1922

The Cerro de Pasco Mining Company's first purchase of mining claims in the central sierra in 1901 marked the end of a long series of attempts by local mine owners to innovate and to develop the industry. From about the 1870s, entrepreneurs had been experimenting with new machinery and technology in order to rationalize and stabilize production. But for a series of reasons, of which a scarcity of capital and the unreliability of the labor supply were the most important, previous efforts had failed. By the end of the nineteenth century, bottlenecks had become so frustrating that many locals were eager to sell out to foreign capital.[17] In the course of their experiments, however, they had already established a tradition of mining work and migration in many peasant villages of the region.

In an industry where production and marketing were unreliable and technology relatively primitive, few mine owners could afford to maintain a permanent labor force. Instead they relied on occasional levies of temporary labor, acquired in the peasant communities by *enganche*. They advanced money to merchants with ties in the villages, who in turn would lend cash or goods to peasants with the condition that the debt be worked off at a set rate per day (*tarea*) in the mining centers.[18]

Since the division of labor in mining work was almost non-existent, peasants easily adapted to the requirements of such work. There were only two categories of workers: the *barreteros*, who extracted the mineral with pick and shovel; and the *apiris* or *japires*, who carried the ore out of the mine in huge bags balanced on their shoulders. In some of the smaller mines, the same workers spent three days a week extracting the ore and the other three days crushing or grinding it for the refining process. In all cases, the owners demanded long hours under poor conditions before they considered a day's *tarea* fulfilled. They did not provide the workers with even the most elementary facilities, such as ventilation or ladders for entering and leaving the mine. By forcing peasants to pay for many necessities, including candles, mine owners also tried to keep them on for longer periods of time before they could pay back the sum of the *enganche*. Indeed, many laborers ended up working *quaraches*, or 36 uninterrupted hours with only 12 to rest before another stint, in an attempt to pay back what they owed more quickly and return to their villages.[19]

Under these conditions, neither the laborer nor the owner considered mining work a permanent employment alternative. From the mine owner's point of view, seasonal labor from the region's communities made it possible to pay below subsistence wages, since the reproduction of a worker's labor power was still bound up in the agrarian household economy. In fact, many migrants arrived at the mining centers in family groups, carrying with them bags of produce or herds of animals to serve as food during their stay. From the worker's point of view, migration to the mines was but one of many seasonal activities in which a peasant household engaged. During slack periods in the agricultural cycle, or in years when there was an emergency need for money, several members of a peasant family would migrate—one to the mines, another to the subtropical sugar estates in the eastern *ceja de selva* zone, perhaps a third to sell some additional handicraft in local markets.[20]

Working in the mines thus was an integral part of the village subsistence economy rather than a proletarian work experience. As long as it provided an additional source of income to pull families through lean times, or even to help accumulate some land, mining work could actually prevent the pauperization of the peasantry. Moreover, given the primitive working conditions and the small size of the production units, peasants easily adapted to mine labor and were not subject to dramatically new social relations as a result of their work in the mines. It is hardly surprising, therefore, that they maintained a household or village orientation during their time in the mining centers, and that resistance to exploitation took the form of running away or evading the *enganchador*, rather than confrontation of the owner in the mining centers.[21]

Things began to change with the arrival of the Cerro de Pasco Mining Company, especially with regard to levels of investment. Between 1902 and 1908, the company bought 730 mining claims in Cerro de Pasco, built a new railroad between Oroya and Cerro to facilitate the transport of minerals, completed the railway to Jauja and Huancayo—important commercial towns in the Mantaro Valley, bought over 100 coal mine claims to the north of Cerro, and began acquiring properties in the Morococha area. The company also instituted important changes within the productive sector. It rationalized the system of mine tunnels, installed cars and elevators for the internal transportation of ores, built a system of iron tubes for ventilation below ground and, on the surface, devised an intricate network of cars and storage facilities that dumped minerals directly on the railroad cars for transportation to the smelter.[22]

And, of course, there was the smelter itself. The product of several years of investment and experimentation at the old mineral hacienda of Tinyahuaraco, it was capable of processing a total of 1,000 tons of ore a day by 1907. When compared to the 100– to 200–ton per day capacity of the next three largest smelters, Tinyahuarco must have seemed huge to Peruvian miners of the day. Equally impressive was the size of the labor force, which at Tinyahuarco alone, reached 1,500 and 2,000 workers in 1908. In an industry where the largest mines had previously employed around 300 people, and where the other smelters had between 100 and 300 workers each, a concentration of 1,500 laborers in one place was quite a transformatiton.[23] But there were also important limits to how deeply the changes went in this early period.

Despite major investments in mines, railroads, and general infrastructure, and despite the much larger size of the work force, the company continued to rely on pre-existing technology and labor relations for the actual extraction of ores. Through the use of *contrata*, the mining itself was often farmed out to individual contractors—usually petty merchants or wealthy peasants with previous experience in the industry—who were paid so much per ton or meter of mineral. The *contratistas* were thus responsible for all aspects of production, using their own tools and methods and obtaining their own labor force. Even where it was impossible, for whatever reasons, to use *contratistas*, the company did not acquire a permanent or stable labor force but simply plugged into the *enganche* networks already developed in the previous period, enlarging and manipulating them for its own ends.[24]

In the final analysis, the Cerro de Pasco Corporation did not radically alter the system of production in the first decades of existence. Like the local miners before it, the company maintained a relatively low organic composition of capital and relied on lengthening the working day, paying low wages, and other strategies in order to extract a high level of surplus from its workforce. The *mercantil*, or company store, became famous in this regard by 1910. Stocked mainly with goods imported from the United States, it sported prices up to 30 percent higher than those in other stores. Because workers were paid only once a month, they usually were forced to get advances on goods from the *mercantil* through a complex system. Every afternoon as they left the mines, they received a metal token which they had to exchange for a cardboard one when they reported to work the next morning. Once they built up a supply of several cardboard tokens, they could exchange them for a receipt from the company cashier and purchase goods at the company store against the next month's wages. Ideally, of course, the system served as a way of further lowering wages, since the company was able to take back up to 30 percent of what it paid out simply by maintaining a monopoly on workers' consumption from one payday to the next.[25]

The Cerro de Pasco Company further increased its profits in this early period by cutting corners on safety standards and production methods. The Railway Company, part of the same firm, was legendary for its delays, the bad quality of its equipment, and the frequency of its accidents—especially when transporting workers and their families. With regard to mining production itself, careless excavation and unsafe disposal or storage of explosives endangered the lives of workers and anyone else in the mining centers. In the coal mines of Goyllarisquisga, for example, the use of dynamite rather than coal-cutting machines, in the presence of high levels of volatile coal gas, caused four major explosions in 1910. The haphazard nature of excavation in Cerro de Pasco, done without refilling the areas dug out, subjected the labor force to landslides and the city dwellers to sinkholes into which houses, animals, and even people disappeared on several occasions. In addition, the unsafe storage of large amounts of dynamite at the nearby Yanacancha site threatened the entire area's population with extinction during the numerous and violent highland electrical storms.[26]

Thus, in its early years, the foreign corporation resisted making the investments necessary to raise its profits through increased productivity in the extraction process. Instead, it took profits out of the workers' hides. Subject to hazardous conditions and the ever-present danger of silicosis, a laborer who worked continuously in the mines, according to calculations made in 1914, could not expect to live more than five years.[27] When a laborer died in an accident or from lung disease, the company did its best to disclaim responsibility, whether by asserting that the accident had been fortuitous, or by insisting that the person had been employed only occasionally and thus it could not be proven that the illness was due to mining work. In those cases, such as Goyllarisquisga, where responsibility in a death could not be avoided, the Peruvian government paid out one *libra peruana* (the equivalent of a British pound or slightly less) to the closest relatives, while the company handled the funeral costs and nothing more.[28]

From the worker's point of view, therefore, there were a number of reasons for maintaining a household or community orientation toward migration and work in the mines. Under conditions where the company paid wages below subsistence and attempted to extract further surplus by monopolizing consumption, migrants struggled against exploitation by using the resources available to them through the village economy. As had been the case in the nineteenth century, people often took animals, bags of vegetables, grain, and other agricultural supplies with them to the mines in an effort to circumvent the high cost of living and break the company store monopoly. In a situation where the illness and death endemic to mine labor were not considered the responsibility of the company, the peasant community fulfilled a vital function as refuge to the widowed or incapacitated. And for those who wished to survive beyond five years, it was not wise to see the mines as more than a seasonal workplace in any case; the village, for reasons of simple survival, remained a person's real home.[29]

In addition to the central role the community played in ensuring subsistence and survival, the nature of labor acquisition and labor relations in the mines also tended to maintain a village orientation. When workers were contracted through *enganche*, their initial relationship was with a merchant who lent them money for needs in the community. Each *enganchado* was expected to declare his village property liable for the debt and to present one or two *fiadores* (guarantors) from the community who would assume the outstanding balance should the *enganchado* default.[30] Thus the wage relationship in the mines was at best of secondary importance to the workers. Much more crucial was the *tarea* or day's shift, which was counted toward the payment of the *enganche*. This was proven in 1908, when the company offered workers the opportunity of laboring six eight-hour shifts per week, rather than nine ten-hour shifts per week, at the same wage. The North Americans simply could not understand it when the workers refused, attributing it to the traditionalism of the local peasantry. "These customs are . . . deeply rooted in the minds of an ignorant people," one North American engineer concluded. "This is merely one example of the stupidity of the native miners."[31] Had he understood the nature of the *enganche* relationship, in which property and friendships in the home village were held hostage for the completion of certain number of *tareas*, it would have become clear why a reduction in the number of *tareas* per week, even if it meant working fewer hours for the same wage, was unacceptable to the mine workers.[32]

Contrata also tended to reinforce the connection to the community. Most *contratistas*, peasants with some experience in mining work, tended to contract the workers they needed through connections in their home villages. As a result, the line between mine and community often blurred as relations of subordination or dependency established in a village context were transferred to the mining centers. This certainly was the case with the Onofre brothers, *contratistas* at the San Francisco mine belonging to the Morococha Mining Company, a subsidiary of the Cerro de Pasco Corporation. Rather than getting involved in production, the Morococha Mining Company simply reaped the benefits of extraction by paying its *contratistas* per ton of mineral. Responsible for the entire production process, the Onofres made large profits through the traditional methods of paying low wages, intensifying work rhythms, and lengthening the work day. They advanced food and other goods to their workers at inflated prices through their stores in Morococha, taking back through commerce much of what they paid out in wages. They used their accumulated earnings to buy land in their village of origin, further strengthening their position as patrons in the rural sector.[33]

The connection between village and mine was further strengthened by the system of labor relations itself. Aside from a few improvements in the transportation system, working conditions in the San Francisco mine remained very similar to what they had been in the nineteenth century. There were only three categories of workers: the *perforadores*, who opened holes in the wall to put in the dynamite; the *lamperos*, who broke up the ore with pick and shovel once the explosion had loosened it; and the *carreros*, who loaded up small railway cars with the pieces of ore, pushing them to the nearest *jaula* (elevator) ready to take the cargo to the surface. The few supervisors or foremen who directed the work were usually close friends or clients of the *contratistas* rather than technically trained personnel.[34]

For many peasants hired through *contrata*, then, relations in the mines simply reproduced those in the community. They worked with people from their village, usually returning several times to work with the same *contratista*. Often ex-*contratados* maintained a relationship of patronage and clientele with their previous bosses when they returned to their communities. Under these conditions, it is easy to see why a village orientation was maintained in the mines. Exploitation was perceived as resulting from the abuses of local *contratistas* rather than emanating from the system of mining production. Resistance took the form of running away or seeking out alternate patrons, rather than confronting conditions or relations in the mining centers themselves.[35]

Yet other tendencies were also beginning to operate in the mining centers at this point. Especially in the newer mines, in the smelter, and on the railroad, labor relations were changing. In the coal mines of Goyllarisquisga, which had not been heavily exploited in the nineteenth century, although the workers were contracted through *enganche*, they were also subject to new work experiences in the crews of 10 to 20 men, usually directed by a foreign foreman.[36] Despite the apparently lax supervision standards, the direct contact with an impersonal technician and the potential solidarity with other workers in the same crew began to set the material conditions within which laborers from different villages could become fully conscious of the company's exploitation. Similar situations were created elsewhere. At the smelter, for example, the very nature of the work necessitated a much more complex division of labor and more intimate contact among large groups of workers, while all the supervisory personnel, with one or two exceptions, were North American.[37] On the railroad, opportunities for contact and solidarity among laborers under new work conditions, combined with the obvious favoritism the company showed to foreigners, set the conditions for a broader consciousness. Overall, then, there were sectors of the corporation's activities in which the creation of community feeling among workers as workers, and the clear presence of the foreign company's representatives in positions of authority, aided in the formulation of a more "proletarian" consciousness and strategy and, as we shall see, facilitated more direct and collective forms of resistance such as strikes.

The same tendencies toward solidarity, moreover, began to appear at the level of the mining communities as a whole. As authors have shown for other parts of the world, the very nature of a mining community tends to throw people together and to make clear a broad commonality of interests.[38] This is true at least in part because of the insular nature of the mining "company town," where almost everything is owned by the company, and everyone's work rhythms and lives—be they mine workers, retailers, housewives, peasants, or others—are governed by the rhythm and needs of the mines. In the central highlands, despite the transient nature of the labor force, this potential solidarity was clear in several ways. In the first place, the carelessness of the corporation, both inside the mine and with relation to the community, created an adversarial relationship. People were understandably concerned about the storage of dynamite so close to the population. They worried that their houses would be the next to fall into the sinkholes generated by random excavation in Cerro de Pasco. The impact of explosions and cave-ins in the mines was great on the entire town's population, as the destroyed bodies of miners were carried out and widows spent days before the company offices demanding some form of compensation. Finally, even the question of daily needs—given the way the company attempted to monopolize consumption through the *mercantil*—tended to pit mining community against corporation and to foment the development of a broader consciousness of the origins of exploitation.

Once workers, their relatives, or other members of the community began to perceive these broader relationships and to consider acting on their perceptions, they found that aid was available from a series of progressive groups and intellectuals. Central among these was the Asociacion Pro-Indigena, a group of Lima-based, middle-class intellectuals who were developing a strong *indigenista* stand against the government. In 1910, for example, the Associacion was instrumental in getting the repeal of the 1903 *Reglamento de locacion de servicios para la industria minera*, a set of regulations passed to support the mining industry by allowing, among other things, political authorities to get involved in chasing run-away workers. The repeal of this law was seen as a direct attack on state aid in labor acquisition and was protested vigorously by local *engancha-dores*. Also in 1910, Pedro Zulen, one of the organization's most notable representatives, traveled to the central highlands to investigate complaints about *enganche* that had been received by congressional representatives in Lima. He talked to scores of *enganchados, fiadores*, and their families, and his report, published in the Lima newspaper *La Prensa*, still constitutes one of the most basic and complete sources on the functioning of the *enganche* system, as well as an influential condemnation of it. Finally, the Associacion also protested the numerous accidents, poor working conditions, and lack of company accountability so obvious in the mining industry, serving as a resource for the families of injured workers seeking compensation, publicizing the more abusive examples of lax safety standards, and so on.[39]

In the final analysis, the development of class and consciousness among workers displayed contradictory tendencies during the first two decades of Cerro's operations. On the one hand, the village-oriented nature of *enganche* and *contrata* maintained the workers' identification with the rural community and the peasant household economy. On the other hand, changing labor relations, a new sense of community solidarity in opposition to the company, and the aid of progressive urban groups all opened up new alternatives for political action and consciousness. Yet there is no evidence that these contradictions resulted in prolonged social stress or confusion. Quite the contrary; similar to what June Nash has shown for Bolivia, laborers were able to creatively use the various cultural, political, and economic alternatives open to them and, depending on the circumstances, meld together aspects of each to find the most successful adaptation to the harsh conditions they faced.[40]

In some cases, workers found that calling on the resources of their villages was their most effective weapon in the battle against exploitation. Most would have been hard-pressed, for example, to survive from one payday to the next without the additional supplies they brought with them. Migration was also a household undertaking in other ways. Groups of relatives migrated together, usually bringing unmarried female family members with them to handle domestic chores for all. Wives or daughters also migrated for brief periods of time to the mining area, taking care of their husbands or fathers or engaging in petty commerce as a supplementary source of revenue for the family. In addition to its economic benefits, migration by village and household provided continuing ties of solidarity and mutual cooperation in a new and possibly hostile environment. As a result, some early forms of protest took on a village tinge.

Thus when peasants from the villages of Chongos working in the Pena Blanca mineshaft in Cerro de Pasco escaped en masse after a major explosion in 1908 and returned to their village, they were simply calling on the cultural tools and traditions available to them to repudiate their condition in the most effective way they could.[41]

Under other circumstances, reactions in the mining centers could take on a more hybrid or transitional orientation. In February 1913, for example, an incident began in Morococha when a police officer intervened in a fight among several workers and attempted to arrest one of them. The laborers reacted by forcing the officer to release their arrested companion and, having gathered a crowd of about 400, marched to the local police station to demand the punishment of the arresting officer. Though the *comisario* (sheriff) tried to calm the crowd by agreeing to their demand, the crowd would not be convinced, and, reinforced by additional people from the mining community, they stoned and attacked the station. After sacking the offices and archive and roughing up the officers, the crowd broke up into several smaller groups and proceeded to loot surrounding stores. Their third target was the local governor's house, where they destroyed archives and stole some personal items. They then moved on to the railroad station, where they only broke a door. The riot was finally stopped by the urban guard, organized on the spur of the moment by the town's merchants. By the next morning, when reinforcements arrived from the nearby provincial capital of Yauli, the sheriff organized a room-by-room search in the workers' quarters and arrested the 30 men and 2 women in whose possession he found stolen merchandise, sending them by train to be imprisoned in Lima.[42]

Given its spontaneous and unplanned nature, the violence in crowd actions of this sort may seem random and arbitrary. Certainly the authorities in Morococha viewed it this way, blaming a few agitators and the drunken credulousness of the crowd.[43] Yet if we look more carefully at the targets selected, there was a sort of rationality. As local authorities, the police and the governor usually sided with the company in any dispute and were directly visible as repressive agents. In a mining center where much of the extraction was still done by *contrata*, it was often the local merchants who took advantage of the workers by charging them high prices on goods and serving as *contratistas*. Finally, most workers and their families had experienced the poor service extended by the railroad. The rapidity with which a crowd gathered, moreover, and the participation of women, make clear that the action was community-oriented. Ultimately, the Morococha riot seems to have been a general mining community reaction to exploitation, attacking its most obvious symbols.

In a sense, it is understandable that such a transitional action occurred in Morococha. One of the older mines, in which the narrowness of the

veins made modernization of production extremely difficult,[44] Morococha continued to operate with little change in labor relations throughout the first decades of the twentieth century. Because they usually worked
for *contratistas* and remained oriented toward their villages, laborers in
Morococha had less chance to develop a broader and more conscious
analysis of the corporation and its relationship to the workforce. On the
other hand, the existence of a mining community with a set of common
grievances based on consumption, the behavior of local authorities, and
the poor quality of urban services could begin to unite people across the
boundaries drawn by village origin or work experience. Thus, the riot
of the Morococha laborers was neither village-oriented nor workplace-
oriented. Instead, it brought people together as members of a mining
community and, even if in a tentative and politically diffuse form, began
to forge bonds of solidarity based on new experiences in an urban
framework.

As mentioned earlier, the situation was quite different among laborers
employed in other sections of the company's operations, where a number
of more defined strikes broke out before 1920. The location of the early
strikes points to the fact that new work experiences, as well as a certain
level of commitment to location, job, and fellow workers, were necessary
before it became reasonable to engage in serious, planned protest. Though
the general population of miners did strike in April 1912, demanding
that the company pay for the carbide consumed by their safety lamps,[45]
the other mobilizations tended to occur among workers in the more
industrialized sectors of the firm's operations, particularly the coal mines,
railroad, and smelter. In all these cases, there seemed to be a higher
level of skill and job stability. In 1909, for example, the stokers at the
Cerro de Pasco Railway Company not only demanded higher wages, but
also a nine-hour day and that the company consider seniority in giving
promotions—hardly the demands of a transient labor force.[46] In 1917,
when the coalminers from Goyllarisquisga and Quishuarcancha, the machinists, stokers, and other workers from the railroad, and the labor
force at the smelter all went out on strike, their delegations demanded,
in addition to higher wages and shorter hours, the extension of free
medical care and the provision of food and other subsistence needs at
cost.[47] Even in those mobilizations with broader participation, the special
position and militance of workers from the more industrialized sections
were evident. When the sheriff of Morococha sent a letter to the prefect
reporting on local plans for a general strike in 1921, he specifically
mentioned that it was being organized, instigated, and led by railroad
workers who, in his opinion, were "an element always disposed toward
that sort of movement."[48]

The use of one form of resistance, be it a return to the village economy,
an urban crowd action uniting the various sectors of a mining com-

munity, or even an organized strike, did not preclude the use of other forms. As the Morococha sheriff's comments bear out, there clearly was communication among the various mining centers and labor forces. All workers, including those in the more traditional mines, participated in the 1912 and 1917 strike movements.[49] Besides, until the 1920s most workers, no matter where they labored, had had direct contact with *enganchadores* and maintained close ties to their communities of origin. Especially in times of stress, such as death, accident, or other calamity, it was to their village and its culture that they turned. In the end, the company itself tacitly agreed to the maintenance of this situation. By relying on *enganche* and *contrata* relationships still rooted in the village milieu, by refusing to pay a living wage, and by shirking its "social security" responsibilities vis-à-vis its workers, the corporation in effect encouraged the reproduction of mixed labor relations and a hybrid village and mining center orientation. Until the situation as a whole changed, the most reasonable adaptation for the workers was to continue mixing strategies in order to resist exploitation in the most rational and effective way possible.

THE SECOND STAGE OF TRANSFORMATION, 1922–30

By 1918, a series of difficulties convinced the Cerro de Pasco Corporation that it had become imperative to change the basis on which the mining industry was organized. Central among these was the problem of labor relations and labor acquisition. With the continued expansion of mining, the *enganchadores* and *contratistas* on whom the corporation relied found themselves competing with one another for a labor pool that was not growing fast enough, and they were forced to resort to ever more violent methods in order to acquire a sufficient supply of laborers. This was true in great measure because other sectors of the regional economy also were expanding and competing for workers, and the peasants, quick to see the changing balance of forces, were becoming quite adept at playing one sector or *enganchador* off against another.[50] This strategy, moreover, often was combined with running away or never reporting at all. In 1910, for example, Pedro Zulen's calculations on *enganche* in Jauja yielded a runaway rate of nearly 50 percent of the total labor force. Precisely because the problem was so pervasive, it was too expensive to prosecute more than a few runaways through the courts.[51] In the long run, therefore, the benefits accruing to the corporation from maintaining *enganche* and *contrata*—including lower levels of capital investment and paying below subsistence wages and benefits—began to be outweighed by the fact that peasant resistance was making labor acquisition an expensive, violent, and embarrassing social war.

There also were more directly technological reasons for bypassing *enganchadores* and *contratistas*. As the sheer size and complexity of the company's operations began to demand increasing rationalization, centralization, and efficiency, the *contratista*'s control of production and the seasonal nature of *enganche* labor became obstacles to further modernization. Not only was it more difficult to centralize operations that were under the direction of *contratistas*, but the nature of *contrata* and *enganche* militated against the creation of a skilled labor force. An acute observer commented as early as 1908:

The system of enganche has, among other inconveniences, the fact that the mines and principally the smelters, cannot form a skilled labor force, because even though the Indian learns rapidly, he leaves once his contract expires, and it is necessary to replace him with more unskilled personnel.[52]

Indeed, even before the 1920s the need for a more stable and skilled labor force was being felt in some sections of the company. In an attempt to meet this demand, the corporation began to hire some workers directly, without going through the *enganchadores*. These workers, called *maquipureros*, were paid a higher wage than the *enganchados*, and the differential increased as time went on in an effort to attract more labor through this method.[53] It was only with the transformations of the 1920s, however, that direct hiring began to overtake *enganche* as a method of labor acquisition.

More than any other single event, the planning and construction of the Oroya smelter between 1918 and 1922 symbolized the changing realities of the central sierra mining industry. As the corporation expanded its holdings, the capacity and location of the smelter at Tinyahuarco became an obstacle to further rationalization and integration. In order to better organize transportation and production and to provide enough smelting capacity for all the ores from Casapalca, Morococha, and Cerro de Pasco, the best solution turned out to be the construction of a new and modern smelter at Oroya, a central location on the highland railway. In 1922, the Oroya smelter was inaugurated.[54]

Reorganizing the flow of minerals and metals and imparting a new rhythm and rationale to the extraction process, the smelter became the technological hub of the company's entire operation. As the efficiency and speed of smelting increased, it became necessary to further rationalize and transform ore extraction. Wherever possible, the corporation modernized relations of production, increasing the division of labor and the supervision of the workforce. This process of modernization increased the need for a skilled and stable labor force and, by the time the 1920s were over, the seasonal migration pattern that had predominated previously had been relegated to a secondary position. *Enganche*, as an organized form of labor acquisition for the mining industry, disappeared altogether. *Contrata* was brought under closer company control and used for more marginal or auxiliary tasks.[55]

The transformation of labor relations in mining was further aided by changes in the peasant sector. Although they had used continued access to family and community resources to resist exploitation in the mines, many seasonal migrants unavoidably became involved in vicious circles of indebtedness due to *enganche* contracts. Over the medium- to long-run, migration to the mines had set into motion a process of pauperization and differentiation at the household and village level, increasing the number of people forced to depend on a wage for survival.[56] This process of pauperization received dramatic impetus from the ecological effects of the Oroya smelter.

Because of financial problems connected with the collapse of copper prices on the international market late in 1920, the corporation had built the smelter in a hurry and without any apparatus to screen the smoke it emitted. Desperate to begin paying back the debts accumulated during construction, the company also very quickly brought the smelter up to full capacity. As a result, between 100 and 125 tons per day of arsenic, sulphur dioxide, lead, bismuth, and other poisons began falling on neighboring villages, and the disastrous effects of the smoke were felt for many miles. By 1924, 30 communities had begun proceedings against the corporation for smoke damage.[57]

Because smoke damage drastically cut into the productivity of village flocks and fields, the construction of the Oroya smelter directly contributed to the proletarianization of the central sierra peasantry. When combined with the previous effects of differentiation at the community level, it generated precisely the type of labor force the newly revamped mining industry needed. More than any decade before it, therefore, the 1920s were a period in which the combined needs of the mining sector and of a changing peasant economy generated a more permanent and skilled work force for the industry. As laborers chose to stay permanently in the mines, experiencing new relationships and loosening traditional social ties with their villages, the scene was set for a major transformation in class consciousness.

As we have already seen, even before the 1920s, workers had been involved in several strike movements that had demonstrated contact among mining centers, as well as a desire to confront the corporation directly as the entity responsible for the exploitation of the workforce. These movements had culminated in 1917–18, when laborers from all mines and other sections of the company's operations struck for higher wages in the context of the struggle for the eight-hour day in Lima. By 1918 the Central Obrera de Mineros del Centro, a recently formed miners' union, had affiliated with the anarchist-inspired Federacion Obrera Local de Lima.[58]

With the structural changes of the 1920s, one would expect that these initial tendencies toward working-class organization would have been strengthened; yet, for a combination of reasons, things worked out somewhat differently during the decade. When Augusto B. Leguia came to power in 1919, he courted the support of the lower classes through a series of seemingly progressive policies. Among these was an effort to provide institutional support for the claims of highland Indians, especially with regard to land. At a government-sponsored congress in Lima in 1921, the Comite Pro Derecho Indigena Tahuantinsuyo was founded, becoming the first national *indigenista* organization with participation by the peasants themselves. Initially it seemed that the mine workers would also benefit from this trend, since in 1923 members of the Comite created the Federacion Obrera Regional Indigena, an anarchosyndicalist organization which began a campaign to protest mining accidents and conditions in the central highlands. In the end, however, Leguia was not interested in real change for the country's lower classes, but simply in manipulating their support in order to consolidate his political position. Once working-class and other popular organizations began to develop some independence, he quickly suppressed them. By mid-decade, much of the miners' organizing activity in the central region had been driven underground, where it would remain until 1929–30.[59]

Despite the poor conditions for organizing, or perhaps in part because of them, laborers dedicated much time in the 1920s to the formation of committees whose purpose was to provide financial support for their home villages. By a monthly contribution of a day's wages, workers helped pay for public works construction in their communities of origin—a fountain in the village square, a library or school, or perhaps even the installation of running water or an electric generator. Because these committees emphasized the continuing importance of community responsibility and solidarity, and because they united migrants from a single village across social and economic lines, they tended to impede the formation of a unified working-class perspective. The district committees were not, however, simply reactionary or backward-looking organizations. Because they could mean very different things to rich and poor migrants from the same villages, the committees could also foment the development of working-class consciousness among the poorer workers.[60]

That the functioning of district committees could increase tensions between the better- and worse-off workers is clear from the examples of the committees formed by migrants from the village of Acolla. In the mining center of Casapalca, it was the poorer Acollinos in the less prestigious jobs who did much of the footwork necessary to start the committee. Not coincidentally, the corporation refused to automatically discount a day's pay from each member's monthly wages, and the delegates were forced to walk many miles each month collecting from room to room, both in Casapalca and nearby Bellavista. As one of the members of the committee's organizing board explained, the workers truly suffered before they were able to collect enough money to donate a bell for their community's church. Only a year later did some supervisors from the same village intercede with the superintendent and get the automatic discount for the committee members approved by the administration.[61] The situation was different in the case of the Morococha committee, which from the start was dominated by well-off workers. When it was founded in August 1923, its members set the monthly contribution at five *soles*, which was a day's wage only for the better-paid employees. The administration granted them the automatic discount immediately. Over the years the Morococha committees donated not only a clock, but a library and an electric generator to their community.[62]

These differences clearly were not lost on the workers. In Morococha, those who found membership in the committee too expensive were bound to note that money seemed more important than village origin. In Casapalca the committee delegates, their feet worn out from walking after a long working day, filed away the fact that all the organizational work and experience they were acquiring could not equal, in the eyes of the administration, the influence of a few supervisory personnel. Not surprisingly, some of these same delegates later would be very sympathetic to the idea of a union.[63]

Whatever the changes in the mining industry, patterns of labor migration, and potential consciousness that occurred in the 1920s, mine workers in the central highlands continued to identify with and return to their communities. While most workers were staying in the mines for years at a time, they left their families behind in the village and called upon community resources to help them survive or even to accumulate a bit of money. Certainly the longer migration patterns tended to erode village or even household solidarity; at least in part the district committees were an effort to reverse that tendency. Whatever the cost of maintaining community ties, however, they still provided great benefits for miners, both materially and culturally. The fact that they were not ready to give that up, even in the context of changing industry, was born out by the 1929–30 strikes.

The 1929–30 battle between the Cerro de Pasco Corporation and its mining labor force was the first instance of extended contact between mine workers and a leftist political party based in Lima. In 1928, after the inundation of several mine tunnels under the Morococha lake had killed at least 28 workers, the group around Jose Carlos Mariategui that published the magazine *Labor* in Lima began to establish contacts with workers in the central mines. In addition to circulating *Labor* in the mining centers, Mariategui and his collaborators began a correspond-ence with several mine workers. By February 1929, this effort led to the founding of the Sociedad Pro-Cultura Popular in Morococha. Naming Ricardo Martinez de la Torre their representative in Lima, the Sociedad continued to communicate with Mariategui's group and to emphasize the importance of workers' education and culture.[64] With the beginning of the world depression, however, this cultural interchange soon took on political overtones.

The precipitous decline of copper prices on the world market after 1929 turned the short-term financial problems of the Cerro de Pasco Corporation into a major crisis as it became impossible to keep up with payments on the loans that it had financed a number of large construction projects during the 1920s. In an attempt to recoup its losses, the company cut production, laid off large numbers of workers, and forced those remaining to take a cut in pay. The dramatic drop in the miners' standard of living greatly facilitated the formation of unions, which sprang up in a number of mining centers between late 1929 and early 1930. Unionization also received an important boost from the successful strike of October 1929 in Morococha, organized by a committee in touch with Mariategui's group (recently reconstituted as the Partido Socialista).[65]

Spurred on by its early successes, the relationship between the Socialist party and the miners' unions continued to flourish. In March 1930 Jorge del Prado, a prominent militant, went up to the mining region to seek work and establish himself among the mine workers. Given the high level of mobilization and dissatisfaction among the workers, unions in a number of centers were formed almost spontaneously, within a 24– or 48–hour period of agitation.[66] Especially between August and September, union representatives in most mines presented lists of demands (pliegos de reclamos) to the corporation. In addition to wage increases, each list included at least some of the following points: that the corporation be made responsible for furnishing workers with the necessary tools and safety equipment (masks and wetgear) and for replacing them when needed, without charge; that the company take on the responsibility for providing certain subsistence items and firewood at cost; that contrata be abolished or severely limited; and that the company provide sufficient precaution against, as well as compensation for, work accidents and other work-related disabilities such as silicosis.[67]

Both the careful organization of the lists of demands presented at the various work centers and the fact that workers were seeking redress in a planned and carefully strategic fashion point to the progress that had been made in the organization of working-class protest. Certainly the presence of contacts from the Socialist party, reorganized as the Communist party during 1930,[68] had aided in bringing this organizational growth to fruition. The level of mobilization also remained high into the latter months of the year, as the corporation repeatedly refused to make good on the agreements it had reached with workers' representatives.[69] Ultimately, however, the class consciousness manifested by the mine workers was still highly frustrating to the Lima militants.

One of the realities the Lima organizers found most difficult to accept was that the workers did not identify the Peruvian state with capitalist exploitation, but saw their condition as more strictly connected to the foreign company and the *gringos*. Jorge del Prado complained from Morococha in July 1930 that the very same people who had organized the victorious strike in that mining center only a few months before had become enthusiastically involved in preparing a large fiesta for Peruvian Independence Day (July 28). "Since capitalism has arrived [here] in its imperialist stage," del Prado commented, "I attribute this [attitude] to the fact that they see their exploitation as a national rather than a class problem."[70] Further proof of these perceptions was provided by the manifesto the Oroya workers circulated a month later. After some familiar phrases about the importance of proletarian class struggle, the document reached some rather surprising conclusions about the nature of Peruvian politics:

Happily, *companeros*, a government of punctilious military men has now begun, who with their steely character and temperate personality will dominate all perverse anarchy, whether through persuasion to work and order, or through the imposition of force. They will leave an exemplary government, full of true honesty and patriotism.[71]

Thus workers in Oroya, while seeing the connection between the North American company and their situation, still placed their trust in the new military government of Sanchez Cerro. Since Sanchez Cerro had ended the 11–year Leguia dictatorship, known for its corruption and "soft" position on foreign capital, and since the new dictator publicly declared his sympathy for the popular sectors, there was perhaps some justification for these hopes.[72] In Morococha as well as Oroya, laborers seemed to put their faith in the government, hoping for new legislation favoring workers as the answer to their problems.[73]

Jorge del Prado saw the source of these attitudes in the way that the miners' hostility toward the foreign corporation lent credence to some of the nationalist arguments of the petty bourgeoisie, most notably members of APRA and the Independent Socialists.[74] But perhaps the explanation is both more complex and less convoluted. As del Prado himself pointed out, the mine workers in the central highlands had experienced capitalism in its imperialist stage through relations with a foreign company. If we consider this fact in terms of the labor process itself, it meant the transition from a situation in which local merchants—as *enganchadores* and *contratistas*—were the most visible exploiters, to one in which foreigners—as foremen and other direct supervisory personnel—became the closest targets for working-class anger. While it seems that this anger had been generalized from the individual *gringos* to the *gringo* company by 1930, in part due to the transformations in the industry during the 1920s, the same had not occurred with regard to the Peruvian state's collaboration in the process of imperialist penetration. This did not make the mine workers "petty bourgeois deviationists," however, but simply reflected the particular development of their consciousness under the conditions they had experienced.

There is yet another possibility. As we have already seen, the more permanent nature of migration in the 1920s did not irreversibly cut mine workers off from their communities of origin. To a certain extent, miners still identified with an indigenous village culture, a tradition which had its own way of maintaining cultural solidarity as well as its own political tools. The hope that the new government might provide some aid against the foreign company was perfectly understandable within the context of communal political traditions. The indigenous peasantry, always among the least powerful sectors of the population, had developed a political style of negotiation vis-à-vis the state that habitually took into account the implications of government changes for the balance of forces at the local level. Rather than signifying a false optimism about the paternal generosity of the government, this political style was the most realistic adaptation peasants could work out in a situation in which other alternatives were closed to them and in which they were extremely vulnerable to repression.[75] As the Oroya Miners' Congress was to show, there was rationality to the mine workers' continued use of communal political styles and strategies.

Held in Oroya between November 8 and 11 and with the participation of delegates from most of the important mining centers and other divisions of the corporation, the Miners' Congress was the culmination of all previous organizational work. Attended by numerous workers and their families, the congress moved quickly toward an anti-capitalist and revolutionary spirit. Much of the sentiment generated seemed spontaneous and frightened the authorities to the point that, during the small hours of the morning of November 11, the prefect gave an order to have the delegates arrested and quietly sent to Lima. Once the workers found out about the arrests, they formed a group of between six and seven thousand and marched to the police station, red flags waving. After a confrontation with over 100 policemen, the crowd retreated into the smelter, taking two company employees hostage. The final result of the conflict was the release of the delegates taken to Lima, in exchange for the freedom of the hostages.[76]

In the aftermath of the confrontation, workers from various other mining centers attempted to reach Oroya to greet the returning delegates. After the police blocked the passage of a group of laborers from Malpaso on a bridge near that center, a riot resulted in the death of over 20 workers. Workers' organizations in Lima called for a general strike in solidarity with those killed, and the response of the government was a state of siege in the departments of Lima and Junin.[77] Under cover of the state of siege, the Cerro de Pasco Corporation provided the authorities with carefully detailed lists of all known agitators and then settled back to weather the Depression, using the circumstances as an excuse to fire large sectors of the labor force.[78]

In the end, the entire series of events proved a blessing in disguise for the company. After a month-long lockout, the corporation rehired only those workers who, both for economic and political reasons, were considered "safe." By 1932, its entire labor force had been reduced from its 1929 size of nearly 13,000 to approximately 4,300.[79] Not only did this allow the corporation to cut its Depression losses, but it also served as a kind of "spring cleaning." Years later, when the firm resumed hiring, it was a great deal more careful and selective. For whatever reason, unions did not reemerge until 1945.[80]

For the mine workers, the results of the 1930 mobilizations are somewhat more difficult to assess. Though both the Lima militants and the local authorities expected them to give free reign to their "proletarian instincts," in practice the laborers' consciousness was much more mixed. Even as they made the transition toward permanent wage labor in the 1920s, most workers—as manifested by the creation of the district committees—sought to maintain one foot in the countryside. Thus when the corporation staged its lockout after the November mobilizations, the majority simply returned to their communities. While it is true that the availability of this alternative blunted their continued militance in confronting the company, it probably was the most reasonable thing to do given the circumstances. Even if party members complained bitterly about this course of action,[81] in the end it was the mine workers who had suffered the brunt of the company's repression. It also was the mine workers who, in the context of the world Depression of the 1930s, found themselves attempting to return to the peasant economy they had left behind a number of years earlier.

In an economy so dependent on the world market that all commercial and productive sectors were affected by the Depression, when a foreign employer fired thousands of laborers without providing compensation, there really was nowhere else to go but back to the rural community. Thus the workers, though militant and proletarian in their actions, had good reason—as workers—to hedge their bets by preserving alternatives in the village and developing a more eclectic approach to consciousness. Ultimately, the events and repression of 1930 made this clear. And in the process of adapting to the particular conditions they faced, mine workers also developed a culturally specific form of proletarian consciousness that would endure for years to come.

CONCLUSIONS

Especially when one analyzes the first generation of proletarianization, it is necessary to develop an approach that can encompass not only the actual events in the new industrial centers, but also the peasant or small-producer perspective from which the new workers come. In the case of the miners of the central sierra, that perspective combined a peasant household approach to migration and an indigenous communal tradition that emphasized the importance of continued collective solidarity and allegiance to the rural sector. Understanding the traditions, motivations, behavior, and symbols of that newly formed labor force, therefore, means analyzing the way in which a village perspective was incorporated into an emerging working-class consciousness. Only then can we "get inside" the process of consciousness formation and understand the various forms it took as it developed.

Between 1880 and 1930, the perspective of miners in the central highlands went through three distinct stages. The first, from 1880 to 1900, corresponded to the final years of the pre-Cerro period. Given the low levels of investment that local mine owners could afford, the technology of mining at this point was quite primitive, and the industry could not afford to maintain a permanent labor force. Mining work thus remained seasonal, generally unskilled, and undifferentiated, and could easily be handled by occasional labor from the area's peasant communities. Consequently, miners remained peasants, integrating short cycles of migration to the mines into their household economies and not engaging in struggles specific to the mining centers themselves.

With the arrival of the Cerro de Pasco Company in 1901, conditions began to change. In its first two decades, the company invested a great deal of capital in buying mines, building infrastructure, and expanding production. As the size of the labor force grew, so did opportunities for the development of new forms of consciousness among workers. But a series of factors militated against this, for the corporation did not invest much in the actual extraction of ores, relying instead on pre-existing labor relations and methods of labor acquisition. The result was a combined mining center and rural village orientation on the part of the laborers, as a mixed *contrata* and *enganche* labor force who experienced new forms of solidarity as a mining community, some differentiation of tasks in the work place, and even occasionally some limited technical supervision.

Depending on the circumstances and on the particular sectors of the company's operations, therefore, the specific course of struggle adopted by the laborers varied enormously during this time. On the one side, many workers continued to identify mainly with their home villages, using resources from the countryside to survive while engaging in mining work and struggling against the exploitation of the *contratista* or *enganchador*, which was rooted, in the last instance, in community relationships. On the other side, workers in the more technologically sophisticated and stable sectors of the firm increasingly began to carry out organized strikes and presented lists of demands manifesting a desire to remain in the mines. In between, a series of hybrid protest forms emerged in which it was clear that workers and their families were forming different kinds of bonds with other members of the mining community, but which did not necessarily correspond with particular kinds of consciousness at the point of production.

The situation was once again altered in the 1920s, when the corporation entered a more industrial phase. The inauguration of the Oroya smelter generated a new pace of production and a reorganization of the industry, with an increased division of labor and a greater need for a more skilled and permanent labor force. As workers remained in the mines on an extended basis, laboring under the closer supervision of company personnel, they tended to develop a more sophisticated and enduring consciousness of their exploitation as mine workers. By the 1929–30 strike movements, these trends culminated in a clear understanding of the foreign company's role in the region and a desire to seek solidarity with other workers.

Despite the tendency for consciousness to change along with the nature of investment, the particular labor relations and conditions, and the nature of confrontation in the workplace, one thing seemed to remain relatively constant throughout the 1900–1930 period. Workers maintained an allegiance to their villages. At the cultural level, miners reproduced some of the folkloric celebrations from the countryside and formed village associations. At the economic level, they continued to be partially dependent on resources from the peasant household economy, saw the village as a refuge in case of accident or retirement, and fulfilled material communal obligations by donations to their village committees. Indeed, a household orientation and village culture became integrated into the forms of struggle the miners developed. In 1930, for example, during the celebration of carnival in Morococha, one of the many traditional folksongs was adapted to commemorate the deaths of workers in the major catastrophe in that mining center two years before.[82] And the company encouraged the maintenance of village culture and village ties by paying low wages and benefits, giving little job security, and minimizing compensation for accidents or work-related illnesses.

Since the mid-1940s, life in the mines has begun yet another stage. As a relatively stable labor force has entered its second and third gen-

erations, unions increasingly have become institutionalized and have
developed organic connections with Lima-based national radical parties.[83] In the rural areas, since 1930, the quickening pace of agrarian
transformation and the proletarianization of the peasantry have tended
to make the village household economy less and less viable.[84] Yet despite
these tendencies, many workers stubbornly have continued to cultivate
a new relationship with their communities.

For some the tie to the village fulfills a more exclusively cultural or
emotional need. One example is a Morococha union leader and revolutionary who, within hours of returning to visit the village where he
was born, altered his language and entire social style in order to integrate
himself into the communal celebrations.[85] For others there is still a
stronger material tie. Many retired miners, for example, spend their last
years in the community, where the lower cost of living, possible access
to a small plot of land, and support from relatives can all help to stretch
a meager pension. These workers also can count on the respect of their
fellow villagers when they return because most of them have, over the
years, helped to pay for schools, libraries, and other projects in the
community with their regular contributions to the district or village committees in the mining centers.[86] Finally, there is a sense in which Andean
culture melds and mixes in the central highlands, whether in the villages
or the mines, city or countryside. On the one hand, miners maintain
religious or folk festivals from the communities, adapting them to fit
new needs. On the other hand, mining paraphernalia such as the wetgear
distributed by the company or the dynamite used in mining work become
integrated into village festivals and folk traditions.[87] In the end, the
cultural and historical perspectives of mine and community have become
inextricably intertwined.

Is this mixture the result of a "transitional" or "immature" working-
class consciousness? I think not. Rather, the combination of proletarian
and village traditions is the result of two historical tendencies. The first
is the specific path toward class formation that workers took in the central
sierra between 1900 and 1930. Given the harsh and insecure working
conditions, the prolonged use of *enganche* and *contrata*, and the slow
transformation of labor relations, workers held on to their village and
household ties, using the community as a refuge and prop in times of
difficulty. By the time objective conditions changed in the mines, village
customs were firmly integrated into an emerging proletarian consciousness, helping workers deal with the premature death and impermanence
of the proletarian condition, providing a language of solidarity and defining the terms under which individuals could integrate themselves into
a historical tradition of struggle that, because it extended backward and
forward in time, could serve as a source of strength and identity.[88]

The second historical tendency that has helped preserve the mixture of village and proletarian perspectives is the form taken by capitalist development in Peru, and by extension in other parts of the Third World. Given the difficulties of capital accumulation and transformation in Third World areas, the development of capitalism often has occurred in alliance with petty household production, weakening and changing it, but not quite eliminating it. When capitalist production enters a crisis, the tendency is for other forms and relations of production to become more important or prominent until capital recovers. Proof that these tendencies continue to operate in the central highlands has been provided in recent years, since the nationalization of the mines in 1974, and particularly with the world recession of the early 1980s. Shortages of capital and crises of production have encouraged the reemergence of more traditional labor relations, such as *contrata*, in the less modern mines,[89] while at the same time more technologically sophisticated forms of production, such as open pit mining, continue to be employed in the newer and more productive centers.[90]

In the final analysis, both the historical and the material conditions of capitalist development in central Peru have favored the emergence and maintenance of a village perspective within working-class consciousness. This does not mean that mine workers are in a transitional, immature, or "false" stage of consciousness that must or will be transformed in the future. Quite the contrary; it is in the very nature of dependent capitalism to generate relations and traditions different from those generated in the "classic" centers of capitalist development. It is a testimony to the creativity, dynamism, and determination of Third World peoples that, when confronted with the penetration of foreign capital and capitalist relations, they struggled successfully to put their own stamp upon them.

NOTES

1. The Second Industrial Revolution (approximately 1873–95) involved, among other things, the development of new fuels and industrial alloys, as well as increasing production for a mass market and the greater use of science in industry. Not coincidentally, the same period witnessed increasing competition for colonies among developed countries as England, France, and Germany competed in Asia and Africa, and the United States expanded direct investment in Latin America. Much investment was dedicated precisely to the exploitation of the new raw materials needed for industry, such as copper, rubber, and so on. For more technological information on this period, see David S. Landes, *The Unbound Prometheus* (New York, 1969), especially pp. 231–358.

2. Adrian DeWind, Jr., "Peasants Become Miners: The Evolution of Industrial Mining Systems in Peru," Ph.D. dissertation, Columbia University, 1977, 1:11 and 1:17; Rosemary Thorp and Geoffrey Bertram, *Peru 1890–1977: Growth and Policy in an Open Economy* (New York, 1978), pp. 81–83.

3. A. J. Laite, "Miners and National Politics in Peru, 1900–1974," *Journal of Latin American Studies*, 12:2 (1980), p. 321.

4. Alberto Flores Galindo, *Los mineros de la Cerro de Pasco, 1900–1930* (Lima, 1974).

5. Josh deWind, "From Peasants to Miners: The Background of Strikes in the Mines of Peru," reprinted in Robin Cohen et al. (eds.), *Peasants and Proletarians: The Struggles of Third World Workers* (New York, 1979), 149–172.

6. A. J. Laite, "Industrialization, Migration and Social Stratification at the Periphery," *Sociological Review*, 26 (1978), pp. 859–888.

7. For an excellent treatment of this point, see E. J. Hobsbawm, "Class Consciousness in History," in Istvan Meszaros (ed.), *Aspects of History and Class Consciousness* (London, 1971), pp. 5–6.

8. Hobsbawm, "Class Consciousness in History," pp. 7–8, and Tom Bottomore, "Class Structure and Social Consciousness," in Meszaros, *Aspects of History and Class Consciousness*, pp. 50–51, emphasize this point not only with regard to Marx's work, but also with regard to Georg Lukacs.

9. The concept of enclave, and how the effects of capitalism could be fragmented within a particular economy, has had a long life in the literature, particularly among some currents of dependency theory. For some basic definitions, see Fernando Henrique Cardoso, *Dependency and Development in Latin America*, trans. Marjory Mattingly Urquidi (Berkeley, 1979), esp. pp. 69–73; and Eric R. Wolf and Edward C. Hansen, *The Human Condition in Latin America* (New York, 1972), esp. pp. 3–27. For a stimulating treatment of the issues of dependency and Marxist theory, and the implications for an analysis of classes, see *Latin American Perspectives*, special issue 30–31 on "Dependency and Marxism," Summer and Fall, 1981.

10. For an introduction to the problem of labor market segmentation and its relationship to consciousness, see Richard Edwards, Michael Reich, and David Gordon (eds.), *Labor Market Segmentation* (Lexington, Mass., 1973), esp. Part 1.

11. See, for example, Sidney W. Mintz, "The Rural Proletariat and the Problem of Rural Proletarian Consciousness," reprinted in Cohen et al., *Peasants and Proletarians*, pp. 173–197; and Florencia E. Mallon, "Peasants and Rural Laborers in Pernambuco, 1955–1964," *Latin American Perspectives*, 5:4 (Fall 1978), pp. 49–70. For an analysis of the effects of populist politics on working-class consciousness, see Kenneth Paul Erickson, "Populism and Political Control of the Working Class in Brazil," in Juan Corradi and June Nash (eds.), *Ideology and Social Change in Latin America* (New York, 1977), pp. 91–127.

12. See, for example, Hobsbawm, "Class Consciousness in History," pp. 9–13; E. J. Hobsbawm, *Primitive Rebels* (New York, 1959); and Charles Tilly, "Collective Violence in European Perspective," in Hugh Davis Graham and Ted Robert Gurr (eds.), *Violence in America: Historical and Comparative Perspectives* (New York, 1969), pp. 4–37.

13. An excellent treatment of this point can be found in Bottomore, "Class Structure and Social Consciousness," pp. 49–64.

14. Recent work which has begun to take this perspective includes June Nash, *We Eat the Mines and the Mines Eat Us: Dependency and Exploitation in Bolivian Tin Mines* (New York, 1979); June Nash, "Worker Consciousness and Union Organization: The Problem of Ideology and Practice in Bolivian Mines," in Corradi

and Nash, *Ideology and Social Change*, pp. 113–141; and Michael Taussig, *The Devil and Commodity Fetishism in South America* (Chapel Hill, 1980).

15. See A. J. Laite, "Miners and National Politics in Peru."

16. Nash, *We Eat the Mines*, esp. pp. 17–209; Nash, "Worker Consciousness and Union Organization," esp. pp. 115–130; June Nash and Manuel Maria Rocca, *Dos mujeres indigenas: Basilia, Facundina* (Mexico, 1976); and Juan Rojas and June Nash, *He agotado mi vida en la mina* (Buenos Aires, 1976).

17. For a more extensive treatment of the nineteenth-century mining industry and its problems, see Florencia E. Mallon, "The Poverty of Progress: The Peasants of Yanamarca and the Development of Capitalism in Peru's Central Highlands, 1860–1940," Ph.D. dissertation, Yale University, 1980, esp. chaps. 2 and 4.

18. For information on the role of merchants in obtaining labor for the mines, see *Exposicion que presenta Carlos Renardo Pflucker al Supremo Gobierno con motivo de las ultimas ocurrencias acaecidas en la Hacienda Mineral de Morococha* (Lima, 1846), pp. 11–12; Universidad Nacional de Ingenieria (hereafter cited as UNI), Tesis #14, Ismael Bueno, "Informe sobre Yauli," 1887, p. 27; Archivo Notarial Flores (hereafter cited as ANF), Expedientes y Libros Judiciales, Libro de Juicios Verbales, Acolla, 1876, Remusgo vs. Villar, Sept. 16, 1876; Protocolos Notariales, Luis Salazar, Book 5; August 25, 1893; and Archivo Prefectural de Junin (hereafter cited as APJ), Letter from the Subprefect of Jauja B. S. Leiva to the Prefect of the Department of Junin, April 2, 1888.

19. On the labor system in the mines in the nineteenth century see Estevan Delsol, *Informe sobre las minas de Salpo, Quiruvilca y Huamachuco, en el Departamento de la Libertad* (Lima, 1880), pp. 30–33; UNI, Tesis #10–12, Federico Villarreal, "Memoria sobre Yauli," 1885, p. 13v; Tesis #13, German Remy, "Informe sobre Yauli," 1885, pp. 5v-6v; Tesis #14, Ismael Bueno, "Informe sobre Yauli," 1887, p. 27; Tesis #16, Rafael Munoz, "Informe sobre Cerro de Pasco," 1887, pp. 2–3.

20. A more complete treatment of migration as part of peasant household economy can be found in Mallon, "The Poverty of Progress," pp. 67–103, 213–227, 366–377.

21. Runaway rates apparently were quite high during the nineteenth century, and certainly high enough to cause mine owners some losses. See *Exposicion que presenta Carlos Renardo Pflucker*, p. 11; UNI, Tesis #14, Ismael Bueno, 1887; and Francisco del Castillo, Tesis #50, "Informe sobre Huarochiri y Yauli," 1891.

22. For the company's acquisition of property and construction of infrastructure in this early period, see A. DeWind, "Peasants Become Miners," 1:11 and 1:17; and Thorp and Bertram, *Peru 1890–1977*, pp. 81–83. For changes in the productive sector, see Ministerio de Fomento, *Boletin del Cuerpo de Ingenieros de Minas* (hereafter cited as BCIM), Carlos E. Velarde, "Reglamentaciones mineras para el Cerro de Pasco" (Lima, 1905), pp. 17–19.

23. For information on the smelter, see Ministerio de Fomento, *BCIM* #61, Comision del Cerro de Pasco, "Informe anual sobre la labor" (Lima, 1907), pp. 38–41. For the comparative size of the various labor forces and the capacity of the other smelters, see Ministerio de Fomento, *BCIM* #67, "Estadistica Minera del Peru en 1907" (Lima, 1908), pp. 40–43; *BCIM* #65, Alberto Jochamowitz, "Estado Actual de la Industria Minera en Morococha" (Lima, 1907); *BCIM* #76,

Carlos P. Jimenez, "Estadistica Minera del Peru en 1908" (Lima, 1909), esp. pp. 70–71; *BCIM* #77, Carlos P. Jimenez, "Estadistica Minera del Peru en 1909 y 1910" (Lima, 1911), esp. pp. 70–71; and *BCIM* #78, Carlos P. Jimenez, "Estadistica Minera del Peru en 1911" (Lima, 1912), pp. 78–79.

24. For a detailed analysis of the company's use of *enganche* and *contrata*, see Mallon, "The Poverty of Progress," pp. 281–289, 299–309.

25. Dora Mayer, *La Conducta de la Compania Minera del Cerro de Pasco* (Callao, 1914), pp. 5–6, 9.

26. On the abuses of the railroad company, see Mayer, *La Conducta*, pp. 13–14. On careless excavation and storage of explosives, see ibid., pp. 14–19, and APJ, "Oficio del Director de Fomento al Prefecto de Junin, sobre la Resolucion Suprema dictada ese mismo dia," Lima, June 5, 1910. On the accidents in Goyllarisquisga, see Mayer, pp. 26, 30–33; APJ, "Expreso de la Comision Especial de investigaciones en Goyllarisquisga al Ministro de Fomento," Goyllarisquisga, Aug. 14, 1910; and "Oficio de la Direccion de Fomento al Prefecto de Junin, informandole de la Resolucion Suprema dictada el 26 de agosto," Lima, Aug. 29, 1910.

27. Mayer, *La Conducta*, p. 59.

28. On attempts to disclaim responsibility for work accidents and on poor compensation, see ibid., pp. 33–35; and Pedro Zulen, "El enganche de indios: Informe del Comisionado de la Asociacion Pro-Indigena," *La Prensa*, Oct. 7, 1910, p. 5.

29. The worker's perspective on migration has been attained mainly through interviews with Fortunato Solis (Acolla, Jan. 20, 1978); Lydia Solis de Maita (Acolla, 1977); Mauricio Huaman (Jauja, Feb. 9, 1978); and German Maita (Acolla, Feb. 7, 1978).

30. Zulen, "El enganche," pp. 4–5.

31. DeWind, "Peasants Become Miners," 3:18–19.

32. Ibid.

33. Interviews with Elias Valenzuela Soto, Oscar Teofilo Camarena, and Francisco Solis Camarena, Tragadero, Nov. 29, 1977; for the Onofres' accumulation of property, see ANF, Protocolos Notariales, Luis Salazar, Book 17: Nov. 18, 1907, pp. 323–324v; Book 18: Mar. 11, 1908, pp. 412–414, Mar. 19, 1980, pp. 428v–430v. Mar. 30, 1908, pp. 450–451v, April 18, 1908, pp. 475v–476v, June 26, 1908, pp. 562v–564, July 28, 1908, pp. 611–612; Book 20: May 17, 1910, pp. 739v-740v; Book 22: Jan. 10, 1911, pp. 20–21v; Book 26: Dec. 10, 1913, pp. 523–524v, April 18, 1914, pp. 750–751v; Book 32: Jan. 23, 1917, pp. 42–43v, April 18, 1917, pp. 220–221v, July 25, 1917, pp. 438–440; Book 33: Aug. 20, 1917, pp. 506v–508, Aug. 20, 1917, pp. 508–510, Jan. 18, 1918, pp. 954–955, Jan. 19, 1918, pp. 956v-958; Book 33–34: Jan. 30, 1918, pp. 1000–1001v.

34. Interview with Oscar Teofilo Camarena (Tragadero, Nov. 29, 1977), who worked with the Onofres at the San Francisco mine, as a foreman and as manager of one of their stores.

35. A more complete treatment of resistance to *enganche* and *contrata* can be found in Mallon, "The Poverty of Progress," esp. pp. 310–315.

36. For the history of Goyllarisquisga, see "Goyllarisquisga: La Mina de Carbon mas Alta del Mundo," in *El Serrano* (Revista publicada por la Cerro de Pasco

Corporation para sus empleados), 18:222 (June 1968), pp. 12–15. For labor relations at the mine, see Mayer, *La Conducta*, pp. 30–33.

37. Mayer, *La Conducta*, pp. 55–58.

38. See, for example, Temma Kaplan, "Class Consciousness and Community in Nineteenth-Century Andalusia," in Maurice Zeitlin (ed.,), *Political Power and Social Theory*, vol. 2 (Greenwich, Conn., 1981), pp. 21–57; Domitila Barrios de Chungara, *Let Me Speak: Testimony of Domitila, a Woman of the Bolivian Mines* (New York, 1979); Dolores Ibarruri, *They Shall Not Pass: The Autobiography of La Pasionaria* (New York, 1966), esp. pp. 11–89; and Nash, *We Eat the Mines*, pp. 87–88.

39. Dora Mayer, *'Un Decreto Libertador': leido ante la Conferencia sobre el enganche organizada por el Centro 'Union Hijos de Cajacay'* (Lima, 1914); Zulen, "El enganche," pp. 4–5; and Mayer, *La Conducta*, pp. 41, 43.

40. Nash, *We Eat the Mines*, p. 121 and passim.

41. Mayer, *La Conducta*, p. 53. For a more extensive analysis of the household migration pattern, based on interviews with migrants, see Mallon, "The Poverty of Progress," pp. 366–398.

42. APJ, "Oficio del Comisario de Morococha Miguel Malpartida, al Subprefecto de la Provincia," Morococha, Feb. 18, 1913.

43. The pioneering study which unmasked this seemingly random violence and demonstrated its underlying political coherence is George Rudé, *The Crowd in History, 1730–1848* (New York, 1964). For commentary on the responsibility of agitators in Morococha and the drunkenness of the crowd, see APJ, "Oficio del Comisario de Morococha," Feb. 18, 1913.

44. The narrowness of the veins in Morococha and the resulting difficulty of modernization are discussed in "Esto es Centromin Peru," Departamento de Relaciones Publicas, Centromin, Lima, n.d., p. 12.

45. Mayer, *La Conducta*, p. 55.

46. Ibid., pp. 53–54.

47. APJ, "Oficio de la Comicion de los Trabajadores de los Talleres de Mecanica de la Cerro de Pasco Railway Company al Prefecto del Departamento de Junin," Cerro de Pasco, May 29, 1917; "Informe del Subprefecto de Pasco al Prefecto del Departamento," Cerro de Pasco, June 1, 1917; "Conclusiones acordadas entre los delegados de los Obreros de la Seccion Minas de la Cerro de Pasco Mining Company y el Representante de Esta," Cerro de Pasco, June 1, 1917; "Conclusiones Acordadas entre los delegados de los obreros de las minas de Goyllarisquisga de la Cerro de Pasco Mining Company y el Representante de Esta," Goyllarisquisga, May 31, 1917; "Conclusiones Acordades entre los delegados de los obreros de la Cerro de Pasco Railway Company de las secciones Casa Redonda y Departamento de Carros y el Representante de la Expresada Compania," Cerro de Pasco, June 1, 1917; "Conclusiones acordadas entre los delegados de los fogoneros, carboneros y brequeros de la linea de la Cerro de Pasco Railway Company y el Representante de esta compania," Cerro de Pasco, June 1, 1917; "Conclusionses acordadas entre los delegados de los obreros de las minas de Quishuarcancha de la Cerro de Pasco Mining Company y el Representante de Esta," Quishuarcancha, June 1, 1917; "Acuerdo entre el Superintendente del Smelter y los delegados nombrados debidamente por los trabajadores," La Fundicion, Nov. 29, 1917.

48. APJ, "Oficio del Comisario de Morococha al Prefecto del Departamento," May 28, 1921.

49. For the sources on 1912, see Note 45; on 1917, see Note 47.

50. For the peasants' adeptness at playing off competing labor needs in the commercial economy, see Mallon, "The Poverty of Progress," esp. pp. 236–249, 331–335. On the use of one *enganchador* against another, see Zulen, "El enganche," p. 4.

51. For the calculations on the runaway rate, see Mallon, "The Poverty of Progress," p. 333. For the problems with prosecuting runaways through the courts, see Zulen, "El enganche," pp. 4–5; APJ, "Solicitud de varios enganchadores al Subprefecto de Jauja," Jauja, May 28, 1910; ANF, Expedientes y Libros Judiciales, "Queja de Pedro Ramos contra el Juez de Paz de Masma, Juan M. Soto, sobre el juicio que Vicente Cairampoma ha instituido contra el primero sobre pago de cantidad de soles provenientes de una fianza," Jauja, May 15, 1903; "Revisorio referente a la demanda verbal seguida ante el Juez de Paz de 2ª Nominacion de esta Cuidad por Don Manuel Nunez Salinas, apoderado de Don Nicanor Galarza contra D. Pablo M. Hinostroza, sobre cantidad de soles," Jauja, 1904–1906; and "Pablo Stucchi contra Francisca Ortega, por cantidad de soles provenientes de una fianza," begun in Jauja, Oct. 12, 1906.

52. Ministerio de Fomento, *BCIM* #72, Celso Herrera, "Estado actual de la mineria en la provincia de Huarochiri" (Lima, 1909), p. 47.

53. For an analysis of the *maquipuro* system, see A. DeWind, "Peasants Become Miners," 3:14–16.

54. Ibid., chap. 1; A. J. Laite, "Industrialisation and Land Tenure in the Peruvian Andes," paper presented at the Symposium on Landlord and Peasant in Peru, Cambridge, England, 1972; and Julian Laite, "Processes of Industrial and Social Change in Highland Peru," in Norman Long and Bryan Roberts (eds.), *Peasant Cooperation and Capitalist Expansion in Central Peru* (Austin, Tex. 1978), pp. 72–98.

55. By the late 1920s, *contrata* seems to have been used almost exclusively for some of the reinforcement work in which laborers installed beams in the shafts to prevent cave-ins. For this as well as other information on the increasing division of labor and complexity of labor relations in the mines, see Ricardo Martinez de la Torre, *Apuntes para una interpretacion marxista de la historia social del Peru* (Lima, 1947), vol. 1, pp. 343–345; and APJ, "Informe de las condiciones de vida i explotacion de los obreros del Cerro de Pasco [Parts I and II]," Cerro de Pasco, Nov. 7, 1930. For the end to *enganche* relationships, I have relied on interviews with German Malta and Fortunato Solis, both workers in the mines in the 1920s; and on William Hutchinson, "Sociocultural Change in the Mantaro Valley Region of Peru: Acolla, a Case Study," Ph.D. dissertation, Indiana University, 1973, pp. 39–40.

56. A more complete treatment of the process of differentiation and pauperization within the peasant village can be found in Mallon, "The Poverty of Progress," pp. 259–398.

57. J. Laite, "Processes of Industrial and Social Change," pp. 81–84; A. DeWind, "Peasants Become Miners," 5:2–9; and Flores Galindo, *Los mineros*, p. 49.

58. A. J. Laite, "Miners and National Politics," pp. 323–324.

59. Sources on Leguia and lower-class mobilization during the period include

Agustin Barcelli, *Historia del sindicalismo peruano* (Lima, 1971), I:172–179; Baltazar Caravedo, *Clases, lucha politica y gobierno en el Peru (1919–1933)* (Lima, 1977); A. J. Laite, "Miners and National Politics," pp. 325–327; Frederick B. Pike, *The Modern History of Peru* (New York, 1967); and Ernesto Yepes del Castillo, *Peru 1820–1920: Un siglo de desarrollo capitalista* (Lima, 1972).

60. Sources on the district committees include interviews with Mauricio Huaman, German Maita, and Fortunato Solis; Hutchinson, "Sociocultural change," pp. 56–57; Archivo Municipal de Acolla, "Libro de Sesiones", and Archivo Municipal de Marco, "Libro de Actas." There is not enough space here to deal more extensively with the differences in consciousness or experience between rich and poor migrants from the same village. For a more detailed treatment, see Mallon, "The Poverty of Progress," pp. 366–398.

61. Interview with Fortunato Solis.

62. Interview with Mauricio Huaman.

63. Interview with Fortunato Solis.

64. A. DeWind, "Peasants Become Miners," 7:8–9; Flores Galindo, *Los mineros*, pp. 78–79; Martinez de la Torre, *Apuntes*, IV:5–6.

65. A. DeWind, "Peasants Become Miners," 7:9–10; Flores Galindo, *Los mineros*, pp. 79, 82–88; Martinez de la Torre, *Apuntes*, IV:6–19.

66. Martinez de la Torre, *Apuntes*, IV:27–36; Flores Galindo, *Los mineros*, pp. 87–100.

67. Martinez de la Torre, *Apuntes*, IV:38–41, 52–61; and APJ, "Informe de las condiciones de vida i explotacion de los obreros del Cerro de Pasco [Parts I and II]," Cerro de Pasco, Nov. 7, 1930; "Pliego de reclamos de los obreros de Goyllarisquisga," Goyllarisquisga, Aug. 29, 1930; "Peticion de los operarios de Cerro de Pasco," Sept. 10, 1930; "Pliego de Reclamaciones formulado por los empleados y obreros de la Cerro de Pasco Copper Corporation que presentan ante la superintendencia de la misma," Cerro de Pasco, September 6, 1930; and "Acuerdo entre los delegados representantes del Sindicato Metalurgico Obrero de Oroya y el Superintendente de la Cerro de Pasco Copper Corporation," Oroya, Sept. 12, 1930.

68. Flores Galindo, *Los mineros*, pp. 86–90, 96–104.

69. APJ, "Informe que presenta el Prefecto del Departamento de Junin, Mayor J. Santivanez, al Senor Ministro de Gobierno, sobre el Congreso minero en Oroya," n.d., pp. 2–8.

70. Martinez de la Torre, *Apuntes*, IV:28.

71. Ibid., p. 35.

72. For the most recent treatment of these events, see Steve Stein, *Populism in Peru: The Emergence of the Masses and the Politics of Social Control* (Madison, Wis., 1980), pp. 83–128.

73. Martinez de la Torre, *Apuntes*, IV:28.

74. Ibid.

75. For a more detailed consideration of peasant and communal political styles, see Mallon, "The Poverty of Progress."

76. APJ, "Informe que presenta el Prefecto del Departamento de Junin, Mayor J. Santivanez," pp. 10–23.

77. For the massacre at Malpaso, see A. DeWind, "Peasants Become Miners," 7:23; Martinez de la Torre, *Apuntes*, IV:111, 113–115; APJ, "Informe que pres-

enta . . . Santivanez," pp. 23–24; and A. J. Laite, "Miners and National Politics," pp. 327–28. For the state of seige see, in addition to the sources just cited, Biblioteca Nacional de Peru, BN-D1130: "Decreto-Ley #6927, Declaracion de Estado de Sitio en los Departamentos de Lima y Junin," Lima, Nov. 12, 1930.

78. On the corporation's collaboration with the repression, see APJ, "Lista de dirigentes huelguistas, Morococha," 1930; "Lista de dirigentes huelguistas, Oroya," 1930; "Lista de dirigentes huelguistas, Cerro de Pasco," 1930; "Lista de dirigentes huelguistas, Malpaso," 1930; "Lista de los activos en la huelga, Goyllarisquisga," 1930; "Lista de los activos en la huelga, Casapalca y Bellavista," 1930; "Otra lista de la Corporation de los activos en la huelga," Morococha, 1930; "Lista de los activos en la heulga, Mahr Tunel e Hidroelectrica," 1930; "Lista general de los activos en la huelga, a nivel de la Compania entera," Oroya, Dec. 5, 1930.

79. A. De Wind, "Peasants Become Miners," 7:9, 7:24.

80. Flores Galindo, *Los mineros*, pp. 107, 114.

81. Martinez de la Torre, *Apuntes*, pp. 114–115.

82. Flores Galindo, *Los mineros*, p. 79.

83. A. J. Laite, "Miners and National Politics," pp. 330–340.

84. Mallon, "The Poverty of Progress," pp. 399–519.

85. Frances Antmann, personal communication, Lima, 1981.

86. Personal observations in the Yanamarca Valley, 1977–78.

87. Personal observations in Acolla and Huaripampa, central highlands, 1977–78.

88. A similar point is made by Nash, *We Eat the Mines*, esp. pp. 121–169.

89. Personal observation by Frances Antmann, Morococha, 1981.

90. "Esto es Centromin Peru," esp. p. 10 (on Cobriza).

Annotated Bibliography

Aminzade, Ronald. *Class Politics and Early Industrial Capitalism: A Study of Mid-Nineteenth Century Toulouse, France.* Albany: State University of New York Press, 1981. An important study of the development of class consciousness among workers in Europe during the first half of the nineteenth century.

Amsden, Alice. *International Firms and Labour in Kenya: 1945–1970.* London: Frank Cass, 1972. Amsden brilliantly if somewhat sketchily argues the impact of the influx of multinational corporations in fundamentally altering the shape of industrial relations in Kenya in the direction of American-style "bread and butter" unionism.

Arenberg, Conrad, and Kimball, Solon. *Family and Community in Ireland.* Cambridge, Mass.: Harvard University Press, 1940. This classic is a beginning for anyone interested in migration and class formation.

Aya, Roderick. *The Missed Revolution: The Fate of Rural Rebels in Sicily and Southern Spain 1840–1950.* A marvelous synthetic essay on the connection between agricultural change and social protest.

Bauer, Arnold J. "Rural Workers in Spanish America: Problems of Peonage and Oppression." *Hispanic American Historical Review.* 59:1 (Feb. 1979), 34–63. A provocative discussion of the various mechanisms with which the propertied classes in Latin America coaxed or coerced the rural poor into the labor force.

Berg, Maxine; Hudson, Pat; and Sonenscher, Michael, eds. *Manufacture in Town and Country before the Factory.* Cambridge, England: Cambridge University Press, 1983. A careful look at labor organization in city and country in the period before the rise of industrial capitalism.

Bertaux-Wiame, Isabelle. "The Life History Approach to the Study of Internal Migration." In *Biography and Society: The Life History Approach to the Social Sciences,* edited by D. Bertaux, pp. 248–265. Beverly Hills, Calif.: Sage Publications, 1981. Oral history investigating the contacts and motives of migrants to Paris from a rural region in the 1930s.

Blanchard, Peter. *The Origins of the Peruvian Labor Movement, 1883–1919*. Pittsburgh: University of Pittsburgh Press, 1982. The most recent summary in English, which focuses mainly on Lima. Though ultimately disappointing, it does introduce the reader to the events of the battle for the eight-hour day (1918–1919), perhaps the most important early struggle by Peruvian workers.

Bolton, D. "Unionization and Employer Strategy: The Tanganyikan Sisal Industry, 1958–1964." In *African Labor History*, edited by P. Gutkind, R. Cohen, and J. Copans, pp. 175–204. Beverly Hills, Calif.: Sage Publications, 1978.

Bryceson, Deborah. "The Proletarianization of Women in Tanzania." *Review of African Political Economy*. 17 (Jan.-Apr. 1980), 4–27.

Calhoun, Craig. *The Question of Class Struggle: Social Foundations of Popular Radicalism during the Industrial Revolution*. Chicago: University of Chicago Press, 1982. A new critique of Thompson which attempts to resurrect the traditional view of social protest in England before 1819. Unlike most other participants in the debate, this book lacks both clearly drawn arguments and new evidence. There is a lot of smoke and heat here but little light.

Chatelain, Abel. *Les migrants temporaires en France de 1800 à 1914*. Lille: Publications de l'Université de Lille, 1976. Surveys the apex and decline of temporary migration by region, summarizing the author's life work.

Chayanov, A. V. *The Theory of Peasant Economy*, edited by Daniel Thorner, Basile Kerblay, and R. E. F. Smith. Homewood, Ill.: American Economic Association, 1966. This is a class interpretation of the logic of peasant families. Recently it has been applied to the families of those engaged in domestic industry.

Chevalier, Louis. *La formation de la population parisienne au XIXᵉ siècle*. Paris: Presses Universitaires Françaises, 1950. Catalogues Parisians' origins, occupations, residence, migration patterns, and enduring regional groupings.

Chirot, Daniel. *Social Change in the Twentieth Century*. New York: Harcourt Brace Jovanovich, 1977. An analysis of the twentieth-century world system that is congruent with Wallerstein's analysis of earlier periods.

Clayton, Anthony. "The 1948 Zanzibar General Strike." *Research Report No. 32*. Scandinavian Institute of African Studies, Uppsala, 1976. The 1948 strike is a little known but important event.

Clayton, Anthony and Savage, D. C. *Government and Labour in Kenya, 1895–1963*. London: Frank Cass, 1974. An overview of labor from the establishment of the colony. Clayton and Savage are particularly concerned with the evolution of official labor policy, although in addition they provide a wealth of detail on working conditions, economic conditions, and employer attitudes in the colony.

Cohen, Gary A. *Karl Marx's Theory of History: A Defense*. Oxford: Clarendon Press, 1978. Of importance to anyone interested in both a Marxist critique of Edward Thompson's codeterminist concept of class and a Marxist analysis of structuralism.

Coleman, D. C. "Proto-industrialization: A Concept Too Many." *Economic History Review*. Second Series. 36:3 (Aug. 1983), 435–488. Critique of the concept of protoindustrialization.

Cooper, F. *From Slaves to Squatters: Plantation Labour and Agriculture in Zanzibar and Coastal Kenya, 1890–1925*. New Haven: Yale University Press, 1980. This is the first history to focus on labor in the former slave-holding region; it is an excellent examination of the particularities of that economy and the responses of ordinary Africans to it.

Corbin, Alain. *Archaïsme et modernité en Limousin au XIXᵉ siècle, 1845–1880*. 2 vols. Paris: Marcel Rivière, 1975. Elucidates the sources and process of change in a poor rural region.

Deere, Carmen Diana. "Women's Subsistence Production in the Capitalist Periphery." Reprinted in Robin Cohen et al., eds., *Peasants and Proletarians: The Struggles of Third World Workers*. New York: Monthly Review Press, 1979. A pioneering and by now classic article on the intersection between male wage labor and female subsistence production, which demonstrates that the exploitation of unpaid female labor through the household unit ultimately cheapens the cost of wage labor for capital.

del Carria, Renzo. *Proletari senza rivoluzione*. Milan: Edizioni Oriente, 1966. An account of what the author sees as the sellout of the revolutionary working class by the leaders of its institutions when faced with government resistance to workers' challenges.

DeWind, Josh. "From Peasants to Miners: The Background of Strikes in the Mines of Peru." Reprinted in Robin Cohen et al, eds., *Peasants and Proletarians: The Struggles of Third World Workers*. New York: Monthly Review Press, 1979.

Dugrand, Raymond. *Villes et campagnes en Bas-Languedoc*. Paris: Presses Universitaires Françaises, 1963. Analyzes regional economic change to account for present day deindustrialization.

Duncan, Kenneth, and Rutledge, Ian, eds. *Land and Labour in Latin America*. New York: Cambridge University Press, 1977. An excellent collection of essays dealing with changing patterns of land ownership and labor recruitment in post-independence Latin America, with particular attention to the impact of the export economies.

Dupeux, Georges. "Immigration urbaine et secteurs économiques: l'exemple de Bordeaux au début du XXᵉ siècle." *Annales du Midi*. 85 (1973), 209–220. Surveys the sector of employment and occupation of migrants in a growing commercial center.

Elkans, Walter. *Migrants and Proletarians: Urban Labour in the Economic Development of Uganda*. London: Oxford University Press, 1960. This is a classic work, but it tends to present the migrant worker as tradition-bound and quiescent.

Fawzi, Saad ed din. *The Labour Movement in the Sudan, 1946–1955*. London: Oxford University Press, 1957. A quite valuable work on a little-known subject.

Flores Galindo, Alberto. *Los mineros e la Cerro de Pasco, 1900–1930*. Lima: Pontifica Universidad Catolica del Peru, 1974. A crucial contribution to the debate on how "radical" the Peruvian mine workers were. The author calls into question not only their radical reputation, but also the extent to which they had developed working-class consciousness at all. Based on primary sources, including company records, and on interviews with former mine workers.

Foster, John. *Class Struggle and the Industrial Revolution: Early Industrial Capitalism in Three English Towns*. New York: St. Martin's Press, 1974. Foster's book presents an imaginative and original interpretation of class conflict in English textile towns during the Industrial Revolution.

Friedland, William. *Vuta Kambi: The Development of Trade Unions in Tanganyika*. Stanford: Hoover Institute, 1969. The most comprehensive work on East Africa outside Kenya. This study presents the emergence of trade unions during the 1950s and 1960s within the conceptual framework of institutional transfer.

Furedi, F. "The Kikuyu Squatters in the Rift Valley: 1918–1929." In B. A. Ogot, ed., *Hadith 5*, (Nairobi: EALB, 1975), 177–194.

Goodman, David, and Redclift, Michael. *From Peasant to Proletarian*. New York: St. Martin's Press, 1982. An argument for looking at Latin American proletarianization as a highly differentiated process within the context of a world system approach.

Gramsci, Antonio. *Selections from the Prison Notebooks*. New York: International, 1971. The idea of "dominant culture" borrows much from Antonio Gramsci's notion of "hegemony." Although the sections on "The Modern Prince" and "State and Civil Society" are most often cited, the section on "Notes on Italian History" is most suggestive.

Grillo, R. D. *African Railwaymen: Solidarity and Opposition in an East African Labour Force*. London: Cambridge University Press, 1973. An anthropological work focusing on ethnic, status, and other personal relationships among one group of fairly stabilized Ugandan workers.

Gutkind, P.; Cohen, R.; and Copans, J., eds. *African Labor History*. Beverly Hills, Calif.: Sage Publications, 1978.

Gutman, Myron P., and Leboutte, Rene. "Rethinking Proletarianization and the Family." *Journal of Interdisciplinary History*. 14 (Winter 1984), 587–607. Summary and important clarification of debate over proletarianization and protoindustrialization.

Hammond, John L., and Hammond, Barbara. *The Town Labourer*. New York: Doubleday, 1968 (first written in 1925 and subsequently revised; last edition in 1938). This is a classic discussion of the industrial working class in the English Industrial Revolution. Its interpretation has been much debated, and while later scholarship makes revision of the Hammonds' work necessary it is still worth reading.

Hartmann, Heidi. "Capitalism, Patriarchy and Job Segregation by Sex." *Signs*. 1:3, part 2 (Spring 1976), 137–169. A provocative and interesting article which traces capitalism and the sexual division of labor within modern industry to "patriarchy."

Hobsbawm, E. J. "Custom, Wages, and Work Load in Nineteenth Century Industry." In *Labouring Men*, edited by E. J. Hobsbawm. New York: Anchor, 1964. Hobsbawm elaborates some fascinating and bold theories concerning the effects of class struggle on industrial relations.

Humphries, Jane. "Class Struggle and the Persistence of the Working Class Family." *Cambridge Journal of Economics*. 1 (1977), 241–258. This is a highly original and interesting attempt to depict the role of the family within working-class protest movement.

————. "The Working Class Family, Women's Liberation, and Class Struggle: The Case of Nineteenth Century British History." *Review of Radical Political Economics*. 9:3 (1977), 25–41.

Hunecke, Volker. *Classe operaia e Rivoluzione industriale a Milano, 1859–1892*. Bologna: Il Mulino, 1982. (original publication: *Arbeiterschaft und Industrielle Revolution in Mailand, 1859–1892: Zur Entstehungsgeschichte der italienischen Industrie und Arbeiterbewegung*. Gottingen: Vandenhoeck and Ruprecht, 1978). Exhaustively researched study of the Milanese working class in the early years of the Industrial Revolution in Lombardy, and its early leadership, the non-Marxist, worker autonomy oriented Partito Operaio.

Iliffe, John. "The Creation of Group Consciousness: A History of the Dockworkers of Dar-es-Salaam." In *The Development of an African Working Class*, edited by R. Sandbrook and R. Cohen. This small gem views the emergence of workers' consciousness from "the bottom up."

Izard, Miguel, et al. *Politica y Economia en Venezuela, 1810–1976*. Caracas: Fundacion John Boulton, 1976. An excellent collection of careful historical essays by authors of various nationalities.

Janmohamed, K. "African Labourers in Mombasa, c. 1895–1940." In B. A. Ogot, ed., *Hadith 5*, (Nairobi: EALB, 1975), 154–176.

Jeanin, Pierre. "Le proto-Industrialization: développement ou impasse?" *Annales ESC* 25 (1980), 52–65. Critique of Kriedte, Medick, and Schlumbohm on early industrialization.

Jerome, Harry. *Migration and the Business Cycle*. New York: National Bureau of Economic Research, 1926.

Johnson, Christopher H. *Utopian Communism in France: Cabet and the Icarians*. Ithaca: Cornell University Press, 1974. A rich study of an early socialist movement that touched French industrial workers.

Jones, Gareth Stedman. "Working Class Culture and Working Class Politics in London, 1870–1900: Notes on the Remaking of the Working Class," *Journal of Social History*. 7 (Summer 1974), 460–508.

King, K. "Education and Social Change: The Impact of Technical Training in Colonial Kenya." In B. A. Ogot, ed., *Hadith 6* (Nairobi: EALB, 1976), 145–164.

Klarín, Peter F. *Modernization, Dislocation and Aprismo: The Origins of the Peruvian Aprista Party, 1870–1932*. Austin: University of Texas Press, 1973. A pioneering study which traces the origins of Peru's greatest populist party to the process of proletarianization generated by the development of a capitalist sugar industry on Peru's northern coast.

Kriedte, Peter; Medick, Hans; and Schlumbohm, Jurgen, eds. *Industrialization before Industrialization: Rural Industry in the Genesis of Capitalism*. New York: Cambridge University Press, 1981. Important series of essays on proletarianization and household formation in Central Europe.

Kruijt, Dirk, and Villinga, Menno. *Labor Relations and Multi-National Corporations: The Cerro de Pasco Corporation in Peru (1902–1974)*. Assen, the Netherlands: Van Gorcum, 1979. The authors treat the development of the mining labor force in Peru as an example of working-class formation in an enclave economy, which responds more to the needs of foreign capital than to the character of internal relations.

Laite, A. J. *Industrial Development and Migrant Labour in Latin America*. Austin: University of Texas Press, 1981. Part of the new tendency in the literature on the working class in Third World countries which focuses on the continuing tie of workers to the rural sector. Though based on a limited amount of data, especially for the rural sector itself, the study concludes that it is necessary to develop a new category, "migrant worker," to account for the differences in consciousness and political action of these rural-urban migrants.

———. "Miners and National Politics in Peru, 1900–1974." *Journal of Latin American Studies*. 12:2 (1980), 317–340. A relatively empirical summary of the various changes in the relationship between Peruvian mine workers and the state during the twentieth century, which sees the workers as adapting relatively pragmatically to the confines placed on political activity by state policy.

Lehning, James R. "Nuptiality and Rural Industry: Families and Labor in the French Countryside." *Journal of Family History*, No. 4 (1983), 333–345. Contribution to discussion over the relationship between protoindustry and fertility.

Lequin, Yves. *Les ouvriers de la région lyonnaise (1848–1914)*. Vol. 1, *La formation de la classe ouvrière régionale*. Lyon: Presses Universitaires de Lyon, 1977. Traces the evolution of the region's urban economies, rural economies, and labor force in order to analyze the connections among the three.

Levine, David. *Family Formation in an Age of Nascent Capitalism*. New York: Academic Press, 1977. An important study of the demographic basis of English proletarianization.

Lis, Catherina, and Soly, Hugo. *Poverty and Capitalism in Pre-Industrial Europe*. Atlantic Highlands, N.J.: Humanities Press, 1979. A provocative effort at large-scale synthesis which describes the proletarianization process on a European scale.

Lombardi, John. *Venezuela: The Search for Order, The Dream of Progress*. Oxford: Oxford University Press, 1982.

Magalam, J. J. *Human Migration: A Guide to Migration Literature Available in English, 1955–1962*. Lexington: University of Kentucky Press, 1968. One of the best general guides with comments about the state of the theory.

Mallon, Florencia E. *The Defense of Community in Peru's Central Highlands: Peasant Struggles and Capitalist Transition, 1860–1940*. Princeton, N.J.: 1983. The author examines both the rural and urban sides of the proletarianization process, exploring their fundamental interdependence and the active role of peasant struggle in defining the nature and outcome of the transition to capitalism.

Marres, Pierre. *Les Grande Causses*. 2 vols. Tours: Arrault, 1935.

Martz, John, ed. *Venezuela: The Democratic Experience*. New York: Praeger, 1977. A collection of North American interpretations of Venezuelan history and political life.

Mata, Hector Malave. "Formacion Historica del antidesarrollo de Venezuela."

In *Venezuela: Crecimiento sin Desarrollo*, edited by D. F. Maza Zavala et al. Mexico, D.F.: Editorial Nuestro Tiempo, 1974.

Meillassoux, Claude. *Femmes, greniers et capitaux*. Paris: Maspero, 1979. An anthropologist discusses the role of women and material production in tribal societies.

Mendels, Franklin F. "Proto-Industrialization: The First Phase of Industrialization." *Journal of Economic History*. 32:1 (1972), 241–261. A widely influential call to reexamine the origins of European capitalist development.

————. "Seasons and Regions in Agriculture and Industry during the Process of Industrialization." In *Region und Industrialisierung, Studien zur Rolle der Region in der Wirtschaftgeschichte der letzten zwei Jahr hunderte*, edited by Sidney Pollard. Gottingen: Vandenhoeven und Ruprecht, 1980. A stimulating discussion of the influence of regional forces on the development of industry.

Merli, Stefano. *Proletariato di fabbrica e capitalismo industriale*. 2 vols. Florence: La Nuova Italia, 1972. Contentious but well-documented argument that the Italian working class was formed (before the post-1900 growth of heavy industry) particularly in the textile factories of the end of the nineteenth century, in response to oppressive conditions. Volume 2 publishes many relevant documents.

Merlin, Pierre. *La Dépopulation des plateaux de Haute Provence*. Paris: La Documentation française, 1969. Analyzes the origins and mechanics of severe rural depopulation of a mountain region.

Moss, Bernard. *The Origins of the French Labor Movement: The Socialism of the Skilled Worker*. Berkeley: University of California Press, 1976. A fine overall portrait of French worker political activity in the course of the nineteenth century.

Murphy, Robert F. *Headhunter's Heritage: Social and Economic Changes among the Mundurucú Indians*. New York: Octagon Books, 1960. This anthropological and historical study traces the impact of the rubber trade (both during and after the boom) on the natives of the upper Tapajoz valley.

Nascimbene, Adalberto. *Il movimento operaio in Italia: La Questione sociale a Milano dal 1890 al 1900*. Milan: Cisalpino Goliardica, 1972. A hasty and poorly documented once-over of the Milanese worker movement and socialism in the last decade of the nineteenth century.

Nash, June. *We Eat the Mines and the Mines Eat Us: Dependence and Exploitation in Bolivian Tin Mines*. New York: Columbia University Press, 1979. An original and pioneering attempt to interpret the culture and political behavior of mine workers. The author displays great sensitivity to the syncretic culture of the indigenous Bolivian workers, and to the human contradictions present in their consciousness and actions. A first-rate example of "urban" anthropology.

Pacheco de Oliveira Filho, João. "O cabocol e o brabo: notas sobre duas modalidades de força-de-trabalho na expansão da fronteira amazônica." *Encontros com a Civilização Brasileira*. 11 (May 1979), 101–140. In an effort to revise the image of the Brazilian tapper population as an undifferentiated mass, the author of this study examines the transition from relatively autonomous to coerced labor in the rubber economy and the way in which this affected "frontier" society in the Amazon.

Paige, Jeffrey. *Agrarian Revolution: Social Movements and Export Agriculture in the Underdeveloped World*. New York: Free Press, 1975. Important interpretation of the relationship between different forms of agriculture and the protest movements they produce.

Petras, James; Morely, Morris, and Smith, Steven, *The Nationalization of Venezuelan Oil*. New York: Praeger, 1977.

Pierrard, Pierre. *La vie ouvrière à Lille sous le Second Empire*. Paris: Bloud & Gay, 1965. A rich and detailed study of working-class life in the north of France under the Second Empire.

Piore, Michael J. *Birds of Passage: Migrant Labor and Industrial Societies*. Cambridge, England: Cambridge University Press, 1979. An economist reexamines the migration process and places it in the social context. This is a very provocative and interesting theory of the forces governing the migration of industrial workers.

Pitié, Jean. *Exode rural et migrations intérieures en France*. Poitiers: Norois, 1971. A close analysis of rural depopulation, followed by case studies.

Popkin, Samuel. *The Rational Peasant*. Berkeley: University of California Press, 1979. The best known critique of Scott's *The Moral Economy of the Peasant.*.

Pounds, N. J. G. *An Historical Geography of Europe 1500–1800*. Cambridge, England: Cambridge University Press, 1979. This book is a fund of information concerning the progress of industrialization across the European continent.

Procacci, Giuliano. *The Italian Working Class from the Risorgimento to Fascism*. Cambridge, Mass.: Center for European Studies, Harvard University, Monograph 1, 1979 (an English-language summary of his *La lotta di classe in Italia agli inizi des Secolo XX*. Rome: Editori Riuniti, 1978). Study emphasizes diversity within the labor force and the importance of non-industrial workers in the Italian worker movement through 1900.

Ragionieri, Ernesto. *Una comune socialista. Sesto Fiorentino*. Rome: Edizioni Rinascita, 1953. Very influential, mostly institutional history in economic and social context.

Rangel, Domingo Alberto. *Los Andinos en el Poder*. 2nd ed. Caracas: Vadell Hermanos, 1974. A well-known Venezuelan Marxist interpretation.

Roberts, Bryan R. "The Bases of Industrial Cooperation in Huancayo." In *Peasant Cooperation and Capitalist Expansion in Central Peru*, pp. 139–162. Edited by Norman Long and Bryan R. Roberts, Austin: University of Texas Press, 1978.

Roseberry, William. *Coffee and Capitalism in the Venezuelan Andes*. Austin: University of Texas Press, 1983.

Ross, Eric B. "The Evolution of the Amazon Peasantry." *Journal of Latin American Studies*. 10:2 (Nov. 1978), 200–210. A brief but useful overview of a non-tribal peasant population in the Amazon, and the ways in which this "peasantry" had adapted to various phases of Amazonian economic history.

Rudé, George. *The Crowd in the French Revolution*. Oxford: Oxford University Press, 1959. A classic statement of the role of artisanal workers in social protest in the eighteenth and nineteenth centuries.

Sandbrook, R. *Proletarians and African Capitalism: The Kenyan Case, 1960–1972.* London: Cambridge University Press, 1975. This is a full and solid study of both the internal politics of the union movement and union-government relations in the 1960s.

————. "The State and the Development of Trade Unionism." In *Development Administration: The Kenyan Experience*, pp. 252–294. Edited by G. Hyden, R. Jackson, and J. Okumu, Nairobi: Oxford University Press, 1970.

Sandbrook, R., and Cohen, R., eds. *The Development of an African Working Class.* London: Longman, 1975.

Santos, Roberto. *História econômica da Amazônia, 1800–1920.* São Paulo, 1980. This impressive survey of Amazonian economic history from the waning years of the colonial period to the collapse of the wild rubber market supplies much-needed information on long-term trends in prices, production, and demographic patterns.

Scott, James C. *The Moral Economy of the Peasant.* New Haven: Yale, 1976. Although Scott makes explicit reference to E. P. Thompson, the use of the idea of moral economy to create a theory of peasant culture and politics is attributable to Scott.

————. "Protest and Profanation: Agrarian Revolt and the Little Tradition." *Theory and Society.* 4 (1977), 1–38, 211–246. This two-part essay makes Scott's allegiance to Robert Redfield explicit.

Scott, Roger. *The Development of Trade Unions in Uganda.* Nairobi: East African Publishing House, 1966.

Seccombe, Wally. "Marxism and Demography." *New Left Review.* 137 (Jan.-Feb. 1983), 22–47. Marxist interpretation of debate over protoindustrialization and proletarianization.

Sewell, William H., Jr. *Work and Revolution in France: The Language of Labor from the Old Regime to 1848.* Cambridge, England: Cambridge University Press, 1980. An original and interesting work that examines continuity and change in attitudes toward work and in the French workers' movement between 1760 and 1848.

Smelser, Neil J. *Social Change in the Industrial Revolution.* Chicago: University of Chicago Press, 1959. A powerful early attempt to synthesize the relationship between working-class families and industrial change in Western European society. Much of the literature in the field, and principally much of Edward Thompson's work, can be viewed as a response to Smelser.

Soboul, Albert. *Les Sans-culottes Parisiens en l'an II.* La Roche-sur-Yonne: Potin, 1958. The classic French statement of the role of the popular masses in social protest during the radical phase of the French revolution in Paris.

Spagnoli, Paul G. "Industrialization, Proletarianization and Marriage: A Reconsideration." *Journal of Family History.* 8:3 (1983), 230–247. Using material based on northern French coal towns, Spagnoli suggests that protoindustrial interpretations of labor force formation will not explain the growth of the working class in this region of France.

Spalding, Hobart A., Jr. *Organized Labor in Latin America: Historical Case Studies of Urban Workers in Dependent Societies.* New York: Harper and Row, 1977. Despite an overemphasis on the role of the Communist parties and of outside ideologies in the formation of the Latin American working classes,

this remains the best general study of the Latin American labor movement
and contains an excellent bibliography.

Spriano, Paolo. *The Occupation of the Factories: Italy, 1920.* London: Pluto Press,
1975. Translated by Gwyn A. Williams. The failure of the machine industry sit-down strike wave seen as illustrative of the lack of will of Socialist
party leadership, and paving the way to Fascism.

———. *Storia di Torino operaia e socialista.* Torino: Einaudi, 1972 (combined edition of two earlier works, first published in 1958 and 1960). A quick look
at working conditions and economic history as the setting of a primarily
institutional history of Turin socialism.

Stearns, Peter N. *Lives of Labor: Work in a Maturing Industrial Society.* New York:
Holmes and Meier, 1975. An important interpretation of the roots of
worker militancy by an influential American labor historian.

Stephenson, Charles. "Migration and Mobility in Late Nineteenth and Early
Twentieth Century America." Ph.D. dissertation, University of Wisconsin,
1980. For those interested in migration particularly, the introduction to
Charles Stephenson's dissertation is very helpful. The dissertation also
provides an interesting application of theory to data on internal migration.

Stichter, Sharon. *Migrant Labour in Kenya: Capitalism and African Response 1895–
1975.* London: Longman, 1982. This work provides an overview of labor
from the establishment of the colony in the 1890s. Stichter examines the
spread of African wage earning alongside the competing growth of peasant economies, and the early history of protest actions by both migrant
and urbanized workers, emphasizing the efforts of workers to exert control over the conditions of their work.

———. "Trade Unionism in Kenya, 1947–1952: The Militant Phase." In *African
Labor History*, edited by P. Gutkind, R. Cohen, and J. Copans, pp. 154–
174. Beverly Hills, Calif.: Sage Publications, 1978.

———. "Workers, Trade Unions, and the Mau Mau Rebellion." *Canadian Journal
of African Studies.* 2 (1975), 259–275.

Sulmont, Denis. *Historia del Movimiento Obrero Peruano (1890–1977).* Lima: Tarea,
1977. The most recent and most analytically sophisticated overview of the
Peruvian labor movement.

Taussig, Michael T. *The Devil and Commodity Fetishism in South America.* Chapel
Hill: The University of North Carolina Press, 1980. An original and in-
triguing attempt to explore the internal logic of emerging working-class
consciousness that compares rural proletarians in Columbia's Cauca Valley
with Bolivian tin miners.

Thomas, Brinley. *Migration and Economic Growth.* Cambridge, England: Cambridge University Press, 1954.

Thompson, E. P. *The Making of the English Working Class.* New York: Vintage,
1966. This classic, first published in 1963, has strongly influenced almost
all studies of class formation and proletarianization.

Tilly, Charles. "Migration in Modern European History." in *Human Migration:
Patterns and Policies*, edited by William H. McNeill and Ruth S. Adams,
pp. 48–74. Bloomington, Ind.: Indian University Press, 1978. A widely
applicable theory and overview of changes in migration patterns that
occurred with urbanization and industrialization.

Trempé, Rollande. *Les mineurs de Carmaux 1848–1914*. 2 vols. Paris: Les editions ouvrières, 1971. Certainly one of the finest discussions of the forces of miner militancy available for any country.

Tugault, Yves,. *La mesure de la mobilité: cinq études sur les migrations internes*. Paris: Presses Universitaires Françaises, 1973. A study measuring internal migration in France during the last century, followed by case studies. It contains a general survey of the French literature.

van Zwanberg, R. *Colonial Capitalism and Labour in Kenya, 1919–1939*. Nairobi: East African Literature Bureau, 1975. Though uneven and sometimes overstated, the book contains useful information for the mid-colonial decades.

Wagley, Charles. *Amazon Town: A Study of Man in the Tropics*. New York: Alfred A. Knopf, 1953. The classic study of village life in a non-tribal area of the Amazon, it includes a description of rubber tapping in the post-boom era as well as frequent historical references.

————, ed. *Man in the Amazon*. Gainesville, Fla.: University of Florida Press, 1974. Although this collection of articles by anthropologists, social scientists, geographers, and others mainly deals with the contemporary Amazon, much of the material has some bearing on the Amazon during the rubber boom.

Wallerstein, Immanuel. *The Modern World System: Capitalist Agriculture and the Origins of the European World Economy in the Sixteenth Century*. New York: Academic Press, 1974. Wallerstein's first and still his best statement of the "world system" perspective.

————. *The Modern World System II: Mercantilism and the Consolidation of the European World Economy, 1600–1750*. (New York: Academic Press, 1980). The second volume in Wallerstein's pathbreaking survey of the roots of capitalism and their ties with state systems.

————, ed. *Labor in the World Social Structure*. New York: Sage, 1983. Soviet and American scholars survey the process of labor formation. Several of the American scholars place their analysis within the framework of a world economy.

Williams, Raymond. *Marxism and Literature*. Oxford: Oxford University Press, 1977. Ostensibly an introduction to basic concepts, this book is more fundamentally a condensation and reinterpretation of ideas Williams has been developing since *Culture and Society*.

Wolf, Eric. *Europe and the People without History*. Berkeley: University of California Press, 1982. Attempt to define and analyze the interrelation between different parts of the world economy.

Index

About the Contributors

MICHAEL HANAGAN is Assistant Professor of History at Columbia University. He is the author of numerous articles and of *The Logic of Solidarity: Artisans and Industrial Workers in Three French Towns, 1871–1914* (1980) and editor (with Charles Stephenson) of *Confrontation, Class Consciousness, and the Labor Process: Studies in Proletarian Class Formation* (forthcoming). Currently he is working on a history of class formation, family formation, and worker militancy in nineteenth-century France.

FLORENCIA E. MALLON is Associate Professor of Latin American History at the University of Wisconsin, Madison; she has taught at Marquette University and at Yale University. She has published several articles on peasant politics and is the author of *The Defense of Community in Peru's Central Highlands: Peasant Struggle and Capitalist Transition, 1860–1940* (1983). She also works on gender and class in the transition to capitalism and currently is researching a comparative project on "Peasants and the National Question in Peru and Mexico, 1850–1900."

FLEMMING MIKKELSEN is Research Fellow at the Institute of Criminal Science, University of Copenhagen and the Institute of Political Science, University of Arhus. He has published articles and books on economic history, working-class culture, climatic change, and methods in social science history. Currently he is writing in the field of collective action and concluding a research project on industrial conflicts in Scandinavia, 1848–1980.

LESLIE PAGE MOCH is Assistant Professor of History at the University of Michigan at Flint. She is the author of *Paths to the City: Regional Migration in Nineteenth-Century France* (1983) and co-editor of *Essays on the Family and Historical Change* (1984). Currently she is engaged in a study of the relationship between migration patterns and social change in modern Europe.

WILLIAM ROSEBERRY is Associate Professor of Anthropology at the New School for Social Research and has taught previously at the University of Iowa and Johns Hopkins University. He is the author of *Coffee and Capitalism in the Venezuelan Andes* (1983). His current research interests involve a comparative analysis of the formation of peasantries in Europe and Latin America.

CHARLES STEPHENSON is an Assistant Professor of History at Central Connecticut State University. He is the author of numerous articles and of *The Real Democrats: The Democrats of Texas in Texas Politics* (1986) and editor (with Robert Asher) of *Life and Labor: The Dimensions of American Working-Class History* (1986) and (with Michael Hanagan) of *Confrontation, Class Consciousness, and the Labor Process* (Greenwood, 1986). He serves as editor (with Robert Asher) of the American Labor History Series for the State University of New York Press. He is completing a study of migration and economic development in America.

SHARON STICHTER is Associate Professor of Sociology at the University of Massachusetts at Boston. She is the author of *Migrant Labour in Kenya: Capitalism and African Response, 1895–1975* (1982), and co-author of *African Women South of the Sahara* (1984). Currently she is working on a study of production and reproduction among urban working women in Kenya.

LOUISE A. TILLY is a professor of History and Sociology at the New School for Social Research and Chair of its Committee on Historical Studies. She co-authored (with Joan Scott) *Women, Work, and Family* (1978), and co-edited (with Charles Tilly) and contributed to *Class Conflict and Collective Action* (1982). Currently she is completing a book on labor-force formation and working-class politics in Milan, Italy, 1880–1900.

BARBARA WEINSTEIN is Associate Professor of History at the State University of New York at Stony Brook and previously was a member of the faculty at Vanderbilt University and a Fulbright Lecturer at the University of Campines (São Paulo). She is the author of *The Amazon Rubber Boom, 1850–1920* and currently is at work on a study of elite strategies for worker assistance and labor control in twentieth-century Brazil.